HOLLYWOOD

her story

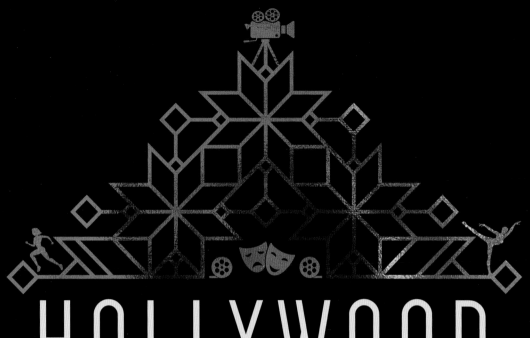

HOLLYWOOD
her story

AN ILLUSTRATED HISTORY OF WOMEN AND THE MOVIES

Jill S. Tietjen, P.E. and Barbara Bridges

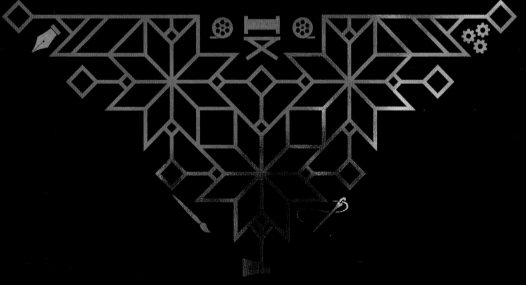

LYONS PRESS · GUILFORD, CONNECTICUT

LYONS PRESS

An imprint of The Rowman & Littlefield Publishing Group, Inc.
4501 Forbes Blvd., Ste. 200
Lanham, MD 20706
www.rowman.com

Distributed by NATIONAL BOOK NETWORK

Book design by Laura Klynstra
Interior illustrations by Shutterstock

British Library Cataloguing in Publication Information available

Library of Congress Cataloging-in-Publication Data available

ISBN 978-1-4930-3705-6 (hardcover)
ISBN 978-1-4930-3706-3 (e-book)

Printed in China, 2019

HALF TITLE: Mary Pickford

TITLE PAGE: Dorothy Dandridge, Anna May Wong, Elizabeth
Taylor, Florence Vidor, America Ferrera; Hattie McDaniel,
Marilyn Monroe, Edith Head, Julia Roberts, Greta Garbo,
Sharmeen Obaid-Chinoy, Louise Brooks

Women editing film at Universal studio, 1920s

To my mother, Bernice (Bee) Stein, who
fostered my love of culture and whose
feminist dreams I embody.

—JILL S. TIETJEN, P.E.

To my mother, Barbara S. Gross, whose love of stories, poetry,
plays and movies influenced me more than I knew.

—BARBARA BRIDGES

CONTENTS

Abigail E. Disney

FOREWORD

History books have a problem. Women have always been approximately 50% of the population, but for thousands of years, they have not been included in much of recorded history. This is not a fair, nor is it an accurate, representation of the truth.

The fact is that women have been left out of the stories we tell ourselves about our past over and over again—written out, rendered invisible. There have been and still are many talented, feisty, wise and witty women who ought to be celebrated. Their stories need to be told and written back into our cultural memories and historical narratives.

When you watch the credits roll at the end of a film, you discover that it takes many people with diverse skills and talents to create the movie you have just seen. Women have filled all of these roles at one time or another—actress, director, stuntwoman, screenwriter, composer, animator, editor and on and on. We can easily see that women's creativity, hard work and flair have helped to create the moving pictures on the screen that entertain and reach our hearts and minds.

This book sets out to document the many women who have been in the film business since its inception. The hidden truth is that women have influenced every facet of the industry since the days when films were a mere flicker of light on the screen. There are more than 1200 women listed in these pages—you'll find many that you know and love. But you will also discover hundreds of women whose names may be unknown to you who have made their contributions to the movie experience in a variety of ways.

Amazingly, women virtually controlled the film industry during the silent film era. Back then they had more opportunities, both behind the camera and on the screen, than they have had at any time since. The highest paid director during the silent film era was a woman. Women screenwriters during that period outnumbered men ten to one. Talent and brains were what mattered, not gender.

Then movies started making money, which attracted more men to the film business. Men took over the studios and assumed almost all of the leadership positions, including director and producer. This cultural dynamic continued after World War II when women were expected to retreat to their homes and leave job opportunities for men.

But still women persisted. Women continued to play all the roles in filmmaking but were more successful in some categories than others. For almost a century, women have endeavored to reclaim the important roles they had once played in film's infancy.

Change toward gender equity has been slow to materialize and exceedingly difficult to achieve. The resurgence of the women's movement in the 1960s saw some doors start to open, and women began to benefit from opportunities to demonstrate their talents for the first time in decades. Some women produced box office successes, such as Julia Phillips, who won an Oscar in 1973 for *The Sting*. Later, a few women became studio heads, starting with Sherry Lansing at 20th Century Fox in 1980.

How have women directors fared since the silent film days? Few female directors were successful between the 1920s and the 1960s. The two who stood out during this time were Dorothy Arzner and Ida Lupino. The major studios were a difficult place for women directors to flourish, with women directing one-fifth of one percent of the films from the 1950s through the 1970s. In fact, it wasn't until 1977, forty-eight years after the Academy Awards were established, that Lina Wertmuller became the first female to be nominated for a Best Director Oscar. Only five women have been nominated over the 90 years of the Academy Awards, with Kathryn Bigelow being the only female to take home the Oscar—and that not until 2010. In the past decade, women have directed an average of 4% of the top 100 grossing films each year.

The Oscars reflect the dearth of women across the disciplines as well. 2018 brought the very first Oscar nomination to a woman for Best Cinematography. The only Oscar awarded to a woman for Best Sound Mixing was in 2010. The first nomination for a female composer occurred in 1974 for Best Original Score, with only a few women receiving the Oscar. More women are represented in the costume design and writing categories at the Academy Awards.

Films tell us stories that help us to understand our world. When they don't reflect real demographics, they give us an inaccurate picture. In the last decade of films, women have made up only 30% of the speaking characters. And we see a female in a leading role only 30-35% of the time. Of those leading women, only 4% are over 40. In fact, of all characters over the age of 40, only about 25% are female. All of this creates a distorted picture of our world. The failure of film to present women in their proper proportion contributes to a culture-wide tendency to dismiss women's power, relevance and autonomy.

One way to increase the number of women on screen or behind the camera is to hire female directors. Women directors are more likely to cast women in their films. They are more likely to hire female leads or women over the age of 40. They are more likely to hire other women in key production roles.

The last few years, however, have seen a massive shift in the visibility of women in Hollywood, especially in light of the Time's Up movement. This movement seeks to make the entertainment industry a safe and equitable place for everyone, where women workers have equal representation, opportunities, benefits and pay. It calls for a significant increase in the number of women in positions of leadership and power.

It is hard to ignore the fact that women have made enormous and important contributions to film once you fully appreciate how many of them have been written out of the record. Women were always there but often invisible, marginalized or minimized. A true history of Hollywood cannot be told without them and their diverse and extraordinary accomplishments. Hopefully these stories will help correct the record, and shift the perception and treatment of women, in the film industry and beyond.

—ABIGAIL E. DISNEY
Filmmaker, Activist and Philanthropist

INTRODUCTION

There is nothing connected with the staging of a motion picture that a woman cannot do as easily as a man, and there is no reason why she cannot completely master every technicality of the art.

—ALICE GUY-BLACHÉ

In 2018, Rachel Morrison became the first female to be nominated for Best Cinematographer in the 90-year history of the Oscars. When we tell this to other women they say "Well, isn't this like other industries where women are just now rising into leadership positions?" The answer is a resounding, "No!" We inform them that in the early days of the industry women did every job as filmmakers, including Alice Guy-Blaché who was the first female movie director. However, we let them know, when movies started making money and became a big business, the men took over. They just nod their heads knowingly.

There is now a movement in Hollywood that says that time's up on the male domination of the film industry. Now is the time for women to reclaim all the roles that they once played, to break in and rise up and be heard. Women helped found the industry and have been involved in every facet of its development. They have been actresses, directors, producers, studio heads, screenwriters, editors, film critics, stuntwomen, and are involved in sound, music, visual effects and animation. It is time to tell not just the male history of Hollywood but the Her Story as well.

The genesis of this book was a series of breakfasts over a couple of years. We got to know each other, talked about our lives, the lack of knowledge of women in history and many other topics that women discuss. Jill's book *Her Story: A Timeline of the Women Who Changed America* was a topic. At one of those breakfasts, Jill mentioned that there would be a series of *Her Story* books. Barbara suggested that the second in the series should be about women and the movies. Suddenly, before the next bite, the seed was planted for this book—a book on women throughout film's existence, a Her Story of the movie industry.

Barbara is engaged in the film industry as the founder of Women + Film, showing films by and about women with the Denver Film Society for over a decade. She has been involved in other film festivals as well as narrative and documentary films. Jill's familiarity with women in the movies was more limited but she had researched prominent women in the film industry for the original *Her Story*. The seed took root and germinated.

We began the research for this book. Over time, we have been amazed by the breadth of women's accomplishments especially in light of the obstacles many had to overcome and the hostilities many endured. Their individual dedication to their craft is evident in their stories.

And now the seed has grown into a tree that is producing fruit. We did some pruning along the way—we are sure we missed some women or couldn't find adequate information about others, especially those from the very early years of the industry. Women are now and have always been found in every corner of the film industry. We are pleased to document their accomplishments in this book.

Come now and enjoy *Hollywood: Her Story*.

—JILL S. TIETJEN AND BARBARA BRIDGES

ICONS KEY

Acting Coach

Composer • Lyricist

Set Decorator • Art Director

Actress

Costume Designer

Sound Mixer/Editor

Agent

Cutter • Film Editor

Studio Executive

Animal Trainer

Director

Studio Photographer

Animator

Journalist • Film Critic

Stuntwoman

Archivist • Film Scholar

Lighting

Technologist

Camera Operator • Cinematographer

Makeup Artist/Hairstylist

Visual Effects

Casting

Producer

Voice Actress

Choreographer

Screenwriter • Scriptwriter

"There is nothing connected with the staging of a motion picture that a woman cannot do as easily as a man, and there is no reason why she cannot completely master every technicality of the art."

—ALICE GUY-BLACHÉ

1890s

SETTING THE STAGE

In 1893, Thomas Edison introduced the Kinetoscope, in which moving film was passed through a peephole for viewing by one person, as a novelty. The public loved it! Being a businessman as well as an inventor, he realized that the public needed motion pictures to view in their Kinetoscopes. To fill that need, he built the first movie studio that same year in West Orange, New Jersey. Believing that the market was going to grow, he also bought the rights to an invention that would project pictures on a large surface. This he named the Edison Vitascope. To put all of the pieces together, he founded the Edison Company and began his filmmaking venture. Edison's first movie, unlike those with which we are familiar today, was less than 30 seconds long and was filmed in 1895. It was titled *The Execution of Mary, Queen of Scots*, but Mary was played by a man. The first Edison movie in which a woman co-starred was the *John Rice–May Irwin Kiss*, which was created in 1896. Not surprisingly, considering the content, it was the first film to cause a stir related to morals.

Edison did not patent his invention and other movie picture companies entered the business including Selig, Vitagraph, Biograph, Kalen, and Essanay. The year 1896 brought the first movie from the first female director in history to use film to tell a story. Produced by French company Gaumont, the film, *The Cabbage Fairy*, was directed by Alice Guy-Blaché, who would later become the first woman to build and operate her own studio. She would open Solax Studios in Fort Lee, New Jersey, the hub of filmmaking in America in its early years.

And the movies began. . .

1893

Inventor Thomas Edison introduces the Kinetoscope as a peep show novelty, and then builds the first movie studio in West Orange, New Jersey. A few years later, he buys the rights to a machine that will project on a large surface (a projector) and calls it the Edison Vitascope.

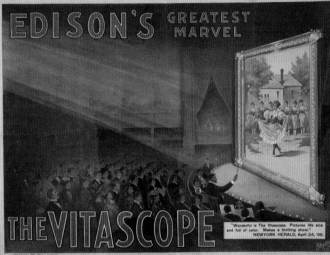

1895

The Edison Company produces its first film *The Execution of Mary, Queen of Scots*, which is a one-half-minute feature. A man plays Mary.

The Biograph Company is founded in 1895 by William Kennedy Dickson, an inventor in Thomas Edison's laboratory. The Company produces more than 3,000 movies until ceasing operations in 1916.

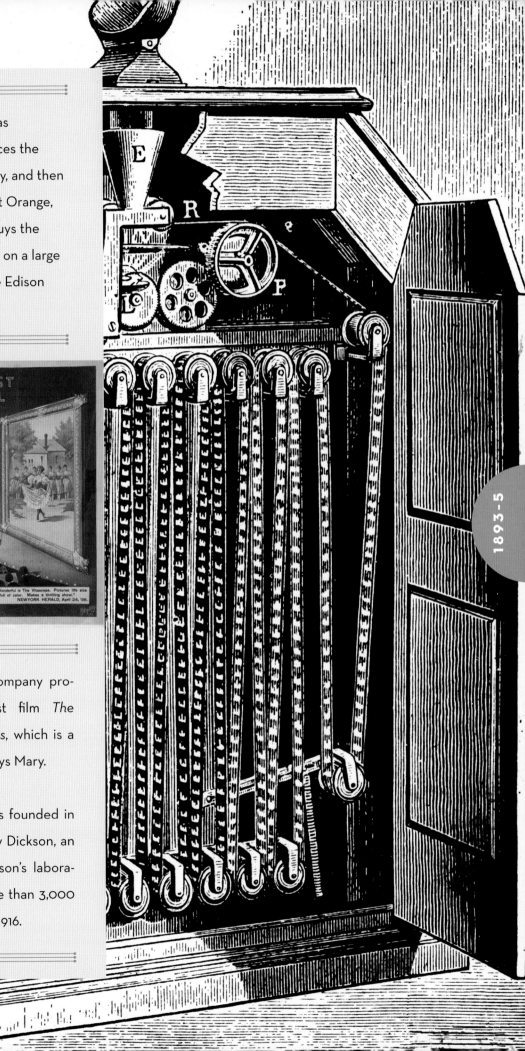

1896

The first female movie director, Frenchwoman **ALICE GUY-BLACHÉ** makes her first film, *The Cabbage Fairy (The Birth of Infants)*. She becomes one of the first individuals to make films on a regular basis. Guy-Blaché develops narrative filmmaking, experiments with sound and employs the first special effects. She innovates films running in reverse, films slowed down or accelerated, stops, double exposures and fade-outs. In 1910, she becomes the first woman to run her own studio. Believed to have made more than 1,000 pictures, the longest of which is thirty minutes, Guy-Blaché is also a producer, writer and cinematographer.

Said of her, "She is never ruffled. Never agitated. With a few simple directions, uttered without apparent emotion, she handles the interweaving movements like a military leader might the manoeuvers of any army." —*Moving Picture World*, 1912.

Said by her: "Gathering up my courage, I timidly proposed to Gaumont [a French company] that I would write one or two short plays and make them for the amusement of my friends. If the developments which evolved from this proposal could have been foreseen, then I probably never would have obtained his agreement. My youth, my lack of experience, my sex all conspired against me."

> Not only is a woman as well-fitted to stage photodrama as a man, but in many ways she has a distinct advantage over him because of her very nature and because much of the knowledge called for in the telling of the story and the creation of the stage setting is absolutely within her province as a member of the gentler sex. She is an authority on the emotions. For centuries she has given them full play while man has carefully trained himself to control them. She has developed her finer feelings for generations. In matters of the heart her superiority is acknowledged, her deep insight and sensitiveness in the affairs of Cupid. . . . It seems to me that a woman is especially well qualified to obtain the very best results, for she is dealing with subjects that are almost second nature to her.

—ALICE GUY-BLACHÉ

1896 The first Edison film in which a woman costars is produced, *John Rice–May Irwin Kiss*, which attracts the attention of censors.

1897 Vitagraph Studios is founded in Brooklyn, New York. By 1907, it is the most prolific studio producing many popular silent films. In 1925, it is purchased by Warner Brothers.

A LA CONQUÊTE DU MONDE
scène vécue
PAR
PATHÉ FRÈRES
1894-19...

Pathé is founded in Paris, France, by the four Pathé brothers in 1896. In the early 1900s, the company is the largest film equipment and production company worldwide. In 1908, the company invents the newsreel. Pathé builds film studios in the U.S. and begins film production in 1914 in New Jersey.

1898 Irish director and cinematographer **MRS. AUBREY LE BLOND** is an early female mountain climber who makes movies of ice skating, tobogganing and mountain climbing.

1896-8

Mary Pickford

1900s

BEFORE
HOLLYWOOD—A TIME
OF EXPERIMENTATION

The infancy of the film industry was a time of experimentation and innovation. Talkies were still decades away. Movies were typically black-and-white silent films on one reel, with a reel holding up to 15 minutes of film. Filmmakers were exploring ways to add interest to their movies using many new techniques, such as sound syncing systems, color tinting, special effects, close-ups, panning shots and artificial lighting.

The majority of the films in this decade, and throughout the silent film era, are lost to us forever. They were made with a film stock that was unstable and needed to be stored properly. This was rarely done, leaving the film to turn to dust. They are also lost to us because the studios didn't value them, especially after the advent of sound. When they needed space, which was expensive, they simply got rid of the older movies, which to them no longer had value.

During this period, gender roles were not prescribed. Whoever could get the job done was welcomed, and women could be found in front of, as well as behind, the camera. Women worked as directors, producers, screenwriters, editors, stuntwomen, camerawomen and actresses.

In those early years, movie actors and actresses were not identified by name. Actresses were identified as "The Vitagraph Girl" or "The Biograph Girl," indicative of the production company with which they were affiliated. The first woman to be identified by her name, thus becoming "The First Movie Star," was Florence Lawrence, who debuted in 1907 in *Daniel Boone*. Florence Turner also became a star once the public knew her name.

One highlight of this decade occurred in 1909 when Mary Pickford first came to the screen. She made 51 movies that year, averaging about one a week. This decade also produced the screenplay adaptation for *Ben Hur*, which was written by female screenwriter Gene Gauntier in two days.

Women were finding their way in the movie business.

1900

One of the first prominent stage actresses to appear in motion pictures, French actress **SARAH BERNHARDT'S** acceptance of film as an entertainment medium legitimizes this new format in the eyes of the public. Her first movie is *Le duel d'Hamlet* in 1900.

1904

What we know today as 20th Century Fox begins when William Fox opens his first movie theater in 1904 in New York City. His movie theaters grow into a movie-making business in 1915 when he establishes the Fox Film Corporation. After the merger of Fox Film Corporation with Twentieth Century in 1935, the company becomes known as 20th Century-Fox.

1907
A founding member of the Essanay Film Manufacturing Company, actor, writer and film director **RUTH STONEHOUSE** performs in comedies and dramas in a silent film era career during which she makes more than 100 films.

FLORENCE TURNER acts in her first movie for Vitagraph Studios in 1907—*How to Cure a Cold*. Known at first only as the "Vitagraph Girl" (no actors are yet identified by name), her name becomes known to the general public in 1910 and she becomes one of the first movie "stars." She starts her own production company (Turner Films) and by 1915 is the top box office star.

"The First Movie Star" and the first film actress whose name is divulged to the public, **FLORENCE LAWRENCE** debuts in 1907 in *Daniel Boone*, among other films that year. She makes almost 300 films over her thirty-year career.

In 1907, **GENE GAUNTIER** writes the screenplay adaptation for *Ben Hur* in two days. She is also an actress, stuntwoman, producer and director. She is credited with playing a critical role in the development of scriptwriting conventions and developing the genre of serials. While at Kalem, Gauntier includes technical language in scenarios that then became something more than the heretofore one-page summaries.

Gauntier says, "It was June 1906 that I literally jumped into the moving pictures, being thrown into a river." Also, "I wrote *Adventures of the Girl Spy*, which embodied all the difficult and dangerous stunts I could conjure up. I played a southern girl disguised as a boy of '61 [1861]. It made a tremendous hit and exhibitors wrote in for more. Thus began the first series made in films. I kept them up for two years until, tired of sprains and bruises and with brains sucked dry of any more adventures for the intrepid young woman, I married her off and ended the [Civil] War. . . . I thought I was finished. But no! The demand for them still came back with one called 'A Hitherto Unrelated Incident of the Girl Spy.' There is always a way in pictures!"

About her stuntwork, she says: "Only youth and a strong constitution could have stood up under it. I was playing in two pictures a week, working in almost every scene, and writing two or three scenarios a week, in the effort to keep up with our production. My screen work was all strenuous, horseback riding for hours each day, water scenes in which I committed suicide or floated on spar in shark-infested waters, climbing trees, coming down on ropes from second-story windows, jumping from roofs or rolling down to be caught in blankets, overturning skills, paddling canoes, a hundred and one 'stunts' thought out to give the action Kalem films demanded. I was terrified at each daring thing I had to do, but for some inexplicable reason I continued to write them. They never seemed so difficult when I was seated before the typewriter in the throes of creating them, but as the moment for performance drew near they assumed unwarranted aspects of terror."

" A 'double' was never even thought of in those days! "

—GENE GAUNTIER

The Kalem Company is founded in 1907 by George Kleine, Samuel Long and Frank J. Marion. Kalem is a blend of the first letters of their last names—K, L, M. After making more than 1500 movies, the company is sold to Vitagraph Studios in 1917.

1907

1908

From *The Film Index* (a trade paper): *Women's chances of making a living here [in the film industry] have been increased by the rise of the cinematograph machine. . . . Many a young actress anxiously awaiting an engagement will agree to this. At the start, when one concern controlled the production of moving pictures in this country, women helpers were not seriously considered in the plans of managers. As a rule when a woman was needed a man donned petticoats and played the part. Even now in a certain class of pictures this is sometimes done, but generally with pretty poor results. Every year there has been an increased demand for women to pose, and indications are that the demand will go increasing, for, instead of one concern in the field, there are now fifteen at least. We have no graded scale of pay, and the woman with a beautiful face gets not more than the plainer woman. Action, not looks, is what recommends a woman for employment with us, and the more experienced the applicant the better chance she has. Ingenues are not popular with managers and novices with no stage experience have not shown at all.*

Actress **LINDA ARVIDSON** performs in her husband D.W. Griffith's debut film *The Adventures of Dollie*.

Actress **FLORA FINCH** appears in her first film *The Helping Hand*, in 1908. She becomes an early comedy star, later forming her own production company. Finch makes the transition to talkies, appearing in her final film in 1939.

1909

Beloved actress **MARY PICKFORD** ("America's Sweetheart" and "The Girl with Curls") is one of the earliest movie stars who is billed under her own name. She appears in 51 movies in 1909. She is the first movie star to own her own film company (Pickford-Fairbanks Studio) and she later helps to found United Artists with D.W. Griffith, Charlie Chaplin and Douglas Fairbanks. Pickford controls the creative output of all of her movies after 1919. She is the first actor, male or female, to become a millionaire. Pickford is one of the 36 founding members of the Academy of Motion Picture Arts and Sciences. She wins the Best Actress Oscar in 1930 for *Coquette*. In 1976, she receives an Honorary Academy Award "In recognition of her unique contributions to the film industry and the development of film as an artistic medium." She says, "I didn't want what happened to Chaplin to happen to me. When he discarded the little tramp, the little tramp turned around and killed him. The little girl made me. I'd already been pigeonholed . . . I could have done more dramatic performances . . . but I was already typed."

When she was sixteen, she said the following to D.W. Griffith, "You must realize I'm an actress and an artist. I've had important parts on the real stage. I must have twenty-five a week guaranteed, and extra when I work extra." She got what she demanded.

> " You may have a fresh start any moment you choose, for this thing that we call 'failure' is not the falling down, but the staying down. "

—MARY PICKFORD

Actress **STELLA ADAMS** appears in many shorts and twelve feature films, primarily during the silent film era. Her first feature film is *In the Sultan's Power* (1909).

Silent film actress **ETHEL CLAYTON'S** thirty-year film career begins with her performance in the 1909 short *Justified*.

Second in popularity as a serial queen to Pearl White (see 1914), **RUTH ROLAND** first appears in film in 1909 in *The Old Soldier's Story*. Hollywood High School's first homegrown movie star, Roland appears in many films and serials, some under the auspices of her own production company. She is not able to make the transition to talkies.

FLORENCE LA BADIE debuts in 1909 in films including the *Politician's Love Story*. She dies of injuries sustained in a car crash at the height of her popularity.

The Thanhouser Company (later the Thanhouser Film Corporation) is founded in 1909 in New York City. It operates until 1920.

A perfect ingénue, actress **VIOLET MERSEREAU** is often cast as a helpless young girl, popular in the films of the time. Debuting in 1908, one of her 1909 films is *The Cricket on the Hearth*.

Silent film actress and an excellent horse-woman who does her own stunts, **EDITH STOREY** signs a movie contract in 1908 with Vitagraph. In 1909, she appears in *Oliver Twist*. She performs in almost 200 movies during her silent film career.

Lillian Gish

1910s

THE SILENT FILM ERA

During the 1910s, experimentation in filmmaking continued in both processes and equipment development. Movies were often shorts, one or two reels. Serials were at their peak of popularity, usually involving beautiful women in trouble. The cliffhanger was developed so that audiences would come back week after week to see if the heroine tied to the railroad track by the villain in the last episode had been saved.

Women virtually controlled the film industry and had more opportunities during the silent film era than at any time since. Women screenwriters outnumbered men ten to one. Many women directors were active in the film industry during this time. Directing was not yet considered "glamorous" and the pay was not high. Filmmaking was fairly casual; budgets and expectations were low. Movies cost about $500 to make.

The most important woman making movies in this period was Lois Weber. She became the highest-paid director of either gender in the silent film era. The first woman to write, direct, produce and star in a movie (seven decades before Barbra Streisand), Weber addressed moral and women's issues of the day including birth control, racial concerns and capital punishment. When she needed a naked statue in her movie and no one else would do it, Weber posed in the nude, spawning moral indignation, free publicity and commercial success for the movie (which earned $3 million at the box office).

Films in this decade included *The Wonderful Wizard of Oz, A Tale of Two Cities* and *The Birth of a Nation*. Like many other films throughout movie history, these films would be made again and again.

Many motion picture companies moved from New Jersey to the Los Angeles area where the workers were non-union, the weather was ideal and the scenery diverse, allowing for filming at nearby locations year-round.

"Hollywood" had found its home.

At the age of 42, **EUGENIE BESSERER** appears as Aunt Em in her first film *The Wonderful Wizard of Oz*. She often is cast as the mother; continuing to appear in silent films and talkies through 1933.

A silent era actress who will appear in hundreds of films, **KATE BRUCE** makes her first movie in 1908 when she is 50 years old. In 1910, she appears in *The Fugitive*. A favorite of D.W. Griffith, she is considered a character actress.

A child actress when she begins her film career in 1910, **BEBE DANIELS** makes the transition to talkies and acts for more than three decades. In 1910, she plays Dorothy in *The Wonderful Wizard of Oz*.

1910

Actress **MARIN SAIS** debuts in 1910. She will continue her career for four decades. Many of the films in which she stars or appears are Westerns. After the transition to talkies, she is often a character actress.

WINIFRED GREENWOOD lands her first movie role in 1910 in *The Wonderful Wizard of Oz*. She plays the role of Momba, which today we know as the Wicked Witch of the West.

The so-called "Madonna of the Screen," actress **ALICE JOYCE** appears in her first film *The Deacon's Daughter* in 1910. She appears in more than 200 films and makes her last movie in 1930.

homas Ince begins his directing career. Known as the "Father of the Western," Ince creates the first major Hollywood studio and develops the assembly-line method of filmmaking.

1911

Actress **LEAH BAIRD** is signed by Vitagraph in 1911. Like many actresses during the silent film era, she later becomes a screenwriter and producer.

One of a trio of acting sisters, actress **NORMA TALMADGE** is one of the greatest film stars of the silent film era. In 1911, she appears in *A Tale of Two Cities* as Mimi—a woman on the way to the guillotine. Talmadge is not able to make the transition to talkies.

After immigrating to the U.S. through Ellis Island in 1905, Swedish-born **ANNA NILSSON** becomes a model and the "most beautiful woman in America." She makes her film debut in 1911 in *Molly Pitcher* and does most of her own stunts.

Silent film actress **DOROTHY PHILLIPS** appears in the first film produced by the company she and her husband found. Unable to make the transition to talkies, she appears mostly in uncredited roles from 1927 forward.

Silent film actress and serial star **ANN LITTLE** appears in her first film in 1911's *The Indian Maiden's Lesson*. She goes on to act in many Westerns, often portraying Native American maidens. In 1925, without providing any reason, she retires from filmmaking while still a popular star.

Silent film actress **MARGUERITE SNOW** appears in her first film in 1911 after accompanying a friend to the studio and being convinced to act in the movie also. Deciding she likes films over the stage, she appears in *The Moth* and *The Buddhist Princess,* among other films, in 1911. She makes serials and features.

The first female Japanese performer to appear in films professionally, actress **TOKUKO NAGAI TAKAGI** has roles in four Hollywood movies for Thanhouser between 1911 and 1914. Anti-Japanese sentiment makes it impossible for her to continue her U.S. film career.

Originally a stage actress, **MABEL TRUNNELLE** is 32 years old when she first appears on the screen. In 1911, she appears in several shorts including *The Battle of Bunker Hill* and *The Star Spangled Banner*. After almost 200 films, her screen career ends in 1923 and she returns to the stage.

1912

Famous Players Company, founded by Adolph Zukor in 1912, releases the first full-length drama. It features Sarah Bernhardt (see 1900) as *Queen Elizabeth*.

> " I suppose that it is still a novelty to see a girl more interested in a mechanical problem than in make-up. "
>
> —FRANCELIA BILLINGTON

Actress **MAE MARSH** gets her big break in D. W. Griffith's *Man's Genesis*. In a fifty-year career, she plays mostly character roles after the advent of talkies. In 1955, she is one of the recipients of the inaugural George Eastman Award presented to recognize individuals for their contributions to the art of film. Other recipients in the inaugural year include Mary Pickford (see 1909), Norma Talmadge (see 1911), Lillian Gish (see 1912), and Gloria Swanson (see 1929).

Actress and crank-turner (camera operator) **FRANCELIA BILLINGTON** is a leading lady in silent films starting in 1912. She is described in *Photoplay* magazine in 1914 as "a brown-haired, gray-eyed, olive-skinned girl of remarkable grace and extreme prettiness standing back of one of the big cameras, turning a crank."

Called "First Lady of the Silent Screen Era" and "First Lady of American Cinema" actress **LILLIAN GISH** (sister of Dorothy Gish—see 1918) is the finest actress of the time. Her first film appearance in an entertainment career that would last 75 years occurs in 1912. In 1971, she receives an Honorary Oscar for superlative artistry and distinguished contribution to the motion picture industry. She is nominated for a Best Supporting Actress Oscar in 1947 for her performance in *Duel in the Sun*. Later in her career, she works to preserve silent films. She is credited with pioneering fundamental film performance techniques and directs one movie.

Gish tells the story of D.W. Griffith's very first close-up (which is of her): "I never had a double or a stand-in. I did it all myself. The blizzard [in *Way Down East*—1920]—I was facing it. The wind on the peninsula was terrible. The snow as it came against my face melted, and on my eyelashes—icicles! And Griffith yelled at the cameraman, 'Billy, Billy get that face!' And he said, 'I will if the oil in the camera hasn't frozen,' and he got that face!"

Griffith said of her: "She is not only the best actress in her profession, but she has the best mind of any woman I have ever met."

1912

Actress **BEVERLY BAYNE** appears in her first films, including *Loan Shark,* in 1912. Later, she is half of one of the first romantic teams in film, paired with her husband Francis X. Bushman.

Probably the first scriptwriter on the staff of a film company, **ANITA LOOS'S** first screenplay, *The New York Hat*, is produced in 1912. It stars Mary Pickford (see 1909) and is directed by D.W. Griffith. She writes the subtitles for Griffith's 1916 epic *Intolerance* and introduces wisecracking to movie subtitles. She later becomes internationally known for her book, *Gentlemen Prefer Blondes*, which becomes a Broadway play and movie. In 1974, at the age of 81, she says: "Helen Hayes, Paulette Goddard, Adele Astaire, we were kids together in New York. I was just a girl who had a writing job. Adele was dancing with her brother. It never occurred to us we'd amount to anything. We were too busy having fun. Well," she giggled, "I'm still doing that."

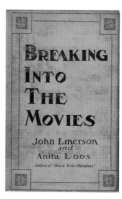

In 1912, the Des Moines (Iowa) *Daily News* announces that writer **GERTRUDE PRICE** (their "moving picture expert") will be writing almost daily columns about the happenings in the new movie picture industry. Her columns appear through 1914.

Actress and producer **HELEN GARDNER** forms her own production company—Helen Gardner Productions—in 1912. She is remembered for the 1912 film *Cleopatra*, one of the first American full-length feature films.

Crank-turner becomes cinematographer: Early moviemaking cameras required the camera operator to turn a crank to advance the film. The nickname for camera operators thus became "crank-turner."

The "Sweetheart of American Movies" before Mary Pickford (see 1909), actress **MABEL TALIAFERRO** begins her movie career in 1912 in *Cinderella*. Cousin of Bessie Barriscale (see 1918), Taliaferro began on the stage at two years old.

Cutter becomes editor: For many years in the film industry, film negatives were actually cut and pasted (or glued) together to make the final film. Thus, early editors were often referred to as cutters. With the advent of digital technology, films no longer need to be physically cut.

> "All I knew was that I wanted to act."

—JEANIE MacPHERSON

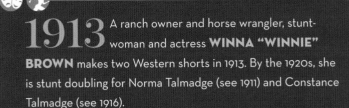

1913 A ranch owner and horse wrangler, stuntwoman and actress **WINNA "WINNIE" BROWN** makes two Western shorts in 1913. By the 1920s, she is stunt doubling for Norma Talmadge (see 1911) and Constance Talmadge (see 1916).

King Vidor, a director, producer and screenwriter in the film industry for almost seventy years, begins his career in 1913. Nominated for five Best Director Oscars from 1929 to 1957, he receives an Honorary Academy Award in 1979 "for his incomparable achievements as a cinematic creator and innovator."

Actress, director and writer **JEANIE MacPHERSON** directs *The Tarantula* in 1913 when she is 27 years old. She serves as Cecil B. DeMille's chief screenwriter from 1915–1945. MacPherson is one of the founding members of the Academy of Motion Picture Arts and Sciences in 1927.

She says, "All I knew was that I wanted to act. Then someone told me about motion pictures, how drama was filmed. I was fascinated. I liked mechanics anyway. I hunted all over New York for a studio—but could not find one. At last a super told me a man named Griffith was doing pictures for the Biograph company. I promptly went there. Mr. Griffith wasn't in. His assistant was. I told him my stage experience. He ignored it, scorned it. . . ." He told me he would see what could be done." She describes her working relationship with DeMille: "I write out every piece of business and almost every gesture and then Mr. DeMille and I will go carefully over it and discuss it from every angle. In addition, a detailed synopsis of the whole thing is prepared, hitting the high spots, for a bird's-eye view of the scenario."

A very popular silent film star in the pre-World War I years, actress **MARGARITA FISCHER** appears in 1913 in *How Men Propose*, written and directed by Lois Weber (see 1916). She appears in *Uncle Tom's Cabin* in both 1913 and 1927.

Actress **ELLA HALL** has the leading role in the 1913 film *Memories*. She appears in 1915 in Lois Weber's (see 1916) film *Jewel*. Her career has faded by the end of the silent film era and she is not able to make the transition to talkies.

Primarily a silent film era actress, **JANE NOVAK** appears in her first film in 1913. She is a highly paid actress during World War I.

1913

A comedienne during the silent film era, actress **BILLIE RHODES** appears in almost 200 films. She begins her career in 1913 acting in the movie *Perils of the Sea* and other shorts.

Action heroine **MARIE WALCAMP**, called "Daredevil of the Movies" and "Adventuress of the Screen," appears in 1913 in *The Werewolf*.

ELEANOR WOODRUFF debuts in Pathé's 1913 movie *The Finger of Fate*. She is cited as one of the highest paid movie stars at Pathé. Woodruff stars with Pearl White (see 1914) in *The Perils of Pauline*.

A popular silent film actress, **MURIEL OSTRICHE** is also the face of Moxie, a carbonated beverage produced in the Northeast and still popular today. Thanhouser sets up a special film division for her, Princess Films. Ostriche makes her last film in 1921.

A star of serials, actress **ARLINE PRETTY** debuts in 1913 in *Love's Justice*. She is unable to make the transition to talkies although she has uncredited bit parts in later movies.

KATHLYN WILLIAMS is one of the most successful of the serial stars of the silent film era. In 1913, she stars in what is considered the first cliffhanger—*The Adventures of Kathlyn*—which inspires women's fashion and hairstyles, a cocktail and a clothing line. Williams says "I really want to direct. Women can direct just as well as men. And in the matter of much of the planning they would be more successful because they often have a keener artistic sense and more of an eye for detail—and so often it is just one tiny thing, five feet of film maybe, that quite spoils a picture, for it is always the little bit of unpleasantness that one remembers . . . women have shown that they can do a great many things that men can—of course, there are some (things) they can't, but then they don't want to—but they have to work hard for all they have achieved."

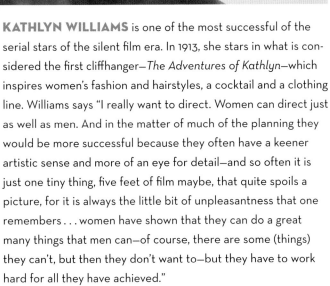

Paramount Pictures, the distribution arm of Famous Players Company (see 1912), is founded. In 1916, Famous Players Company merges with The Jesse L. Lasky Company and becomes Famous Players-Lasky Corporation. When they both merge with Paramount Pictures to form Paramount Famous Lasky Corporation, the predecessor to the Paramount Pictures that we know today is formed.

1913

1914

Director and producer Cecil B. DeMille releases his first film, *The Squaw Man*, in 1914, which is the first feature film shot in Hollywood. He is remembered for his epic productions including *The Ten Commandments*, *Samson and Delilah* and *Cleopatra*, among others.

GRACE KINGSLEY starts in her position as motion-picture columnist and editor at the *Los Angeles Times* in 1914. She continues in that position until 1933, covering the industry's transition from the silent film era to talkies. Kinglsey is credited with introducing Gary Cooper to Hollywood. She continues to write movie reviews until she is 80. Said of her, "She would not touch scandal in any way, no matter how juicy it might be. She reported picture doings only, not bedroom escapades, brawls, separations or desertions. Her idea of picture news was to tell who was doing what, where, when and for how long. This sort of information was vital to freelance actors, cameramen and technicians. It gave them a daily guide to where jobs were open or were about to open. Her section of the *Times* was a sort of trade paper, read by everyone in the business as the first thing to do every morning."

The first film credited to British scriptwriter **MARY MURILLO** is the 1914 movie *A Strand of Blond Hair*, produced by Vitagraph, starring Flora Finch (see 1908). After working for Norma Talmadge (see 1911) Productions, Murillo returns to England in 1923.

Actress and writer **BESSIE LEARN** writes *Her Grandmother's Wedding Dress* and plays the lead in 1914.

Silent film actress **FAY TINCHER** is discovered by D.W. Griffith in 1913. In 1914, she appears in *The Battle of the Sexes*. When it becomes apparent that her talent is in comedy, she moves into that film genre and is touted as "the Female Chaplin". She does not make the transition to talkies.

Comedienne **MINTA DURFEE** co-stars in many films with her husband Roscoe "Fatty" Arbuckle. She appears with Charlie Chaplin in his first Hollywood film *Making a Living* in 1914.

A highly popular star of the silent film era, actress **CLARA KIMBALL YOUNG'S** career blossoms after the release of the 1914 film *My Official Wife*. She is the top box office draw for 1918–1921.

Comedienne **PHYLLIS ALLEN** appears with Charlie Chaplin in three shorts in 1914 during a film career that spans a decade.

Probably the first Asian-American leading actress in the movies, **TSURU AOKI** plays the leading role in a successful and well-critiqued film, *The Wrath of the Gods*. Her last film appearance is in 1960.

A silent film actress second only in popularity to Mary Pickford for a time, **MARGUERITE CLARK** appears in her first films in 1914—*The Crucible* and *Wildflower*.

Actress and screenwriter **MARY FULLER** is a popular film star by 1914. Eight of her screenplays are made into movies.

British-born actress, writer and producer **OLGA PETROVA** makes her U.S. film debut in 1914 in *The Tigress*, directed and produced by Alice Guy-Blaché (see 1896). She writes several scripts. Later, Petrova moves to Broadway and becomes a playwright.

Canadian actress **MINNIE DEVEREAUX** (also known as "Indian Minnie" or "Minnie Ha-Ha") stars alongside Roscoe "Fatty" Arbuckle in the 1914 movie *Fatty and Minnie He-Haw*. She experiences much discrimination and is often typecast due to both her size and her ethnic heritage.

Writer and editor **EVE UNSELL** writes almost 100 films starting in 1914. In 1925, she writes the screenplay and the story for *The Ancient Mariner*.

Actor, director, screenwriter, producer and animal trainer **NELL SHIPMAN** insists her female characters be strong protagonists. She makes history in 1914 when the movie she writes, *Shepherd of the Southern Cross,* becomes the first film shot on location in Australia.

Actress **BESSIE EYTON** appears in over 200 films including *The Spoilers* in 1914.

Bessie Eyton (left) and Kathlyn Williams, in *The Spoilers*

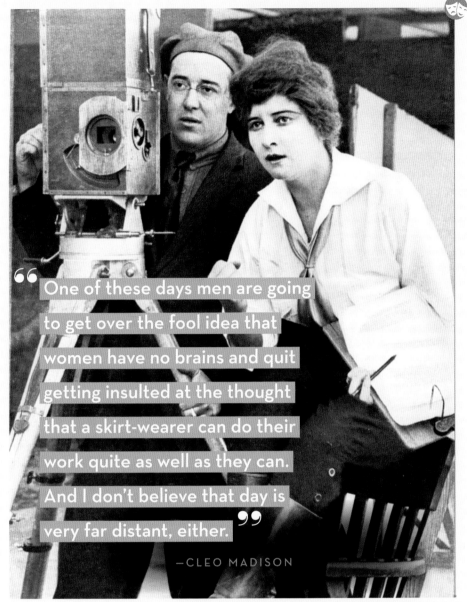

Actress, director, producer and screenwriter **CLEO MADISON** is an early female director during the silent film era. One of the many movies that she makes in 1914 is *The Trey O' Hearts* in which she plays the lead—twin sisters Judith and Rose Trine. Madison said to *Moving Picture World*: "Every play in which women appear needs the feminine touch. Lois Weber's productions are phenomenally successful, partly because her woman creations are true to the spirit of womanhood. I believe in doing most of the work before the camera is called into action. It should never be necessary, except in the case of accident, to retake a scene."

Asked if she had been scared on her first day of directing, she replied, "Why should I be? I had seen men with less brains than I have getting away with it, and so I knew that I could direct if they'd give me the opportunity."

> "One of these days men are going to get over the fool idea that women have no brains and quit getting insulted at the thought that a skirt-wearer can do their work quite as well as they can. And I don't believe that day is very far distant, either."
>
> —CLEO MADISON

1914

LOUELLA PARSONS writes a movie gossip column and is one of the first columnists to cover Hollywood, starting in 1914. Earlier, Parsons begins her film career as a story editor and appears in several films. After she is hired by William Randolph Hearst, her column appears worldwide in 400 newspapers. She founds the Hollywood Press Club and her feud with columnist Hedda Hopper (see 1938) is the stuff of legends. Her daughter, Harriet Parsons (see 1948) becomes a producer.

> "I created my own standard of fun."
> —MABEL NORMAND

Screenwriter, actress, director and producer **MABEL NORMAND** is the "Queen of Comedy" in the silent film era. Normand has her own movie studio and production company and appears in many successful films with Charlie Chaplin and Roscoe "Fatty" Arbuckle. She often writes and directs or co-writes and co-directs the Chaplin films. Normand mentors Chaplin as well and many of The Tramp's traits are borrowed from her. The 1914 film *Mabel's Strange Predicament* is the first film where Chaplin plays the Tramp and she is the leading lady. Normand said "Since all previous laughs had been achieved through the spoken word, and in our early days, through slapstick hokey, I had to cleave a path of laughter through the wilderness of industry's ignorance and inexperience. I created my own standard of fun. [I simply let] spontaneity and my inborn sense of what is mirth-provoking guide me, for no director ever taught me a thing . . . I had no precedent, nothing to imitate."

The queen of the railroad serials along with Pearl White (see 1914), **HELEN HOLMES** acts in numerous movies during the silent film era, most notably *The Hazards of Helen* (serial) in 1914. In her many action-centered roles, Holmes does her own stunts. After her retirement from acting, she and her husband serve as Hollywood animal trainers.

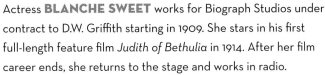

Actress **BLANCHE SWEET** works for Biograph Studios under contract to D.W. Griffith starting in 1909. She stars in his first full-length feature film *Judith of Bethulia* in 1914. After her film career ends, she returns to the stage and works in radio.

MILDRED HARRIS appears in *The Magic Cloak of Oz*. A veteran actress who begins her film career at age 11, she is a leading lady in silent films throughout the 1920s, but is not able to make the transition to talkies. She is also remembered as the first wife of Charlie Chaplin.

The "Queen of the Serials," actress **PEARL WHITE** is known for doing her own stunts. After her debut in 1910, she hits her stride in 1914 with the serial *The Perils of Pauline*. A number of other serials follow including *The Exploits of Elaine*, *The Romance of Elaine*, *The Lightning Raider* and *Plunder*. In the various serials, her stunts include flying airplanes, racing cars and swimming across rivers.

Cecil B. DeMille directs the first feature-length film, *The Squaw Man*, in 1914. Known for producing many epic movies, DeMille helps Paramount Pictures become a successful studio. Jeanie MacPherson (see 1913) is his main writer and Anne Bauchens (see 1941), his editor. As reported by Bison Archives: Bauchens is "the only film editor up until that time written into a director's contract. DeMille wouldn't make a move without these indispensable women by his side."

1914-5

PRINCESS RED WING has the leading actress role in 1914 in *The Squaw Man*, written by Beulah Marie Dix (see 1917). The first well-known Native American star, Red Wing began appearing in short films in 1908.

Credited with originating the phrase "the butler did it," screenwriter and author **MARY ROBERTS RINEHART** writes screenplays for both silent films and talkies. The first films using her stories are released in 1914.

Writer and director **MARGUERITE BERTSCH** is said to be one of the most powerful women working at Vitagraph by 1914. Among the scripts she writes in 1914 is *A Florida Enchantment*. After demonstrating success as a scriptwriter, she has the opportunity to direct. Bertsch also writes a book titled *How to Write for Moving Pictures: A Manual of Instruction and Information* (1917) which is used by many scenario writers and screenwriters.

1915 The Sennett Bathing Beauties are first selected in 1915 and begin to appear in movies and at promotional events. These actresses appear in bathing suits although they are not individually featured or named. The program continues through 1928.

> "You know, I never wrote a picture that I did not mentally direct. Every situation was as clear in my mind as though the film was already photographed."
>
> —MARGUERITE BERTSCH

Actress **LOTTIE PICKFORD**, sister of Mary Pickford (see 1909), gives her best-known performance in the 1915 film *The Diamond from the Sky*. Her silent-film career, begun in 1909, will last almost twenty years.

One of the first female professional camerawomen, **KATHERINE BLEECKER** owns her camera equipment and contributes to prison reform by filming conditions at prisons including Sing Sing. She later makes society films and then manages a theater during World War I.

Screenwriter and actress
OUIDA BERGERE
begins writing scenarios
for movies in 1915.

An opera singer and film actress **GERALDINE FARRAR** appears in her first movie, *Carmen*, in 1915.

One of the first actresses from Broadway to work in Hollywood, **MARY ALDEN** plays her most popular role in the movie *The Birth of a Nation*. She also appears in *Intolerance* in 1916. She makes the transition to talkies and appears in movies through the early 1930s.

Having first appeared in films in 1912, actress **MIRIAM COOPER** is in the cast of the 1915 film *The Birth of a Nation*.

Actress **JOSEPHINE CROWELL** is most prominently remembered for her role as the mother in *The Birth of a Nation*.

1915

Actress **PAULINE FREDERICK** debuts in *The Eternal City* in 1915. Between 1915–1917, she appears in almost twenty feature films.

One of the silent era's best character actresses, **MAUDE GEORGE** debuts in 1915. She writes scenarios for two movies in 1917.

JUANITA HANSEN appears in six films in 1915 working for D.W. Griffith. Later, she appears in serials.

A top-billed star, actress **DOROTHY DALTON** plays a vamp in the 1915 film *The Disciple*. Her vamp is viewed as untraditional and it is said about her "Not because she wanted people to think she was a full-fledged shatterer of hearts before the camera did she make pulses beat hard and fast, but because she couldn't help it." Dalton herself said "I guess I just must have been born that way."

Director, writer and producer D.W. Griffith is credited with pioneering many modern filmmaking techniques. Two of his blockbuster movies are *The Birth of a Nation* in 1915 and *Intolerance* in 1916. He makes approximately 500 movies over his career and helps found the Academy of Motion Picture Arts and Sciences.

Actress and writer **SEENA OWEN** debuts in 1915 in the movie *A Yankee from the West*. She appears in *Intolerance* in 1916 and other movies until the advent of talkies. Unable to make the transition to talkies as an actress, she works as a screenwriter. Her scripts include two movies starring actress Dorothy Lamour (see 1940). One of those scripts is co-written by Owen with her sister Lillie Hayward (see 1943).

 Silent era actress **FANNIE WARD** makes her film debut in 1915 in Cecil B. DeMille's *The Cheat*. Seemingly young in appearance, she is called "The Youth Girl." After her retirement from the film industry, she opens a beauty shop in Paris called "The Fountain of Youth."

 An actress who makes the transition from silent films to talkies, **GERTRUDE ASTOR** becomes a contract actor for Universal after appearing in a short for Biograph, released in 1915. She is believed to be the first actress to sign a contract with Universal. She acts in movies through the 1960s.

 Actress and director **CAMILLE ASTOR** serves as uncredited assistant director for the 1915 movie *Chimmie Fadden Out West* in which she also acts and Jeanie MacPherson (see 1913) writes.

HOLLYWOOD: *Her Story* 51

Considered the first American professional stuntwoman, horsewoman
and actress **HELEN GIBSON**
performs many stunts for the
Hazards of Helen (starring Helen
Holmes—see 1914) and acts in two
episodes when the star is taken ill.
The serial is renamed *Helen* after
Helen Holmes leaves and stars
Helen Gibson. Gibson appears in
her last movie in 1961.

Mr. and Mrs. Sidney Drew

Actress, screenwriter, director and producer
LUCILLE McVEY is also known as Mrs. Sidney
Drew of the comedy duo Mr. and Mrs. Sidney Drew.
Their first success, in 1915, is *Playing Dead*. The
September 1917 issue of *Photoplay* includes the
following comment: "Just between ourselves, I give
Mrs. Drew 75 percent of the credit for the concep-
tion of the Drew comedies. That is, she is the team
member who selects an idea and builds on it. Mr.
Drew has the actor's discernment to understand
her mental processes and to perfect it on the
screen. To him goes the credit for putting the
idea over."

Written by historian Robert Grau in 1915: *In no line of endeavor has a woman made so emphatic an impress than in the amazing film industry, which has created in its infant stage a new and compelling art wherein the gentler sex is now so active a factor that one may not name a single vocation in either the artistic or business side of its progress in which women are not conspicuously engaged. In the theaters, in the studios and even in the exchanges where film productions are marketed and released to exhibitors, the fair sex is represented as in no other calling to which women have harkened in the early years of the twentieth century.*

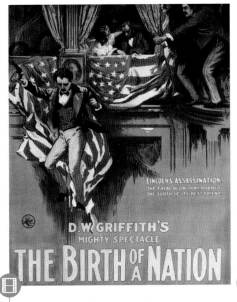

An editor at the Biograph Company, **ROSE SMITH** is known for her work on D.W. Griffith's 1915 film *The Birth of a Nation*. Smith serves as chief editor on Griffith's 1916 *Intolerance*, an epic that costs $400,000, a staggering sum at the time. She edits her last film in 1934.

A leading lady during the silent film era and later a character actress, **MYRTLE STEDMAN** appears in the 1915 film *Hypocrites*, directed by Lois Weber (see 1916). Stedman appears in more than 200 films during her career.

Actress **EDNA PURVIANCE** debuts in 1915 in *A Night Out*. She appears in more than 33 Chaplin films, often as his leading lady.

1916

Primarily a silent film era actress, **ALMA RUBENS** has a bit part in the 1915 film *The Birth of a Nation* before her appearance in the 1916 *Half Breed* makes her a star. Although she makes the transition to talkies, she tragically dies at a young age.

Alma Rubens and John Gilbert in *The Masks of the Devil*,

A film producer and journalist, **MABEL "MIMI" CONDON BIRDWELL** owns the Mabel Condon Film Exchange. She writes articles about filmmaking, thus educating the public of this new technology, and interviews top stars. In 1916, she writes the story for *The Man Who Would Not Die*. A talent agent, she gives Boris Karloff his start. She retires after her marriage in 1923.

Director, writer and producer **JULIA CRAWFORD IVERS** is the General Manager of Bosworth Studios in 1915. A print of the 1916 film *A Son of Erin*, which she writes and directs, is now housed at the Library of Congress.

The "Kodak Girl," who is the "most photographed girl in the world," actress **EDITH JOHNSON** joins Universal in 1916 before moving to Vitagraph two years later.

An actress who makes the transition from silent films to talkies, **MARY MacLAREN** appears in more than 130 films during her over thirty-year career. She is known for her appearance in *Shoes* in 1916.

One of three sisters who find fame as silent film stars (see Viola Dana—1917 and Shirley Mason—1917), actress **EDNA FLUGRATH** (pictured center) appears in the 1916 film *De Voortrekkers*.

HOLLYWOOD: *Her Story* 54

> 66 I'll never be convinced that the general public does not want serious entertainment rather than frivolous. . . . If I can sow a few helpful seeds in my pictures, which will appeal to some man or woman in my audience, I shall be satisfied. That is why I want to go on with this work, I want to present my ideas and again, that is the reason I cannot be happy to direct someone else's story— that would be only half a creation. 99
>
> —LOIS WEBER

The most important female director of silent films as well as the first American female director, **LOIS WEBER** is the second person to experiment with synchronizing sound to film action—the first being Alice Guy-Blaché (see 1896). Weber has her own production company and is the first woman to direct a full-length feature film in the U.S. In 1916, she is the highest paid director in the world. Weber becomes the first and only woman asked to become a member of the Motion Picture Directors Association (precursor to the Directors Guild of America). She is a significant mentor to other women in the film industry. In addition to directing and producing, Weber acts and writes screenplays. As one encyclopedia states: *Not only was she . . . the most important female director the American film industry has known, but unlike many of her colleagues up to the present, her work was regarded in its day as equal to, if not a little better than that of most male directors. She was a committed filmmaker in an era when commitment was virtually unknown.*

Weber says "Now I can preach to my heart's content. And with the opportunity to write the play, act the leading roles and direct the entire production, if my message fails to reach someone, I can blame only myself.

"The public as a whole is sentimental and . . . unless you give them what they want you're not going to make any money. And let those who set themselves up as idealists chatter as much as they please about their art, the commercial side cannot be neglected. We're all in business to make money. You can pander to the whim of the moment; or you can build with an eye to the future. Personally, I prefer the latter."

1916

Actress **NELLIE GRANT** appears in *The Innocence of Ruth* in 1916. Later, she becomes a studio manager.

The first major child film star, **BABY MARIE (MARIE OSBORNE YEATS)** debuts in 1915 and appears in her best remembered movie, *Little Mary Sunshine,* in 1916. After she retires from acting in 1950, she becomes a costume designer and later a costume supervisor.

Actress, director and producer **ALLA NAZIMOVA** makes her screen debut in 1916 in *War Brides.* She later produces and writes movies in which she plays the leading role. The god-mother of future First Lady Nancy Reagan, she coins the term "sewing circle" as code for lesbian or bisexual actresses.

At age 21, **MARION WONG** (above left) establishes the Mandarin Film Company, the only Chinese production company in the industry. She writes, produces, acts in and directs its first feature film, *The Curse of Quon Gwon,* and designs the costumes and the scenery.

 Writer and editor **HETTIE GREY BAKER** edits her first film for Fox Film Corporation in 1916, *A Daughter of the Gods*. It is Hollywood's first film with a million dollar budget. Of her role, she says "[it] was the first time that a woman's name ever appeared on the screen as an editor." She describes her role as production editor at Fox saying, "I take all the parts of the film which the film editors have considered unnecessary or unsatisfactory and have those run off for me on the screen. I pick a piece here and insert it there, clip a part from here and substitute it for another. Finally, I have the whole film run off as I have revised it. Then, if it looks almost censor-proof and yet retains enough interest and spice to hold the public, I let it go." By 1938, she is a studio executive serving as censor representative for 20th Century Fox. Her opinion of censorship is expressed as "If it [a film] is so fixed that it *will* pass the censors—Lord help the people. It is usually so slow and stale that a church deacon would have a hard time not imagining that he is listening to the minister's sermon, and you find him sound asleep—mouth open and all." In 1914, she is a co-founder of what would become the Screen Writers Guild.

One of a trio of acting sisters, **CONSTANCE TALMADGE** appears in her first major role in the movie *Intolerance*, for which she does her own stunts. Her friend, screenwriter Anita Loos (see 1912), writes many screenplays for her.

A real-life baroness, Danish ballerina and silent film actress, **VALDA VALKYRIEN**, who made her U.S. debut in 1914, appears in the 1916 film *Hidden Valley*.

Hollywood's first Latina actress, **MYRTLE GONZALEZ** stars in silent era films from 1913 to 1917. In 1916, she appears in *Her Great Part*.

Actress, director and screenwriter **MARGERY WILSON** is best remembered as Brown Eyes in D.W. Griffith's 1916 movie *Intolerance*. Wilson has starring roles in other movies and directs movies in the early 1920s. She describes her first experience as a director shooting at the Robert Brunton Studios in Hollywood: "When I went over to Mr. Brunton, who had handled all the sets, etc. for Thomas Ince. . . and that was where I met him—he had always been very friendly to me. . . he tried to discourage me from producing and directing. He said it would be bedlam, and that the actors and even the grips would just do as they pleased. But when he saw that he couldn't move me, he began to cooperate. He fixed up existing sets for my story and made it all possible, still shaking his head and saying I would lose my shirt, break my heart, and my health, etc.

"The first day on the set I called everybody together and told them the story and what I expected of each of them. I didn't know Mr. Brunton was eavesdropping. I told my group that if they had suggestions of any kind to give them to me *now* for after we started shooting I wanted not a single interruption. Everything went like clockwork—everybody was so interested we even forgot about lunch—but when we did go over to the commissary to eat, Mr. Brunton came over to the table and silently extended his hand, which I shook gravely.

"When the picture [*That Something*] was finished, I took it over and ran it for Mr. [Frank] Woods, who had given me my first chance in Hollywood and was now at Paramount. When the lights came up, he said 'It's excellent. Who directed it for you, Margery?' In surprise, I said, 'Why, I did. Didn't you see the title—directed by Margery Wilson?' 'Yes, I saw that,' he said. 'But Margery, no woman directed that picture. No woman has that much clarity of mind. That is a man's job.'

"Tears of rage welled into my eyes, I remembered the other times that sound thinking had been termed 'a man's thinking.' And there would be repetitions in the future. Years later, after a speech before the Rotary Club, I went down in the elevator with Ham Beal, the great publicity man, and he asked me, 'Who wrote your speech, Margery?' I said, 'Nobody, I spoke extemporaneously. I plotted it out a little.' He patted my shoulder, 'All right, dear, have it your way—but no woman on earth wrote that speech. Women don't think that way.'"

1916

Camera operator **MARGERY ORDWAY** emerges from obscurity when pictured in *Photoplay* magazine in 1916 during the filming of the movie *Her Father's Son*. Her picture in *Photoplay* is titled "This is the new fall style in camera 'men'" and the caption below the picture reads "Meaning, the style you could fall for. Nor is this a masquerade get-up. Margery Ordway, regular, professional, licensed, union crank-turner at Camp Morosco, has gone into camera work as nonchalantly as other girls take up stenography, nursing, husband-stalking."

Australian actress **ANNETTE KELLERMAN** is the first swimmer to become a movie star and one of the first women to appear nude in a movie. Kellerman's nude scene is in 1916 in *A Daughter of the Gods*. A prize-winning swimmer in her native country, she popularizes the one-piece bathing suit and has her own fashion line of swimwear, performs her own stunts and often designs and makes her own costumes.

R obert Brunton is a Scottish film producer and production designer who works for a time in Hollywood and runs a studio.

Producer and director **MADAME E. TOUSSAINT WELCOME**, together with her husband, make a film in 1916 titled *Doing Their Bit*, featuring the participation of African-American soldiers in U.S. military efforts.

Actress, writer and producer **MARION DAVIES** appears as an actress in the film *Runaway Romany* for which she writes the script and titles. She makes films until 1937, under the sponsorship of William Randolph Hearst, with whom she has a decades-long affair.

Silent era actress **VIOLA DANA** (sister of Shirley Mason (see 1917) and Edna Flugrath (see 1916)) performs in over 100 films including *The Girl Without a Soul* and *Blue Jeans*, both in 1917. She begins her career with Edison in New York City and becomes a star. Dana then moves to California to escape the flu pandemic and acts through the 1920s. One of her last films is Frank Capra's first film for Columbia Pictures, *That Certain Thing* (1928).

Silent film actress **MARJORIE DAW** makes several movies in 1917 and is one of Hollywood's golden people until the advent of talkies. She is a leading lady in films with Douglas Fairbanks including *The Knickerbocker Buckaroo* (1918) and *His Majesty the American* (1919).

1917

1917

One of the top ten serial queens of the silent era, actress **NEVA GERBER** makes her film debut for Kalem in 1912 and appears in her first serial in 1917. She makes many adventures and serials with actor and director Ben Wilson. Her career stalls after his death in 1930.

Film critic **DELIGHT EVANS** begins working at *Photoplay* magazine in late 1917. In 1924, she joins *Screenland* to write movie reviews which are described as the "most widely read and quoted screen criticisms." She becomes editor, a position that she holds until she leaves *Screenland* in 1948.

Actress **OLIVE THOMAS** who made her film debut in 1916, makes four films in 1917 including *A Girl Like That*. Prior to her tragic death, she makes a total of twenty films over four years.

Phil Dunham, Alice Howell, and Frank Coleman

Actress **ALICE HOWELL** displays her comic talents and timing in silent film and has her own production unit for the L-Ko Komedy Company. In 1917, she tells the *New Jersey Tribune*, "The days are not so far in retrospection when I was glad to do any kind of work and I have not forgotten how it feels to stand in line waiting for a chance to do extra work. I wanted the money so badly that I offered to wear any eccentric sort of make-up or take any chances so long as there was a pay check at the end of the week. I often felt then like the down-trodden, put upon, much abused 'slavies' that I struggle to portray humorously today. Most of my scenes are broad farce, but when I get the opportunity I try to register faithfully the character of such a girl."

A writer with over 100 credits over a thirty-five year career, **ELIZABETH (BETTY) BURBRIDGE** begins her career during the silent film era with shorts and stories in 1917. She transitions to talkies and later writes Westerns for television.

> I read pulp Westerns until I was bored to tears. But that's how I learned the story racket—that and talking to the movie cowboys on the set. When I began doing these things, I'd take my plots from New York state plays that I had seen. I'd simply change the setting to the wide-open spaces, put the characters on horses, work in a couple of chases with a sheriff and a posse—and there would be a screen story.

—ELIZABETH (BETTY) BURBRIDGE

Francis X Bushman, Warner Oland, Grace Darmond in *The Marriage Clause*

A silent film era actress **GRACE DARMOND** stars in the 1917 movie *The Gulf Between*, the first Technicolor film.

The U.S. enters World War I. Employment opportunities for women expand significantly as so many men leave to support the war effort.

1917

Often called "Mother" Warrenton, actress and director **LULE WARRENTON** is at one time the only woman in the world to have her own studio. An advocate for the young women coming to Hollywood to find their fortune, she works to establish housing which leads to the Hollywood Studio Club. She acts for ten years, and directs during the years of 1916–1917, including the 1917 film *A Bit o' Heaven*.

HELENA SMITH DAYTON is one of the first female animators experimenting with stop motion and clay animation. The first public screening of her film *Romeo and Juliet* using claymation is in 1917. A review in *The Moving Picture World* says, "This mere lump of clay under her magic touch takes on the responsibilities of life, and love and sorrow which the play requires, and finally grasps in desperation the dagger with which it ends its sorry life, falling in tragic fashion over the already lifeless body of its Romeo."

One of the great beauties of the silent screen era, actress **VOLA VALE** stars in *Each To His Kind* alongside actor Sessue Hayakawa.

Writer, director, producer and actress **GRACE CUNARD** is a serial queen during the silent screen era. The 1917 short *Unmasked* which is a Francis Ford/Grace Cunard production is stored in the National Film Registry (see 1988). She and Francis Ford are credited with what today we call cliffhangers; audiences would come back week after week to see what happened to the heroine.

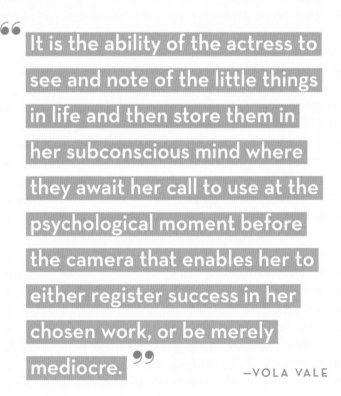

> " It is the ability of the actress to see and note of the little things in life and then store them in her subconscious mind where they await her call to use at the psychological moment before the camera that enables her to either register success in her chosen work, or be merely mediocre. "
>
> —VOLA VALE

1917

One of the most popular actresses of the silent film era, **THEDA BARA** becomes one of the first sex symbols. Denoted as a femme fatale, her nickname becomes "The Vamp." Her 1917 film *Cleopatra* is one of her biggest hits. Bara has been featured on a U.S. postage stamp.

The top silent screen comedienne **LOUISE FAZENDA** appears in hundreds of films including *Maggie's First False Step* in 1917.

A silent film era actress who makes the transition to talkies, **LEATRICE JOY** will be credited with starting the bobbed hair fashion trend during the 1920s. In 1917, she appears in the Mary Pickford (see 1909) film *The Pride of the Clan*.

Silent era film actress **SHIRLEY MASON,** who makes her film debut in 1911, is cast in thirteen movies in 1917 including *The Awakening of Ruth*. She is one of a trio of acting sisters (see Edna Flugrath (1916) and Viola Dana (1917)).

An actress whose career spans six decades **MADGE KENNEDY** begins making movies for Goldwyn in 1917. She is a very popular star during the 1920s.

PRISCILLA DEAN, who makes her stage debut at four and her screen debut at fourteen, becomes famous after her appearance in the 1917 movie *The Gray Ghost*. Signed by Universal Pictures, she makes films for them for two decades, but is unable to make the transition to talkies.

Actress **CLAIRE DU BREY** appears in hundreds of films over four decades. Her 1917 films include *Anything Once*. Although she makes the transition to talkies, most of her roles after the advent of the sound era are small ones. Her final films are in the late 1950s.

Camera operator **DOROTHY DUNN** is one of three known women working in that field in 1917. She gives up acting to become a woman staff photographer.

1917

Actress **RUTH CLIFFORD** becomes a star after appearing in *A Kentucky Cinderella* in 1917. Later she is the voice for Minnie Mouse and Daisy Duck.

> "When the women directed the films, the other directors, the men were very cooperative. And the actors didn't resent it at all because a woman was directing. They took direction just the same as if it were a man directing. Everyone cooperated. It was like a big happy family at the studio—the same players were there, the same directors, and the same women directors."
>
> —RUTH CLIFFORD

Actress and ballroom dancer **IRENE CASTLE** appears in silent era films including *Patria* in 1917. She is a fashion icon and helps popularize the bobbed haircut. The story of her life with her husband Vernon is made into a movie starring Fred Astaire and Ginger Rogers (see 1941) in 1939 titled *The Story of Vernon and Irene Castle*. She serves as an advisor to the film.

A silent film era actress, **FLORENCE VIDOR** makes her film debut in 1916. Her performance as Mimi in the 1917 film *A Tale of Two Cities* vaults her to leading lady status. She is not able to make the transition to talkies.

Author and screenwriter **BEULAH MARIE DIX** writes her first scripts in 1917. During a career that spans the silent film era and talkies, she writes more than fifty scripts. She says, "One learned quite quickly what could and couldn't be done with a camera. . . .It was

all very informal in those early days. Anybody on the set did anything he or she was called upon to do. I've walked on as an extra, I've tended lights and anybody not doing anything else wrote down the director's notes on the script. I also spent a good deal of time in the cutting room."

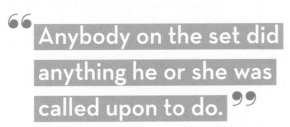

> **Anybody on the set did anything he or she was called upon to do.**
>
> —BEULAH MARIE DIX

A popular actress during World War I, **MABEL BALLIN** signs to make her first film in 1917. She enters the film industry to earn money for the family as her husband is having little success with his painting efforts. Her popularity wanes after World War I and she retires from film-making in 1925.

In addition to starring in over thirty films, actress and director **ELSIE JANE WILSON** begins her solo directing career in 1917 and produces a number of films in that year. She continues to direct until 1919, primarily films that have what is viewed as "female and children" themes.

1917-8

Writer and director **IDA MAY PARK** is one of Universal's most important female directors during the silent film era. In 1917, Park directs her first solo film *The Flashlight*.

Hired as a writer in 1909, Park writes 50 films during her career of which she says, "It was because directing seemed so unsuited to a woman that I refused the first company offered me. I don't know why I looked at it that way, either. A woman can bring to this work splendid enthusiasm and imagination; a natural love of detail and an intuitive knowledge of character. All of these are supposed to be feminine traits, and yet they are all necessary to the successful director. Of course, in order to put on a picture, a woman must have broadness of viewpoint, a sense of humor and firmness of character—there are times when every director must be something of a martinet—but these characteristics are necessary to balance the others.

"It has been said that a woman worries over loves, and works for her convictions exactly as though they were her children. Consequently, her greatest danger is in taking them and herself too seriously. . . . Directing is a recreation to me, and I want my people to do good work because of their regard for me and not because I browbeat them into it. I believe in choosing distinct types and then seeing that the actor puts his own personality into his parts, instead of making every part in a picture reflect my personality."

1918 **HELEN KELLER** establishes a production company to make a movie about her life, titled *Deliverance*. *Deliverance* is preserved at the Library of Congress. In 1955, she is the inspiration for the Oscar-winning Best Feature Length Documentary titled *Helen Keller in Her Story* (originally titled *The Unconquered*). Keller has been featured on a U.S. postage stamp and has been inducted into the National Women's Hall of Fame.

Writer and director **RUTH ANN BALDWIN,** who directed a number of silent films in the 1910s, writes twelve screenplays in 1917.

A stage actress who becomes a film actress, **BESSIE BARRISCALE** films *The Heart of Rachel* in 1918. She is a major star throughout the 1910s and sets up her own production company.

A silent film actress who appears in more than 100 films, **EILEEN SEDGWICK'S** big break comes in 1918 when the star of *Lure of the Circus* becomes sick and Sedgwick acts in this serial instead. Sedgwick performs in many more serials until the advent of talkies.

A leading lady during the silent film era, **ANITA STEWART** also produces. Her first production, in which she also acts, is the 1918 film *Virtuous Wives*.

1918

Silent film actress **DOROTHY DEVORE** specializes in comedy roles such as she plays in the 1918 movie *Know Thy Wife*. A talented comedienne, she is named a WAMPAS Baby Star (see 1922) in 1923. She retires from the film industry in 1930 unable to make the transition to talkies.

A silent film actress who makes the transition to talkies, **ROSEMARY THEBY'S** career-defining movie is the D.W. Griffith film *The Great Love*. She makes almost 250 films during her thirty-year career.

Actress **DOROTHY GISH** (sister of Lillian Gish, see 1912) appears in the first of her 100 films in 1912. A major movie star of the silent film era, Gish appears in *Hearts of the World* in 1918. Her film career will span 50 years.

An author of books for children and a film producer, **MADELINE BRANDEIS** writes and directs the film *A Star Prince*, which is released in 1920 as *Twinkle, Twinkle Little Star*. She founds The Little Players' Film Company which features casts comprised primarily of children.

A former child star, actress **PAULINE CURLEY** performs in several films in 1918 including *Bound in Morocco*. Her movie career lasts 16 years and she leaves the film industry shortly after the advent of talkies.

A silent film actress and leading lady, **LILA LEE,** nicknamed "Cuddles," debuts at age seventeen in 1918 in *The Cruise of the Make-Believes*. She is named a WAMPAS Baby Star (see 1922) in the inaugural class of 1922 and is a leading lady through the silent film era. She makes the transition to talkies and is able to maintain her leading lady status through 1930, when ill health takes its toll. She appears in small roles thereafter.

1918

Milburn Morante and Gale Henry
in *No Babies Allowed.*

"The Elongated Comedienne," **GALE HENRY,** appears in hundreds of films during the silent film era. She is believed to be the model for Olive Oyl of the *Popeye* comic strip. In 1918, she starts her own production to make two-reel comedies. Later, she and her husband train dogs, including Skippy who plays Asta in *The Thin Man*.

Screenwriter **JUNE MATHIS** is the first female executive at Metro/MGM and the highest paid executive in Hollywood. She is remembered for discovering Rudolph Valentino and writing such well-known movies as *The Four Horsemen of the Apocalypse* (1921) and *Blood and Sand* (1922). In 1926, she is said to be the third most powerful woman in Hollywood after Mary Pickford (see 1909) and Norma Talmadge (see 1911). She writes more than 100 movies.

Mary Pickford, Charlie Chaplin, Douglas Fairbanks, and D.W. Griffith form Universal Artists Corporation, an independent film studio. "The company built by the stars" later becomes part of Metro-Goldwyn-Mayer (see 1924).

1919 Actress **FAIRE BINNEY** (sister of Constance Binney—see 1920) is a popular film flapper who appears in *Open Your Eyes* in 1919.

A vaudeville and stage actress, **KATHLEEN CLIFFORD** turns to film and appears in silent films including the 1919 film *When the Clouds Roll By*. She is a leading lady opposite Douglas Fairbanks and others. Her last silent film is made in 1928 and she appears in one talkie in 1932.

Silent film actress **VIVIAN MARTIN,** who makes her film debut in 1914, signs with the Famous Players Film Company and makes four films in 1919. Later, she has her own production company and distributes her films through Goldwyn. Some of the early movies in which she appears are in the collection at the Library of Congress.

One of the leading vamps in the silent film industry, **VIRGINIA PEARSON** acts in and produces *The Bishop's Emeralds* in 1919.

A Sennett Bathing Beauty (see 1915), actress **MARIE PREVOST** debuts in 1916. She appears in over 100 films in her career, including the 1919 film *Yankee Doodle in Berlin.*

PAULINE STARKE, the "Glad-Sad Girl," appears as a lead in the *Eyes of Youth* and other films. An actress who premieres in a bit role in the 1916 film *Intolerance,* she is selected as one of the first WAMPAS Baby Stars (see 1922), and will go on to become a prominent actress.

A silent film actress who makes the transition to talkies, **BETTY COMPSON** is also a film producer. Her breakout performance in 1919 in *The Miracle Man* launches her career. She is nominated for a Best Actress Oscar in 1930 for her role in *The Barker.*

A silent film actress who debuts in 1911, **DOLORES CASSINELLI** appears in *The Virtuous Model* in 1919. Called "The Cameo Girl of the Movies," as she has roles in 69 films between 1911 and 1925, she appears in several World War I dramas and retires from the industry in 1925.

Actress **MARY MILES MINTER,** a teenager, appears to acclaim as Anne Shirley in *Anne of Green Gables.*

An actress with over 200 credits, **ZASU PITTS** begins in the silent film era and makes the transition to talkies. Discovered by Francis Marion (see 1931), Pitts first appears in *The Little Princess,* a film starring Mary Pickford (see 1909). Her first lead performance is in King Vidor's 1919 movie *Better Times.* Her maxim for life is, "If you believe it, it can be so." She has been featured on a U.S. postage stamp.

The American Society of Cinematographers is founded. It will admit its first woman member in 1980, Brianne Murphy (see 1982).

Actress, writer, director and costume designer **PAULA BLACKTON** (pictured right) writes, directs and acts in the 1919 movie *The Littlest Scout*. The movies she writes and directs generally feature her children and are produced by her husband.

Actress **HELEN JEROME EDDY** stars in the 1919 movie *The Turn in the Road* which is King Vidor's first full-length feature. Eddy makes the transition to talkies but becomes a real estate agent after a pay dispute.

A founding member of the Screen Writers Guild in 1933, screenwriter **ADELE BUFFINGTON** will write more than 100 films and transition successfully from silent films to talkies. She sells her first script, *L'Apache*, in 1919, and has a forty-year screenwriting career.

LILLIAN GREENBERGER is the casting director for Universal.

"The time came when I realized that my very power of helping others was limited by the limitations I placed upon myself.

—PAULA BLACKTON

1919

Anna May Wong

1920s

HOLLYWOOD BECOMES BIG BUSINESS

In the mid- to late-1920s, movies became big business. Full-length films could now cost as much as $200,000 apiece to produce and an epic could run to $1 million. Movie production became the most significant industry in Los Angeles. The small, independent film companies, many of them run by women, were put out of business.

Business structures and processes, similar to those that had been adopted in manufacturing industries, were applied in the film industry. Studios were organized into departments (such as story, camera, wardrobe, set, props and publicity) with an assembly-line mentality. Men headed the departments and directed the films. They didn't wear multiple hats like the pioneering men and women before them.

As the structures developed, roles became gendered. Many studios unionized, and the labor unions would not accept women as members. Women film producers all but vanished as did women film editors and camerawomen. Those female editors who did hang on excelled and became the role models for the resurgence of women in the film industry in the second half of the twentieth century. The same was true of screenwriters. At a time when very few women were directing, Dorothy Arzner was able to achieve success as a female director between the late 1920s and the early 1940s.

The films themselves changed dramatically in this decade, too. Sound was introduced. The first "talkie" was released in 1927. This mode of movie production required different skills from actors and actresses than had silent films. Many silent film era stars were not able to bridge the transition.

Instead of writing scripts for a particular actress or actor as they had done previously, studios now created scripts first and then looked for cast members who would play the parts. Audiences had grown beyond the novelty of motion pictures and were looking for actors and actresses with sex appeal and movies with more realistic plots. Stars were looked to as fashion plates and many a fashion trend was started by the clothing or hairstyle of a particular actress.

Another spotlight shown on the stars with the founding of The Academy of Motion Picture Arts and Sciences in 1927. The first Academy Awards, not yet nicknamed Oscar, were presented in 1929 with a ceremony that lasted a mere 15 minutes.

The foundation had been prepared for Hollywood's glamorous golden years.

Character actress **MARY CARR** exemplifies her motherly (later grandmotherly) roles in the 1920 Fox movie *Over the Hill to the Poorhouse*. Her film career lasts for four decades and she has more than 150 credits.

A femme fatale and vamp, actress **LOUISE GLAUM** is well remembered for *Sex* in 1920. She appears in more than 100 movies from 1912 to 1925 and is nicknamed "The Spider Woman" or "The Tiger Woman." She returns to the stage and vaudeville after leaving the film industry.

Known within the black community as "The First Lady of the Screen," **EVELYN PREER** is the first black actress to achieve celebrity and popularity. After debuting in 1919 in the film *The Homesteader*, she appears in 1920 in the film for which she is most well-known *Within Our Gates*.

1920

One of the trio of Talmadge sisters, actress **NATALIE TALMADGE** has a short movie career including a part in *Yes or No* in 1920.

An actress active in the film industry for five years, **CONSTANCE BINNEY** is considered the ideal flapper and appears in *39 East* in 1920.

Actress **CAROL DEMPSTER** appears in her first film in 1915. She acts in a number of D.W. Griffith films including *The Love Flower* in 1920.

"The most beautiful girl in New York City," silent film era actress **MARTHA MANSFIELD** is best known for her performance in *Dr. Jekyll and Mr. Hyde* in 1920.

W ith the ratification of the Nineteenth Amendment, women gain the right to vote.

LOUISE LOWELL is a camerawoman for Fox News in 1920 shooting film for newsreels shown in movie theaters. She is known for specializing in aerial footage.

Six years into her film writing career, **OLGA PRINTZLAU** writes the scenario for *Why Change Your Wife?* (written with Sada Cowan—see 1920). It is directed by Cecil B. DeMille and stars Gloria Swanson (see 1929) and Bebe Daniels (see 1910).

Screenwriter **DOROTHY YOST** has her first script produced in 1920. A writer who bridges the silent film era and talkies, Yost writes four of the Fred Astaire-Ginger Rogers (see 1941) screenplays.

Screenwriter **SADA COWAN'S** first film is produced in 1919. In 1920, *Why Change Your Wife?* (written with Olga Printzlau—see 1920) is released. Cowan works on many films with DeMille over the course of her career and becomes one of his top and highest-paid writers.

Editor and writer **LILLIAN CHESTER** (often called Mrs. George Randolph Chester) writes the titles and screenplay and edits the 1920 silent film *Dead Men Tell No Tales*.

A screenwriter for over twenty years who makes the transition from silent films to talkies, **FRANCES GUIHAN** is the writer for the Ruth Roland (see 1909) movie *Ruth of the Rockies*.

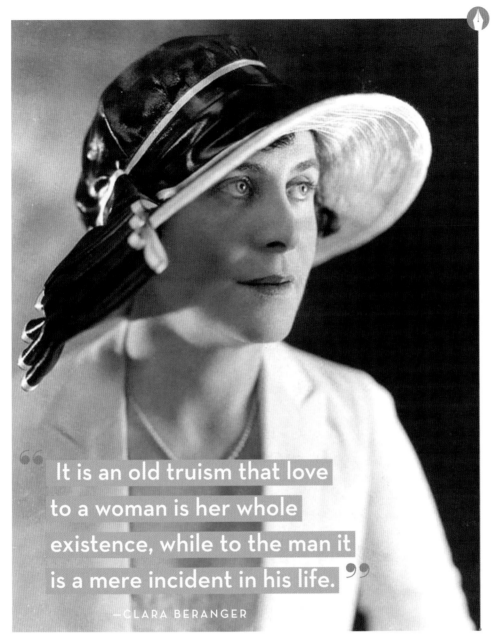

> ❝ It is an old truism that love to a woman is her whole existence, while to the man it is a mere incident in his life. ❞
>
> —CLARA BERANGER

A screenwriter for two decades, **CLARA BERANGER** is an original faculty member at the University of Southern California's School of Cinematic Arts along with Mary Pickford (see 1909). In 1950, she will write a popular textbook *Writing for the Screen*. In 1920, she writes the scenario for *Dr. Jekyll and Mr. Hyde*. Beranger said in *Moving Picture World* in 1918: "It needs no cursory glance at the current releases and those of even six months ago to prove that there are more writers among the feminine sex than the male persuasion.

"The heart throb, the human interest note, child life, domestic scenes and even the eternal triangle is more ably handled by women than men because of the thorough understanding our sex has of these matters. It is an old truism that love to a woman is her whole existence, while to the man it is a mere incident in his life. This is one of the reasons why a woman writing drama for the screen gives to her story the sincerity no man can lend. With this sincerity the audience gets plausibility and probability. Men writers in developing their story have to create artificial emotions which they delude themselves into believing is inspiration."

1920

One of the first female costume designers in the film industry, **CLARE WEST** works on the clothing for the silent film epics *The Birth of a Nation* and *Intolerance*. In 1920, she is the costume designer for *Something to Think About*.

Actors on the set of *Intolerance*

1921

The Motion Picture Relief Fund is incorporated in 1921 with Mary Pickford (see 1909) as vice president. Its president is Joseph M. Schenck, and Reverend Neal Dodd is administrator. Its objective is to provide assistance to individuals in the motion picture industry with needs. In 1932, Mary Pickford conceives of the Payroll Pledge Program for those at or above a certain income level. In 1971, the Motion Picture Relief Fund changes its name to the Motion Picture and Television Fund.

Silent film era writer **MARY H. O'CONNOR'S** last work is *Dangerous Lies* released in 1921. She is an early member of the Screen Writers Guild and its social club, The Writers. O'Connor writes the title cards for the 1916 epic *Intolerance*.

African-American actress and writer **DORA MITCHELL** is best known for her 1921 movies, *The Ten Thousand Dollar Trail* and *By Right of Birth*. She wins a writing contest when she is eleven and often writes screenplays, short stories, and other types of materials under pseudonyms.

Writer, director and producer **MAY TULLY** handles all three roles in her 1921 movie *The Old Oaken Bucket*.

1921

Writer and actress **BARBARA LA MARR** begins as a screenplay writer for Fox Film in New York and goes to Hollywood to pursue an acting career. She appears in several movies in 1921 including *The Three Musketeers*. Later, actress Hedy Lamarr (see 1938) will take her last name.

Known for her role as Lady Diana Mayo in *The Sheik* opposite Rudolph Valentino, actress **AGNES AYRES** has her heyday during the silent film era.

An actress who makes the transition from silent films to talkies, **BETTY BLYTHE** is known for her roles in exotic silent films, particularly *The Queen of Sheba* in 1921.

Actress, editor and director **ALICE TERRY** gains renown as Marguerite in the *Four Horsemen of the Apocalypse*, released in 1921.

One of the Sennett Bathing Beauties (see 1915), silent film era actress **MARY THURMAN** performs in comedies and melodramas. In 1921, she makes several films, including *A Broken Doll* and *Leap Year*.

Spotted by director Lois Weber (see 1916) and signed to a contract with Paramount Pictures, silent film era actress **CLAIRE WINDSOR** stars in Weber's 1921 film *The Blot*. Named one of the inaugural WAMPAS Baby Stars (see 1922), Windsor is a leading lady during the 1920s and sets fashion trends. She is unable to make the transition to talkies.

A silent film actress who does her own stunts in her early movies, **LOUISE LORRAINE** becomes the third woman to play Jane when she stars in 1921 in *The Adventures of Tarzan*. She is named a WAMPAS Baby Star (see 1922) in the inaugural class.

A stage actress and vaudeville performer, **ANITA BUSH** appears in two all-black Westerns in 1921 and 1922 both filmed in the predominantly black town of Boley, Oklahoma. *The Bull-Dogger* is released in 1921 and *The Crimson Skull* in 1922. In her later years, Bush serves as the secretary of the Negro Actors Guild.

Actress **MARGARET McWADE** makes her film debut in 1914. In 1921, she stars in the movie *The Blot*, written, produced and directed by Lois Weber (see 1916). She makes the transition to talkies, often playing spinsters, mothers, aunts and later grandmothers.

1921

Author and screenwriter **ELINOR GLYN** specializes in romantic fiction in print and on the screen. In 1921, she writes the story for *The Great Moment*. She originates the concept of "It"—"a human characteristic that draws others with magnetic force." She is one of the richest and most influential writers in Hollywood, equated with glamour, mystery and anything Forbidden. She is amused by the anonymous poem written after the release of *Three Weeks*: "*Would you like to sin/with Elinor Glyn/on a tiger skin?/Or would you prefer/to err with her/on some other fur?*" She later lamented the Hollywood process: "The blatantly crude or utterly false psychology of the stories as finally shown upon the screen was on a par with the absurdity of the sets and clothes, but we were powerless to prevent this. All authors, living or dead, famous or obscure, shared the same fate. Their stories were rewritten and completely altered, either by the stenographers and continuity girls, or by the assistant director and his lovelady. . . . Even when at last, after infinite struggle, a scene was shot which bore some resemblance to the original story, it was certain to be left out in the cutting room, or pared away to such an extent that all meaning which it might once have had was lost."

" Romance is the glamour which turns the dust of everyday life into a golden haze. " —ELINOR GLYN

Documentary producer and director **OSA JOHNSON** and her husband specialize in exotic adventures and animals. She produces and directs the 1921 documentary *Trailing African Wild Animals*.

" Unexpected difficulties, I think, are at once the challenge and the charm of the lives of all explorers. "

—OSA JOHNSON

Regarded as one of the most beautiful women in film, actress **MARGUERITE COURTOT** becomes famous for her work in the 1919 serial *Bound and Gagged*. She appears in her most important feature-length film, *Down to the Sea in Ships*, in 1922. After falling in love and marrying her co-star from that movie, she retires from the movie industry.

Regarded as one of the finest character actresses of the silent film era, **GLADYS BROCKWELL** appears as Nancy in *Oliver Twist* in 1922.

Actress **NITA NALDI** is usually cast as the femme fatale/vamp starting with her 1920 breakout role in *Dr. Jekyll and Mr. Hyde*. In 1922, she plays opposite Rudolph Valentino in *Blood and Sand*, considered the silent film era's last epic production.

┤ 1 9 2 2 ├

1922

Actress **LILYAN TASHMAN,** who makes her film debut in 1921, appears in Mabel Normand's (see 1914) film *Head Over Heels* in 1922. She is known more for being a fashion icon than being a movie star.

The first Chinese-American entertainment star to be recognized internationally, actress **ANNA MAY WONG** has a forty-year career through the silent film era, talkies, radio and television. In 1922, she stars in *The Toll of the Sea* written by

Frances Marion (see 1931).
A popular leading lady in the silent film era, **MADGE BELLAMY** comes to public attention with her title role in the 1922 film *Lorna Doone*.

Screenwriter and Broadway playwright **MARION FAIRFAX** forms her own production company, Marion Fairfax Productions. In 1922, *The Lying Truth* is released and recognized as a master-piece. Her last movie, *The Blonde Saint*, is released in 1926. In 1921, she says, "I truly believe there is a specific place for the combination of literary achievement and stage presentation. . . . An author's place in the presentation of a motion picture, to my mind, is just as important to the screen as it is in the presentation of a play to the stage drama. It is my ambition to make my stories . . . human and clean, my characters natural, people that really exist in our own lives."

Marion Fairfax with her husband, Tully Marshall

Nicknamed "The Joy Girl," silent film actress **OLIVE BORDEN** is named a Sennett Bathing Beauty (see 1915) in 1922 and a WAMPAS Baby Star (see 1922) in 1925. Her breakout role is in *3 Bad Men* in 1926. A major star by 1927, she walks out on her contract when the studio cuts her salary.

The WAMPAS Baby Stars program debuts in 1922. Sponsored by the Western Association of Motion Picture Advertisers, the program highlights and promotes a group of young (early adult) actresses each year who are believed to be on the threshold of stardom. 1934 is the last year of the program (although the program does not select actresses in 1930 or 1933).

Douglas Fairbanks and
Enid Bennett in *Robin Hood*

A native of Australia, actress **ENID BENNETT** stars in 23 films from 1918 to 1921. She is best remembered for her role as Maid Marian in *Robin Hood* (1922) opposite Douglas Fairbanks.

Costume designer and set decorator **NATACHA RAMBOVA** is remembered for bringing Art Deco to Hollywood, as well as being married to Rudolph Valentino. In 1922, she is art director, writer and costume designer for *Salomé*.

One of the earliest African-American women to have directed a movie, **TRESSIE SOUDERS** writes, directs and produces the 1922 film *A Woman's Error*.

> " A man and a woman, working together on the story, can hit a better emotional angle. "
>
> —DOROTHY DAVENPORT REID

1923

1923 Actress and stuntwoman, **DOROTHY DAVENPORT REID** co-produces *Human Wreckage*, which deals with the dangers of narcotic addiction and which she takes on a roadshow engagement. In her 40-year career, she also directs, writes a screenplay and serves as dialogue director for a number of films. She bills herself as Mrs. Wallace Reid to capitalize on the fame—and scandal—associated with her husband, who dies of substance abuse.

"She can use the fact that she *is* a woman to motivate things. That is, to take deliberate advantage of the theory that women must have a certain consideration not accorded men. Then, it is up to her to follow through with what she has to give. She simply uses the feminine viewpoint for her approach, but she must go from there to masculine attack and execution.

Before this, my experience had been with my own money. What I said had to go. Now I must work that much harder to convince that my slant is sound. I believe it takes a woman to believe in a woman's motives, and every story intended for the screen should have a woman working on it at some stage, to convince the audience of women. Later, also, everything a man does on the screen is done to please a woman or women. Actors say to me, 'You tell me what you think in this scene.' Where, if they were asking a man, they would be more apt to say, 'Tell me what to do.' A man and a woman, working together on the story, can hit a better emotional angle. For example, a man only knows that he gets fed up with a woman, but he doesn't know *why*. A woman, writing the story, has feminine vision into all the little irritations that cause it."

Most well-known for the 1923 film *The Hunchback of Notre Dame*, actress **PATSY RUTH MILLER** is a 1922 WAMPAS Baby Star. A protégé of Alla Nazimova (see 1916), she later becomes an award-winning writer of short stories, novels, plays and radio scripts.

Discovered when she is nineteen-months old, child actress **"BABY PEGGY" MONTGOMERY** appears in nearly 150 short films between 1920 and 1923, including *The Darling of New York* in 1923. Considered a predecessor to Shirley Temple (see 1935), Baby Peggy also appears in nine feature films before her career ends when she is eight years old.

LUCILLE RICKSEN, who debuts as a child star in 1920, plays the leading female role in *The Rendezvous* at the age of 13. Named a WAMPAS Baby Star (see 1922) in 1924, she tragically dies of tuberculosis in 1925 prior to her 15th birthday.

1923

An actress whose popularity sets fashion trends, **COLLEEN MOORE** has her breakthrough in the 1923 film *Flaming Youth*. She was also named a 1922 WAMPAS Baby Star (see 1922). In 1927, she is the top box office draw. Moore makes the transition to talkies, making her last movie in 1934.

LILLIAN DUCEY writes and directs the 1923 film *Enemies of Children* (alternatively titled *Youth Triumphant*). She writes movies through 1930.

From the magazine *The Business Woman*: "Excluding acting, considering solely the business possibilities, the positions are held by women in the Hollywood studios as typists, stenographers, secretaries to stars and executives, telephone-operators, hair-dressers, seamstresses, costume-designers, milliners, readers, script-girls, scenarists, cutters, film-retouchers, film-splicers and other laboratory work, set-designers, librarians, artists, title-writers, publicity writers, plaster-molders, casting-directors, musicians, film editors, executives and department-managers, directors and producers."

JOSEPH P. KENNEDY
presents
ALICE
The LUMBER JACK
6y WALT DISNEY

A WINKLER PICTURE

An ALICE Comedy
TRADE MARK REG. U.S. PAT. OFF.
WINKLER PICTURES

DISTRIBUTED BY GREATER FBO

1924

Initially a secretary at Warner Brothers, **MARGARET WINKLER** starts her own film distribution business, which becomes Winkler Productions. She distributes "Felix the Cat" cartoons starting in 1922. Thus, Winkler becomes the first woman to produce and distribute animated films. Working under the name of M.J. Winkler (to avoid discrimination due to her gender), Winkler likes the "Alice's Wonderland" submission of a young man named Walt Disney who has an idea for an animation series called "Alice Comedies". Even though her studio is bankrupt at the time, she signs Disney to a long-term contract. She edits all of the *Alice* cartoons including the 1924 *Alice's Wild West Show*. She is the subject of a feature film titled *Walt Before Mickey*.

Metro-Goldwyn-Mayer (MGM) is formed in 1924 through the merger of Metro Pictures, Goldwyn Pictures and Louis B. Mayer Productions.

A Polish film star who is invited to Hollywood, actress **POLA NEGRI** arrives in the U.S. in 1922. In 1924, she appears in the critically acclaimed movie *Forbidden Paradise*. She goes on to enjoy a fifty-year movie career.

Actress **AILEEN PRINGLE'S** break-through role is in the 1924 film *Three Weeks*. She will continue to make films after talkies but generally is cast in smaller roles.

Called "The American Venus," actress **ESTHER RALSTON** plays Mrs. Darling in the 1924 film *Peter Pan* and is one of the highest paid silent film stars.

1924

Actress **BETTY BRONSON'S** fame skyrockets when she is selected to play Peter Pan in the 1924 movie. Unable to capitalize on that success, she retires in 1933.

Actress **ELAINE HAMMERSTEIN** appears in her first movie in 1915. In 1924, she appears with William Haines in *The Midnight Express*. She loves extravagant costumes and becomes known off-screen as a style leader.

A silent film and talkies actress, **DORIS KENYON** stars with Rudolph Valentino in the 1924 movie *Monsieur Beaucaire*. Her entertainment career lasts almost fifty years.

An actress who stars in action serials and does many of her own stunts, **ALLENE RAY** hits her stride in 1924 with Pathé. She does not make the transition to talkies as she has a high, squeaky voice.

Tim McCoy and Allene Ray in *The Indians Are Coming*

Actress **DOROTHY MacKAILL** stars in silent films in the 1920s and makes the transition to talkies. She becomes a leading lady in 1924 in *The Man Who Came Back*. Also in 1924, she is named a WAMPAS Baby Star (see 1922).

Writer and occasional actress **MARIAN CONSTANCE BLACKTON,** pictured with her father, J. Stuart Blackton, works on fifteen films over the course of her short career. In 1924, she writes *The Clean Heart* directed by her father for the Vitagraph Company, which he helped found.

Nicknamed "The Sweetest Girl in Pictures," actress **MARY BRIAN** appears in *Peter Pan* as Wendy and makes the transition from silent films to talkies. She is named a WAMPAS Baby Star (see 1922) in 1925.

KATHRYN McGUIRE, remembered for being one of the first actors to be an animal's leading lady in the 1921 movie *The Silent Call* with Strongheart the Dog (see Jane Murfin, 1932), co-stars in two popular 1924 Buster Keaton movies, *Sherlock Jr.* and *The Navigator*. A WAMPAS Baby Star (see 1922) in 1922, her film career has ended by 1930.

1924

1925

In November 1925 *Motion Picture* Magazine editorializes: "Among the greatest 'cutters' and film editors are women. They are quick and resourceful. They are also ingenious in their work and usually have a strong sense of what the public wants to see. They can sit in a stuffy cutting-room and see themselves looking at the picture before an audience. Women writers may also be said to dominate the scenario field. There is a deep scientific reason for this. Some years ago a series of psychological experiments were made in a German university town—long before motion pictures were heard of. School children of both sexes were required to write fiction stories. One fact was established as a result of the experiment; the girl children were not so logical in their plots; they didn't bother so much how they 'got there;' but they showed a superior sense of picturization to the boy children. Also their stories had more interesting detail and more sentiment and more emotion.

"So it would seem that women were naturally fitted for the work of writing for the screen. Experience of motion picture companies has shown that the combination of a woman, with her quick, alert sense of invention and her ability to 'see in pictures,' and a director with a logical sense of construction, is the ideal working team for movies."

Writer and editor **KATHERINE HILLIKER** writes the titles for the silent film *Ben-Hur: A Tale of the Christ.*

Screenwriter **FREDERICA SAGOR MAAS** begins her career in 1925 with *The Plastic Age.* Her autobiography, *The Shocking Miss Pilgrim: A Writer in Early Hollywood,* is viewed as a good reference for the film industry's early history.

The most photographed movie star of 1925 and for a time the leading serial star, actress **EDNA MURPHY** made her film debut in 1918.

Primarily a silent film actress, **MARY PHILBIN** debuts in 1921 in *The Blazing Trail*. She is named a WAMPAS Baby Star (see 1922) in the inaugural class. In 1925, Philbin stars in one of her best-remembered roles in *The Phantom of the Opera*.

Looking older than her years, actress **BELLE BENNETT** often plays mothers, as she does in *Stella Dallas* in 1925.

1925

Actress **DOROTHY DWAN** is known for her role as Dorothy in the 1925 *Wizard of Oz*.

Larry Semon, Dorothy Dwan, and Oliver Hardy in *Wizard of Oz*

An actress who comes to Hollywood from her native France, **RENÉE ADORÉE** is best known for her role in *The Big Parade* which becomes one of MGM's all-time biggest hits and is considered by film historians to be the best movie of the silent film era.

"The Hungarian Rhapsody," actress **VILMA BÁNKY** is signed by Samuel Goldwyn in 1925. Her thick accent hinders her success once talkies are introduced.

Actress **DOLORES DEL RIO,** an early Latin film star, debuts in the 1925 movie *Joanna*. Named a WAMPAS Baby Star (see 1922) in 1926, she is not able to transition into talkies in Hollywood but does later become a famous movie star in her native Mexico.

A femme fatale who makes her first film appearance in 1922, **JETTA GOUDAL** performs in *Salome of the Tenements* and the *Coming of Amos* in 1925.

1925

Called "The Girl with the Bee-Stung Lips" and "The Gardenia of the Screen," actress, dancer, producer and screenwriter **MAE MURRAY** appears in the 1925 film *The Merry Widow*. Her transition to talkies is not successful.

Actress **CARMEL MYERS,** who has her breakthrough role in the 1917 film *Sirens of the Sea*, is best remembered for her role as the seductress in the 1925 film *Ben Hur: A Tale of the Christ*. Her cousin is Ruth Harriet Louise (see 1925).

A silent film era actress who makes the transition to talkies, **IRENE RICH** appears in 1925 in *Lady Windemere's Fan*. She also works in radio for more than a decade.

Actress **VIRGINIA VALLI** makes her film debut in 1916. The peak of her popularity, and most of her films, occur during the mid-1920s. In 1925, she stars in Alfred Hitchcock's first American film, *The Pleasure Garden*.

Screenwriter **ETHEL DOHERTY'S** first script is for *The Vanishing American* in 1925. She writes scripts for ten years.

Actress **MAY McAVOY,** who reaches star status for *Sentimental Tammy* in 1921, appears in her best known silent film, *Ben Hur: A Tale of the Christ,* in 1925. McAvoy co-stars in Hollywood's first talkie, *The Jazz Singer,* in 1927. She also stars in England's first talkie, the 1928 film *The Terror.* She returns to the screen in bit parts in the 1940s and 1950s. Her last part is in the 1959 remake of *Ben Hur.*

A leading lady during the silent film era, **CARMELITA GERAGHTY** has a starring role in *The Pleasure Garden*, the first film directed by Alfred Hitchcock, in 1925. She is named a WAMPAS Baby Star (see 1922) in 1924.

(see 1922)

Carmelita Geraghty and John Stuart in *The Pleasure Garden*

1925

Professional photographer **RUTH HARRIET LOUISE** serves as chief portrait photographer at MGM starting in 1925. She takes more than 100,000 photographs of stars, contract players and hopefuls. She holds the job for five years. Her cousin is Carmel Myers (see 1925).

(see 1925)

Writer and director **ELIZABETH PICKETT (CHEVALIER)** titles and edits the 1925 film *Kentucky Pride*.

Screenwriter **AGNES BRAND LEAHY'S** first movie is in 1925, *Go Straight*.

The editor of *Motion Picture Magazine*, **FLORENCE M. OSBORNE** writes an editorial titled "Why are there no women directors?"

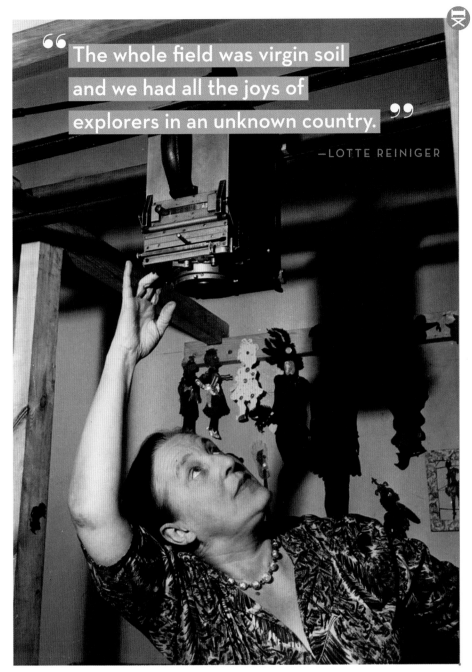

> " The whole field was virgin soil
> and we had all the joys of
> explorers in an unknown country. "
>
> —LOTTE REINIGER

1926

A pioneer in silhouette animation, German director and animator **LOTTE REINIGER** creates and produces a fully animated feature film ten years before Walt Disney. From 1923 to 1926, she works to produce *The Adventures of Prince Achmed* using a technique, known as silhouette animation, that she pioneers. In the process of making the film, she also develops the predecessor to the multiplane camera. When she is approached to produce a feature length animated film, she remembers, "We had to think twice. This was a never heard of thing. Animated films were supposed to make people roar with laughter, and nobody had dared to entertain an audience with them for more than ten minutes. Everybody to whom we talked in the industry about the proposition was horrified." She says, "Animation was in its infancy; there was just Felix the Cat, Fleischer's cartoons, and Mickey Mouse was far away in the future. For the filmmakers of this period, those were the days: with each film we could make new discoveries, find new problems, new possibilities, technical and artistic. . . . The whole field was virgin soil and we had all the joys of explorers in an unknown country."

1926

Director, writer and actress **LOIS WILSON** stars as Daisy in *The Great Gatsby*. Mentored by Lois Weber (see 1916), who gives her a small part in the 1916 movie *The Dumb Girl of Portici* and grooms her for Hollywood, she becomes a WAMPAS Baby Star (see 1922) in the inaugural year. She directs two films and is a scenario writer.

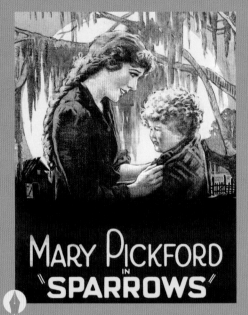

Screenwriter **DOROTHY FARNUM** writes the scenario for *The Temptress* in 1926. She is one of the top writers at MGM during the silent film era.

Nicknamed "The Goddess of the Silent Screen," actress **DOLORES COSTELLO** stars in *The Sea Beast* in 1926, and is named a WAMPAS Baby Star (see 1922) in the same year.

One of the youngest writers in Hollywood at the start of her career, screenwriter **WINIFRED DUNN** works in both silent films and the talkies. In 1926, she writes the story for Mary Pickford's (see 1909) movie *Sparrows*.

─┤ 1926 ├─

A silent film actress who successfully makes the transition to talkies, **LAURA LA PLANTE** is best known for the 1926 film *Skinner's Dress Suit*. She is named a WAMPAS Baby Star (see 1922) in 1923. She retires from making movies in 1935.

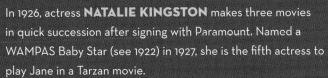

In 1926, actress **NATALIE KINGSTON** makes three movies in quick succession after signing with Paramount. Named a WAMPAS Baby Star (see 1922) in 1927, she is the fifth actress to play Jane in a Tarzan movie.

An actress who makes the transition from silent film to talkies, **JULIA FAYE** appears in many Cecil B. DeMille productions including, in 1926, *The Volga Boatman*, which secures her popularity.

In 1926, **FRANCES HYLAND** is the first woman to be hired as a gag writer by Universal. She writes stories, dialogue and screenplays for twenty years, making the transition from the silent film era to talkies.

1926

VIRGINIA LEE CORBIN begins as a child star and progresses to adult roles. In 1926, she is in *Hands Up!* but is not able to make the transition to talkies and retires from the film industry in the early 1930s.

Billie Dove and Kenneth Thomson
in *The Other Tomorrow*

1927 After appearing in the 1927 movie of the same name, actress **BILLIE DOVE** is dubbed "The American Beauty" and at the height of her fame is a significant box office draw.

The Academy of Motion Picture Arts and Sciences is established.

Screenwriter **AGNES CHRISTINE JOHNSTON** writes more than 85 screenplays, and transitions between the silent film era and talkies. She writes the screenplay for the 1927 movie *The Enemy* starring Lillian Gish (see 1912).

Richard Barthelmess and Molly O'Day

After appearing in her first film in 1926, actress **MOLLY O'DAY** wins an audition against 2,000 other hopefuls to be cast in the 1927 movie *The Patent Leather Kid*. She is named a WAMPAS Baby Star (see 1922) in 1928.

The first "talkie"—*The Jazz Singer*, starring May McAvoy (see 1925) and Al Jolson—is produced.

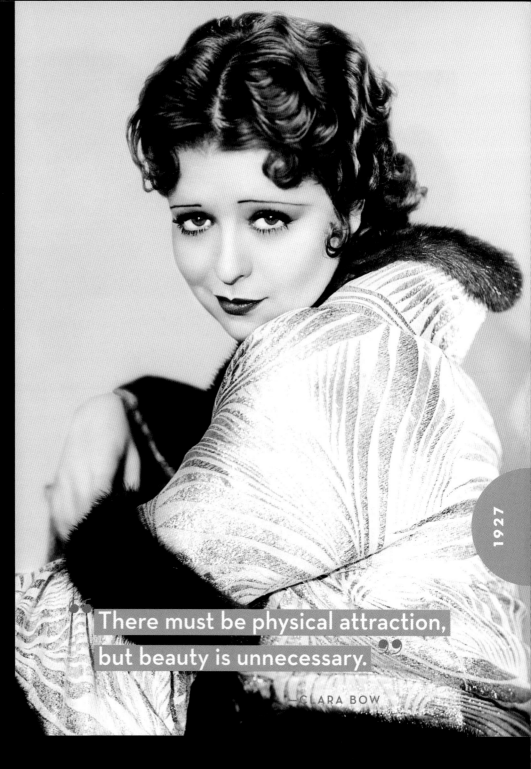

Actress and sex symbol in the 1920s (and a WAMPAS Baby Star (see 1922) in 1924), **CLARA BOW** becomes known as "The It Girl" after her performance in the 1927 movie *It*. Bow is the first or second box office draw in every year from 1927 to 1930. At one point, she receives 45,000 fan letters in a month. She successfully makes the transition to talkies but retires in 1933 to ranch with her husband. Bow has been featured on a U.S. postage stamp. A description of "It" from Elinor Glyn's (see 1921) book *It, and Other Stories* (1927): "To have 'It' the fortunate possessor must have that strange magnetism which attracts both sexes; he or she must be entirely unselfconscious and full of self-confidence, indifferent to the effect he or she is producing, and uninfluenced by others. There must be physical attraction, but beauty is unnecessary. Conceit or self-consciousness destroys 'It' immediately. In the animal world, 'It' demonstrates in tigers and cats—both animals being fascinating and mysterious, and quite unbiddable."

1927

There must be physical attraction, but beauty is unnecessary.

—CLARA BOW

SUE CAROL'S acting career begins in 1927. Named a WAMPAS Baby Star (see 1922) in 1928, she later establishes a talent agency. Her major find is actor Alan Ladd, who becomes her husband.

A very popular actress in the silent film era, **VERA REYNOLDS** is a Sennett Bathing Beauty (see 1915). A WAMPAS Baby Star (see 1922) in 1926, she appears in *Almost Human* and *The Main Event* in 1927.

1928

The RKO (Radio-Keith-Orpheum) holding company is formed. Its first movies are released in 1929. Its last movies include *While the City Sleeps* and *Beyond a Reasonable Doubt*, both released in 1956.

Sister of Dorothy Spencer (see 1940), editor **JEANNE SPENCER** serves as the editor for the 1928 film *Ramona*.

One of the few female producers during the 1930s, **FANCHON ROYER** produces her first film in 1928—*Life's Like That*. *Death in the Air*, which she produces in 1937, is the first film she produces for her company, Fanchon Royer Features, Inc.

Editor **JANE LORING** works on movie trailers before becoming a film cutter at Paramount. Her debut movie as an editor is in 1928 when she works on *Gentlemen Prefer Blondes*, written by Anita Loos (see 1912). She later moves to RKO.

1928

An actress for a decade, **MARCELINE DAY** is well remembered for her role in the 1928 movie *The Cameraman*. In 1926, she is named a WAMPAS Baby Star (see 1922). She appears in Westerns and in dramatic movies. Although she makes the transition to talkies, the quality of roles offered to her diminishes and she retires from the film industry in 1933.

Josephine Lovett with her husband John S. Robertson, 1924

JOSEPHINE LOVETT is nominated for an Academy Award for Writing for the 1928 movie *Our Dancing Daughters*. The movie features Joan Crawford's (see 1946) breakthrough role.

One of the few female directors working during the 1930s in Hollywood, **DOROTHY ARZNER** is also a writer and editor. The first woman to be given a screen credit as an editor, Arzner is also the first woman to join the Directors Guild of America. She invents the boom microphone when she has her crew attach a microphone to a fishing rod, although she does not file for a patent. In 1928, she directs *Manhattan Cocktail.* Of her long career in film, Arzner says, "if one was going to be in the movie business, one ought to be a director.

"My philosophy is that to be a director you cannot be subject to anyone, even the head of the studio. I threatened to quit each time I didn't get my way, but no one ever let me walk out.

"You see, I was not dependent on the movies for my living, so I was already ready to give the picture over to some other director if I couldn't make it the way I saw it. Right or wrong, I believe this was why I sustained so long—twenty years.

"Men think analytically. Women rely on what they call intuition and emotion . . . but those qualities do not help anyone in directing. A director must be able to reason things out in logical sequence."

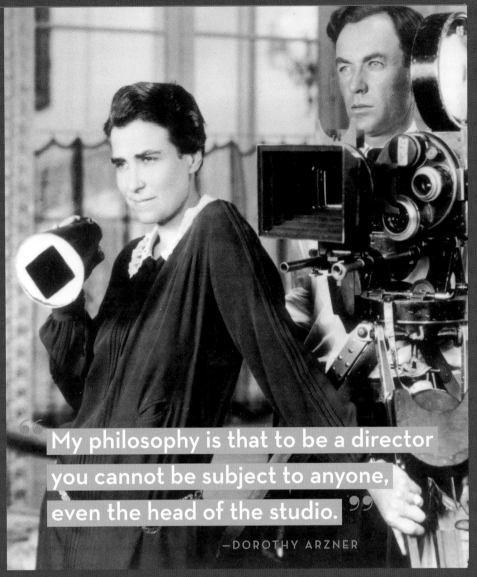

> My philosophy is that to be a director you cannot be subject to anyone, even the head of the studio."
>
> —DOROTHY ARZNER

1928

On the lack of women directors: "I don't honestly know. Maybe producers felt safe with men; they could go to a bar and exchange ideas more freely. But I made one box-office movie after another, so they knew they could gamble a banker's money on me. If I had a failure in the middle, I would have been finished. Today, of course even the stars are all men. When men do put women in pictures, they make them so darned sappy, weeping all over the place, that it's disgusting.

Over her six-decade career, **CONSTANCE COLLIER** evolves from a stage actress to an acting coach. Her arrival in Hollywood from England in the late 1920s coincides with the need of many actors to make the transition to talkies. With her stage background, Collier is able to provide training in voice and diction. She also appears in films in the 1930s and 1940s. Her coaching clientele includes Audrey Hepburn (see 1954), Vivien Leigh (see 1940), Marilyn Monroe (see 1959), and Katharine Hepburn (see 1934).

Silent film era actress **HELENE COSTELLO** begins as a child actor and is named a WAMPAS Baby Star (see 1922) in 1927. In 1928, she co-stars in the first talking full-length feature film *Lights of New York*.

1928

After emigrating from Russia, **OLGA BACLANOVA** finds success with *The Docks of New York* in 1928. Her thick Russian accent is an impediment in talkies and her career declines after the silent film era ends.

Actress **EVELYN BRENT** stars in Paramount Pictures' first talkie, *Interference*. She begins her career in 1915 and is named a 1923 WAMPAS Baby Star (see 1922).

![Eleanor Boardman portrait]

Known as the "Eastman Kodak Girl," actress **ELEANOR BOARDMAN** appears in films for over a decade with her biggest success in King Vidor's *The Crowd* in 1928. She is a WAMPAS Baby Star (see 1922) in 1923.

1929 The first Oscars are awarded.

Joan Bennett and Anthony
Bushell in *Disraeli*

Coming from an acting family and appearing in movies from a young age, actress **JOAN BENNETT** has her first leading role in *Bulldog Drummond* in 1929 with Ronald Colman. She will appear in film and television movies into the 1980s.

Singer and actress **JEANETTE MacDONALD** performs in musicals and other films in the 1930s and 1940s, four of which are nominated for Best Picture Oscars. Her most frequent co-stars are Maurice Chevalier and Nelson Eddy. Her first movie, *The Love Parade*, co-starring Maurice Chevalier and filmed in 1929, is one of the films receiving a Best Picture nomination. She is the top moneymaker in 1936.

Jeanette MacDonald and
Maurice Chevalier in *The Love Parade*

In 1929, choral director **EVA JESSYE** serves as the choir director for the King Vidor movie *Hallelujah!,* which has an all-black cast. She complains about the discriminatory treatment she receives while on the set of the film. *Hallelujah!* is selected for preservation in the National Film Registry (see 1988) at the Library of Congress.

Known for her role as "Chick" in the 1929 movie *Hallelujah,* which has an all-black cast and is an all-sound musical, actress **NINA MAE McKINNEY** fights against the stereotypes of the time. She has more success in Europe and on the stage and she is called "The Black Garbo."

The onset of the Great Depression; with the poor economic situation, many women find it necessary to work.

African-American actress **ROBERTA HYSON** appears in the first black talkie shorts in 1929—*The Melancholy Dame* and *Music Hath Harms* (in which she also sings).

Regarded as *the* flapper of the 1920s, actress **LOUISE BROOKS** helps popularize the bobbed haircut and is best known for the 1929 movie *Pandora's Box*.

1929

Actress and producer **GLORIA SWANSON** is nominated for an Academy Award for Best Actress in 1929 for her performance in *Sadie Thompson*. Swanson produces some of the films in which she stars through her own production company. Her career spans almost six decades and she is probably best known for her role as Norma Desmond in the 1950 movie *Sunset Boulevard*.

1929

> " I adore work, lots of work. I am perfectly miserable when I am not working even for a couple of days. I go down on the lot and watch the others, or visit my stage friends' shows. . . anything to keep in the atmosphere of my beloved work. "
>
> —LINA BASQUETTE

An entertainer who begins her 75-year career when she is nine years old, **LINA BASQUETTE'S** most well-known performance is the role of Judith in *The Godless Girl* in 1929. She is named a WAMPAS Baby Star (see 1922) in 1928.

Screenwriter **DORIS ANDERSON** begins her movie screenwriting career in 1925. In 1929, she writes the dialogue, screenplay and story for *The Wolf of Wall Street*. In a career that spans twenty-five years, she writes more than 60 scripts. Several of her screenplays are produced by Dorothy Arzner (see 1928) and she collaborates with Zoe Akins (see 1933) as well.

The University of Southern California's (USC) School of Cinematic Arts is established. It is a collaborative effort of USC and the Academy of Motion Picture Arts and Sciences.

Janet Gaynor signs an autograph in Washington D.C.

The first actress to win the Academy Award for Best Actress, **JANET GAYNOR** is recognized for her performance in three movies: *7th Heaven*, *Street Angel* and *Sunrise*. Gaynor is named a WAMPAS Baby Star (see 1922) in 1926.

Greta Garbo in *Grand Hotel* in 1932

1930s

TALKIES, TECHNICOLOR AND THE GREAT DEPRESSION

During the Great Depression, movies were seen as a release from the cares of the day. Whether it was Shirley Temple's musicals, Mae West's comedies or Bette Davis's dramas, people were transported to another world.

Technicolor had been experimented with for two decades. By the early 1930s, Technicolor had been greatly improved and the cost reduced. It became the most widely used color process in Hollywood. During the 1930s, films like *The Wizard of Oz* (1939) and *Gone with the Wind* (1939) popularized the technique.

At the end of the 1920s, the studios had experimented with ways to add sound to the movies. By the 1930s, many obstacles had been overcome. With these improvements, it became clear that sound was more than a fad and the studios moved forward with talkies.

Actors' and actresses' voices were now important. Heavy accents or squeaky voices would not do. Famous silent star Norma Talmadge couldn't make the transition. Greta Garbo, in spite of her accent, was still successful. Her first talkie, *Anna Christie* (1930) was advertised as "Garbo Talks!"

More women worked as screenwriters in this decade than in any other and talkies gave them more freedom to write dialogue with humor or realism and to create more intricate plotlines. The scripts often focused on intelligent and independent women.

Although many women editors had been pushed out, those who remained had prominent roles and edited some of the most significant films of the decade. These women were able to capitalize on the evolution of editing from "cutting" films to actually telling stories.

Actresses felt the need to create their own individual looks, as many were not only movie stars, but sex symbols as well. This was the advent of costume designers, an area of expertise where women found the door open. Movie stars, with the help of those costume designers, created fashion trends for the public, and department stores carried copies of the fashions the stars wore on screen.

And so the movies, with their dancing, singing, fashions and adventures, provided a place of escape from daily routines.

BERYL MERCER, who has filled mostly motherly roles since her debut in 1916, plays Lew Ayres' mother in *All Quiet on the Western Front.*

A Sennett Bathing Beauty (see 1915), actress and comedienne **POLLY MORAN** teams with Marie Dressler (see 1931). Among their movies together is *Chasing Rainbows* in 1930.

Nicknamed the "Little Brown Wren" due to her small size, actress **BESSIE LOVE** has an almost seven-decade long career in the film industry. She is named a WAMPAS Baby Star (see 1922) in the inaugural class. Beginning in the silent film era, she transitions to talkies and receives an Academy Award nomination for Best Actress in 1930 for her role in the movie *Broadway Melody.*

1930

An actress whose career spans half a century starting in 1930, **JOAN BLONDELL'S** first movies included *Sinners' Holiday.* A WAMPAS Baby Star (see 1922) in 1931, she is nominated for a Best Supporting Actress Oscar in 1952 for her work in *The Blue Veil.*

Actress and writer **BESS MEREDYTH** is nominated for two Best Writing Academy Awards in 1930 for *A Woman of Affairs* and *Wonder of Women.* She is one of the founding members of the Academy of Motion Picture Arts and Sciences in 1927.

Silent film actress and screenwriter for both silent films and talkies, **BEATRICE VAN** writes the dialogue for the 1930 movie *No, No Nanette.*

1930 The Motion Picture Production Code, which spells out moral guidelines for movies, is put into effect by the Motion Picture Producers and Distributors of America (MPPDA), later known as the Motion Picture Association of America (MPAA). It remains in effect until 1968 when it is replaced by the MPAA film rating system.

Nicknamed the "Orchid Lady of the Screen," silent film era actress **CORINNE GRIFFITH** is considered to be the most beautiful actress of the silent screen, as well as being quite popular. She is nominated for the Best Actress Oscar in 1930 for *The Divine Lady*.

Sex symbol and actress **JEAN HARLOW**'s first major appearance is in the 1930 movie *Hell's Angels* directed by Howard Hughes. By the mid-1930s, she is one of the biggest movie stars in the U.S. A cocktail is named for her.

> "It's consoling to know how many women gave me real aid when I stood at the crossroads"
>
> —FRANCES MARION

1931 The highest paid screenwriter for two decades, **FRANCES MARION** makes the transition from the silent film era to talkies and earns her first Oscar in 1931 for *The Big House*. She wins the Oscar again for *The Champ* and receives two more nominations. The "First Lady" of screenwriting, Marion writes many of Mary Pickford's (see 1909) most successful films. She is trained by Lois Weber (see 1916) on the craft of making movies. Pickford's second husband says "It was Frances who was responsible for coining the multi-million dollar image of 'America's Sweetheart.'" On seeing the decline of female power in the film industry, Marion says (in the 1950s): "I don't think Hollywood will ever again be as glamorous, or as funny, or as tragic, as it was during the teens, the twenties and the thirties. But that's what everybody says about the past as he grows older and looks back on the days of his youth, when everything was new and exciting and beautiful. Was it really that way? Frankly, too often, all I can remember are the heartbreak and the hard work."

"While it's perfectly true that many important men. . . helped and encouraged me, it's consoling to know how many women gave me real aid when I stood at the crossroads. Too many women go around saying that women in important positions don't help their own sex, but that was never my experience . . . In my case . . . the list is endless, believe me!"

The first person to be nominated five times, **NORMA SHEARER** wins the 1931 Best Actress Oscar for *The Divorcee*. She is also nominated for Best Actress that year for *Their Own Desire*.

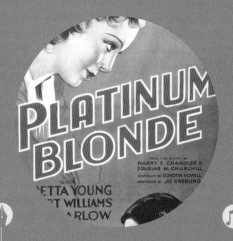

A screenwriter for thirty years, and one who makes the transition from the silent film era to talkies, **DOROTHY HOWELL** helps write *Platinum Blonde* and *The Miracle Worker* in 1931.

Music composer and lyricist **DANA SUESSE** is referred to as "the girl Gershwin." Her musical compositions include "Ho-Hum" which is part of the musical score to several movies in 1931 including *Monkey Business*.

Actress and voice actress **MAE QUESTEL** provides the voices for Betty Boop and Olive Oyl starting in 1931. Between 1931 and 1939, she voices 150 animated shorts for Betty Boop. She bases the voice she uses for Olive Oyl (whom she voices for twenty years) on the voice of actress ZaSu Pitts (see 1919). Later, Questel has bit roles in *Funny Girl* and *National Lampoon's Christmas Vacation*.

1931

Primarily a comedic actress, **THELMA TODD** is best remembered for movies such as 1931's *Monkey Business* (with the Marx Brothers) and *The Maltese Falcon*.

British actress **HEATHER ANGEL** moves to Hollywood and stars in the 1931 movie *Hound of the Baskervilles*. During the 1950s, she provides voices for Disney movies.

Screenwriter **MAUDE FULTON** writes the screenplay and dialogue for the 1931 movie *The Maltese Falcon*.

Swedish-born actress **GRETA GARBO** is nominated for Best Actress Oscars for two films *Anna Christie* and *Romance*, in 1931. A Swedish-born actress who appears in her first American-made film, the *Torrent*, in 1926, she will receive two more Best Actress nominations over her career. In 1955, she receives an Honorary Oscar for her unforgettable screen performances. Throughout her movie career and her life, she avoids social functions and is extremely averse to publicity. She becomes very closely associated with a line from the movie *Grand Hotel*, "I want to be alone, I just want to be alone." Although, she insists, "I never said 'I want to be alone'. I only said 'I want to be left alone.' There is all the difference." She has been featured on a U.S. postage stamp.

Called the ninth-greatest female screen legend by the American Film Institute (see 1999) and the highest paid actress of her time, **MARLENE DIETRICH** debuts in 1931 in *Morocco*, for which she is nominated for the 1932 Best Actress Oscar.

1931

After a career in theater and a severe bout of influenza, **MAUDE ADAMS** works with the General Electric Company to improve stage lighting and with the Eastman Company to develop color photography. Adams receives a patent for her illuminating device in 1931.

1932 Stuntwoman **FRANCES MILES** performs stunts for *Scarface*. She later looks back on the beginning of her career: when she shows up on the set for the first day of filming of *The Hunchback of Notre Dame* in 1923, she realized she was responsible for the horses used in the movie. She says "It was rugged. I took a lot of pushing around, but my real fate in Hollywood was settled that day, although I didn't realize it then. I worked in fifty-two two-reel Westerns, and then graduated into five reelers with guys like Hoot Gibson, Jack Hoxie and Buck Jones. I've done all the falls, fights, chases you could ever think of. When Westerns began to go sissy with banjos, guitars and quartets I branched out into features."

> " I've doubled for lots of stars, but I wouldn't be one for love or money "
>
> —FRANCES MILES

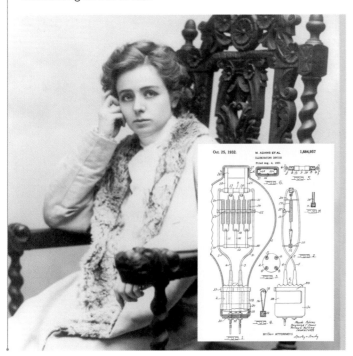

A theater performer and silent film actress, **MARIE DRESSLER** begins making talking films at the age of 59 and wins the Academy Award for Best Actress in 1932 for *Min and Bill*.

Greta Garbo (left) and Marie Dressler in *Anna Christie*

KATHRYN DOUGHERTY is the editor of *Photoplay* magazine from 1932 to 1935.

Actress **IRENE DUNNE** receives her first of five Oscar nominations for Best Actress for *Cimarron*.

1932

" It's better to be looked over than overlooked. "

—MAE WEST

In the entertainment business for seventy years, actress and writer **MAE WEST** is a sex symbol named by the American Film Institute (see 1999) as 15th among the greatest female actresses of classic American cinema. Her first movie role, a small part in the 1932 movie *Night After Night*, becomes famous—she not only steals the scene, she also demonstrates her wit and the double entendres for which she becomes famous. She writes her own material and changes how Americans view sex. For her part, West seemed to enjoy her role as provocateur, saying, "I believe in censorship—I made a fortune out of it."

A silent film era actress in serials and Westerns who makes the transition successfully to talkies, **DOROTHY GULLIVER** appears in *The Last Frontier*. She is named a WAMPAS Baby Star (see 1922) in 1928 and is a popular heroine of the 1930s "cliffhangers."

First a film critic and later an ardent supporter of film preservation, **IRIS BARRY** begins her career in England and moves to the U.S. in 1930. She founds the film study department at the Museum of Modern Art in New York City in 1932. Her efforts make her one of the founders of the film preservation movement. She writes two books on the film industry.

MARIAN NIXON stars in *Rebecca of Sunnybrook Farm* in 1932. The actress, who has her first major role in the 1923 film *Cupid's Fireman*, is also named a WAMPAS Baby Star (see 1922) in 1924.

1933 One of the highest paid screenwriters in Hollywood in the 1930s, **MARGUERITE ROBERTS'S** debut film is *Sailor's Luck* in 1933. Blacklisted for nine years during the 1950s, she returns to Columbia Pictures in 1962 and writes the screenplay for the 1969 movie *True Grit*. In 1968, she says "I was weaned on stories about gunfighters and their doings, and I know all the lingo too. My grandfather came West as far as Colorado by covered wagon. He was a sheriff in the state's wildest days. And my father was a town marshal. He never carried a gun, but all the bad men were afraid of him. He was short and stocky, but some people said he was the strongest man in Colorado, and nothing scared him."

RUTH ROSE writes the screenplay for *King Kong*. She is credited with writing the lines "Oh, no. It wasn't the airplanes. It was Beauty killed the Beast." Her screenplay served as the basis for two of the remakes of the original *King Kong* movie—one released in 1976 and one released in 2005.

Screenwriter, producer and director **JANE MURFIN** is nominated for Best Writing, Original Story in 1933 for *What Price Hollywood?* In the early 1920s, she owns her own production company for which she writes scripts for movies featuring Strongheart, her dog and the first canine star. She is the first woman supervisor at RKO (see 1928) in 1934.

Comedienne **GRACIE ALLEN** appears in *International House* with W.C. Fields. Explaining her comedic character, Allen said "Gracie isn't really crazy. She makes sense in an illogical sort of way. She's off-center. Not quite right really, but nearly right." Allen and her husband George Burns were a team until her death. They are featured on a U.S. postage stamp issued in 2009.

Originally an actress during the silent movie era and a WAMPAS Baby Star (see 1922) in the inaugural class, **HELEN FERGUSON** becomes a very successful publicist in Hollywood. She begins her publicity work in 1933 and represents many big stars for over 30 years.

Journalist, novelist and screenwriter **ADELA ROGERS ST. JOHNS** shares the nomination for the Best Writing, Original Story Oscar in 1933 for *What Price Hollywood?*

1933

A Pulitzer Prize-winning playwright who begins working in the film industry in the mid-1920s, **ZOE AKINS** writes the screenplay for *Morning Glory*, for which Katharine Hepburn (see 1934) wins the Best Actress Oscar.

The first tap dancing movie star, **RUBY KEELER** is particularly remembered for the 1933 movie musical *42nd Street*.

One of the first successful Latinas in the U.S. film industry, actress **LUPE VELEZ** makes her film debut in the U.S. in 1927. She is named a WAMPAS Baby Star (see 1922) in 1928. Known in the media as "The Mexican Spitfire" one of her most successful movies is the 1933 film *Hot Pepper*.

One of the first "scream queens," actress **FAY WRAY** is most noted for playing Ann Darrow in the 1933 movie *King Kong*. After working mostly in Westerns during the silent film era, she is named a WAMPAS Baby Star (see 1922) in 1926. Wray has an almost sixty-year entertainment career during which she makes the transition from the silent film era to talkies and television.

Stunt double for Vivien Leigh (see 1940) in *Gone with the Wind*, Margaret Hamilton in *The Wizard of Oz* and Fay Wray (see 1933) for *King Kong*, accomplished horsewoman **ALINE GOODWIN** is a stuntwoman and an actress for just over twenty years. Of the self-importance stars feel, she says, "We [stuntwomen] don't. I got the break of my life when I lost out as an actress. When sound came in, my voice wasn't right. And am I glad! It's not the money stars earn that you look at, it's what they keep. Chances are, we keep much more."

A stuntwoman during the 1930s and 1940s, **NELLIE WALKER** performs stunts in 1933 for *Tarzan the Fearless*.

Categorized as the first African-American filmmaker, writer, director and actress **ELOYCE KING PATRICK GIST** is known for the 1933 film *Verdict Not Guilty*.

Five men and one woman, Lila Finn (see 1939), form the Screen Actors Guild (SAG) to represent actors and stunt players who appeared in front of the camera. SAG is recognized as the collective-bargaining representative for actors.

During her eighty-year entertainment career, stage and film actress **HELEN HAYES** wins two Oscars—almost forty years apart. In 1933, she wins the Best Actress Oscar for *The Sin of Madelon Claudet*. In 1971, she wins the Best Supporting Actress Oscar for *Airport*. She is known as the "First Lady of American Theater," and is one of the few people to have won an Oscar, Emmy, Tony and Grammy. She is also a recipient of a Presidential Medal of Freedom and has been inducted into the National Women's Hall of Fame.

1934 Screenwriter **SARAH Y. MASON** makes the transition from the silent film era to talkies. In 1934, she shares the Best Writing, Adaptation Oscar for *Little Women*.

Stuntwoman **"LUCKY" MARY WIGGINS** doubles for Claudette Colbert (see 1935) in 1934 in the movie *It Happens One Night*. A daredevil who begins her stunting career by joining a traveling carnival after high school, Wiggins learns to parachute after discovering that those stunts pay more. She signs up as a member of the Women Air Force Service Pilots during World War II.

 Screenwriter **KAREN DE WOLF** writes stories and screenplays for more than twenty years. In 1934, she writes the screenplay for *The Countess of Monte Cristo*.

 Screenwriter and director **WANDA TUCHOCK** is one of two women to be credited as a director on a Hollywood movie during the 1930s. She writes the screenplay and directs the 1934 movie *Finishing School*.

 Animator **LAVERNE HARDING** begins her career in 1934 with several shorts. She specializes in Woody Woodpecker cartoons, designing the character used for more than forty years. By the time she retires, Harding has amassed hundreds of credits over more than fifty years as an animator. In 1980, she receives the Winsor McCay Lifetime Achievement Award (see 1972).

A Hollywood leading lady for over 60 years, **KATHARINE HEPBURN** receives the first of her four Best Actress Oscars in 1934 for *Morning Glory*. Nominated another eight times for the Best Actress Oscar, Hepburn is considered the greatest female movie star of classic Hollywood cinema (see American Film Institute, 1999). She has been featured on a U.S. postage stamp. She says, "If you obey all the rules, you miss all the fun." She also says, "If you always do what interests you, at least one person is pleased."

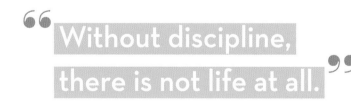

" Without discipline, there is not life at all. "

—KATHARINE HEPBURN

A costume designer with almost 400 movie credits, **VERA WEST** designs primarily gowns for twenty years as the chief costume designer at Universal Pictures. In 1934, one of the many movies in which she is involved is *Great Expectations*.

Animator **LILLIAN FRIEDMAN (ASTOR)** is hired in 1930 by Fleischer Studios, after being rejected by Disney. Promoted to animator in 1933, she works on several Betty Boop cartoons in 1934.

An actress who makes thirty films during the 1930s, **ADRIENNE AMES** is known as a clotheshorse and glamour queen. Her most successful movie is *George White's Scandals* in 1934.

1934

A producer and screenwriter with wide experience in the film industry, **VIRGINIA VAN UPP** writes the screenplay for the 1934 movie *Pursuit of Happiness*. She also works as a casting director and agent. In 1945, she is named Executive Producer of Columbia Pictures. It will be over three decades until another woman holds this position.

Child star **JANE WITHERS** makes her mark co-starring with Shirley Temple (see 1935) in the 1934 movie *Bright Eyes*. The transition to adulthood in films is difficult although she is remembered for her role in the 1956 film *Giant*.

Austrian-born dancer and choreographer **ALBERTINA RASCH** choreographs movies for fifteen years. A naturalized American citizen, she forms her own dance troupe and choreographs and directs the dancing in the 1934 movie *The Merry Widow*.

At a time when blacks are limited to roles as slaves or as domestic help, actress **LOUISE BEAVERS** lands her first film roles in the 1920s. She appears in *Imitation of Life* in 1934.

MYRNA LOY, who makes her film debut in the 1925 silent film *What Price Beauty?*, stars in *The Thin Man* (behind the scenes photograph below). Her 1991 Honorary Oscar is "In recognition of her extraordinary qualities both on screen and off, with appreciation for a lifetime's worth of indelible performances."

Promotional photograph for the film *The Thin Man* starring Myrna Loy and William Powell

1935 A prolific writer of Westerns, **DORIS SCHROEDER** writes the screenplay for *Hop-a-Long-Cassidy* in 1935.

A major film star of the 1930s and 1940s, actress **JEAN ARTHUR** makes the transition from silent movies to talkies and is named a WAMPAS Baby Star (see 1922) in 1929. Her role in the 1935 film *The Whole Town's Talking* became the type of role she would play for most of the rest of her career—a tough working woman who had a heart of gold.

1935

Hollywood's number one draw from 1935 to 1938, child actress **SHIRLEY TEMPLE (BLACK)** sings and dances her way into American's hearts during the Great Depression. After debuting in 1932 (at age three), she wins a 1935 Juvenile Award Oscar "in grateful recognition of her outstanding contribution to screen entertainment during the year 1934."

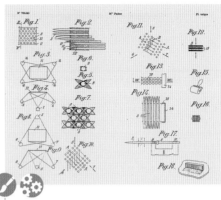

Screenwriter **MARY C. McCALL JR.** writes the screenplay for *A Midsummer Night's Dream* in 1935. She serves as the first female president of the Writers Guild of America and helps found the Screen Writers Guild.

During the years that actress and screenwriter **SALKA VIERTEL** is under contract to MGM (1933 to 1937), she writes scripts featuring her good friend Greta Garbo (see 1931). One of those is the 1935 movie *Anna Karenina*.

A pioneering animator, engineer **CLAIRE PARKER** receives a patent in 1935 for the Pinscreen. This grid of metal rods creates shaded and lit areas that are then filmed frame by frame. These elements are later called pixels. She and her husband produce two movies and her Pinscreen technique is used in the opening title sequence for the 1962 Orson Welles' movie *The Trial*.

Screenwriter **FRANCES GOODRICH** receives the first of her four Oscar nominations in 1935 for *The Thin Man*, in the category of Best Writing, Adaptation. Her other three Oscar nominations, all shared with her husband, Albert Hackett, are for Best Writing, Screenplay (*After the Thin Man*, 1937; *Father of the Bride*, 1951; and *Seven Brides for Seven Brothers*, 1955). She says of their working collaboration: "Each of us writes the same scene. Then each looks at what the other has done and we try to decide which of us has done the better. We advise each other and then go back at it again. We argue but we don't quarrel. When a scenario or play is finished, neither of us can recognize his own work."

1935

> "I know what's best for me, after all I have been in the Claudette Colbert business longer than anybody."
> —CLAUDETTE COLBERT

A movie actress for over twenty years, **CLAUDETTE COLBERT** wins a Best Actress Oscar for her performance in *It Happened One Night*. She will receive two more nominations.

Clark Gable and Claudette Colbert in *It Happened One Night*

Marion Morgan dancers on a Washington, D.C. Beach in 1923

An American-born screenwriter who spent much of her life in England, **GLADYS UNGER** writes the screenplay for the 1935 movie *Sylvia Scarlett* which stars Katharine Hepburn (see 1934).

Newspaper columnist **FLORABEL MUIR** writes about Hollywood celebrities from the 1920s through the 1960s. She writes the screenplay for the 1935 movie *Fighting Youth* produced by Universal Studios.

Choreographer, writer and editor **MARION MORGAN** works with Mae West (see 1932) on the script for West's 1935 film *Goin' to Town*. Morgan and Dorothy Arzner (see 1928) have a long-term business and romantic relationship.

1936 **KAY BROWN BARRETT** is most remembered for bringing *Gone with the Wind* to David O. Selznick. As a talent scout, she is responsible for the American careers of Ingrid Bergman (see 1945) and Alfred Hitchcock. Barrett advocates for Vivien Leigh (see 1940) to be Scarlett O'Hara and she makes Anne Baxter (see 1947) a star. After leaving Selznick, she becomes one of Hollywood's most powerful agents.

About *Gone with the Wind*, she says, "We heard a lot about the book before it was published, but no one could get their hands on a copy. Leland Hayward, the agent, said he could steal me one. Of course, Miss [Edna] Ferber knew nothing about this. I loved what I read and RKO gave me the go-ahead to buy. How do you buy the rights to a purloined book? Leland and I, we did it." Later, she says: "I never felt like a pioneer or like the only woman in a man's world. All I can say is that it was the Depression, and I was happy to have a job. Not to mention a job I loved." She also says, "I thought it shrewd to befriend Hitch on his home turf in London first, to show that we would go to him instead of waiting for him to come to us . . . But I'm given far too much credit for Hitch and not enough for [Vivien] Leigh. Hitch was well known and only required my diplomacy, Leigh was a real discovery."

1936

MARGARET (GLEDHILL) HERRICK becomes librarian for the Academy of Motion Picture Arts and Sciences in 1936. She serves as interim executive director of the Academy during World War II and officially becomes Executive Director in 1945. She serves in that position until 1971. The Margaret Herrick Library, named in her honor, is the primary repository for materials held by the Academy of Motion Picture Arts and Sciences, particularly those related to the Oscars.

An inker and painter in the animation industry for over fifty years, in 1936, **MARTHA SIGALL** is a painter on *Porky's Poultry Plant*. In 2004, she receives the June Foray award (see 1995) for her lifetime of work in animation. Her 2005 autobiography is titled *Living Life inside the Lines: Tales from the Golden Age of Animation*.

A major star at Paramount in the 1940s, **PAULETTE GODDARD'S** most notable role is arguably as Charlie Chaplin's leading lady in the 1936 movie *Modern Times*. She is also married to Charlie Chaplin for a short time. In 1944, she is nominated for a Best Supporting Actress Oscar for *So Proudly We Hail!*

Charlie Chaplin, Paulette Goddard and Henry Bergman, on the set of *Modern Times*

Named one of the greatest actresses in movie history (after Katharine Hepburn (see 1934) by the American Film Institute (see 1999)), **BETTE DAVIS** wins two Best Actress Oscars over her career and is nominated another nine times. Her first win is in 1936 for *Dangerous* and the second is in 1939 for *Jezebel*. She was the first female president of the Academy of Motion Picture Arts and Sciences. The first woman to achieve a Lifetime Award from the American Film Institute, she often plays unsympathetic characters.

Primarily a Broadway musical actress, **ETHEL MERMAN** acts and sings in many movies during the 1930s. Known for her booming voice, she is remembered for the 1936 film *Anything Goes*. Her last movie appearance is in 1980. Merman has been featured on a U.S. postage stamp.

An editor or "cutter" as it was known in the early days of the film industry, **MARGARET BOOTH** is nominated for the 1936 Best Film Editing Oscar for *Mutiny on the Bounty*. She is supervising editor at MGM from 1937 to 1964 where she approves every film before it leaves the studio. "They liked me because I was fast. I was always very fast cutting everything I did. And boy, was I tough." In 1978, she receives an Honorary Academy Award "For her exceptional contribution to the art of film editing in the motion picture industry." Booth also receives the American Cinema Editors Career Achievement Award in 1990. She says, "I loved it. I loved everything about it—the studio, the cutting room—everything. I'd work night you know, and not get paid. I was a workaholic. I never felt I was mistreated. I was always happy about my work. I'd do it all again."

1937 An accomplished horsewoman, **BABE DeFREEST** doubles all of Republic Pictures' serial actresses. In 1937, she performs stunt work for *Gunsmoke Ranch* and *The Painted Stallion*.

A Hollywood screenwriter for two decades, **GERTRUDE PURCELL** is credited with the dramatization (or adaptation) for the 1937 movie *Stella Dallas* with a screenplay written by Sarah Y. Mason (see 1934).

Stuntwoman and actress **JEWELL JORDAN (MASON)** begins her career as an extra when she is eight years old. She serves as an extra, a double and a stunt double during the 1930s and 1940s, suffering numerous injuries along the way. In 1937, she is the stunt double for Luise Rainer (see 1937) in *The Good Earth*. Her niece is Gale Anne Hurd (see 1984).

A screenwriter for thirty years, **ADELE COMANDINI** is nominated in 1937 for Best Writing, Original Story for *Three Smart Girls*.

During her thirty-year career in the movie industry, actress **JOYCE COMPTON** performs in more than 200 films. Named a WAMPAS Baby Star (see 1922) in 1926, in 1937, she appears in *The Awful Truth*.

After a twenty-two year career, acclaimed actress **LUCILLE LA VERNE** works on her final film, *Snow White and the Seven Dwarfs* (Disney's first animated film) in which she voices both the Queen and the Witch.

The highest paid movie star in the late 1930s, actress **CAROLE LOMBARD** wins the Best Actress Oscar in 1937 for *My Man Godfrey*. Today, she is considered one of the greatest female stars of classic Hollywood cinema (see 1999).

1937

Luise Rainer (center) in *The Great Ziegfeld*

The first actress to win back-to-back Oscars and the first to win more than one, **LUISE RAINER** wins the Best Actress Oscar in both 1937 and 1938. Her 1937 Oscar is for *The Great Ziegfeld* and she is honored in 1938 for *The Good Earth*.

Librettist and lyricist **DOROTHY FIELDS** is an early successful female Hollywood songwriter who enjoys a career of almost five decades. She shares the Best Music, Original Song Oscar in 1937 for the song "The Way You Look Tonight" from the movie *Swing Time*. She was nominated in 1936 as well in the same category for the song "Lovely to Look At" from the movie *Roberta*. She has been featured on a U.S. postage stamp.

Arthur Schwartz and Dorothy Fields work on the score of *A Tree Grows in Brooklyn*

LUCILLE BALL has a major role in the 1937 movie *Stage Door*. She will become beloved as Lucy in the *I Love Lucy* television series and own her own production studio. Ball has been featured on a U.S. postage stamp and inducted into the National Women's Hall of Fame.

Described as one of the most talented character actresses, **GALE SONDERGAARD** wins a Best Supporting Actress Oscar in 1937 for *Anthony Adverse*. Her second nomination in the same category comes in 1947 for *Anna and the King of Siam*.

"Preparing the animators' vision for camera required the inking and painting of thousands of fragile, combustible cels with perfect refinement. During *Snow White*, it was not at all unusual to see the 'girls'—as Walt paternalistically referred to them—thin and exhausted, collapsed on the lawn, in the ladies' lounge or even under their desks. 'I'll be so thankful when *Snow White* is finished and I can live like a human once again,' Rae Medby wrote after she recorded 85 hours in a week. 'We would work like little slaves and everybody would go to sleep wherever they were,' said inker Jeanne Lee Keil, one of the two left-handers in the department who had to learn everything backward. 'I saw the moon rise, sun rise, moon rise, sun rise.' Painter Grace Godino, who would go on to become Rita Hayworth's studio double, also remembered the long days merging into nights: 'When I'd take my clothes off, I'd be in the closet, and I couldn't figure it out: am I going to sleep or am I getting up?'"

—PATRICIA ZOHN, *Vanity Fair*, March 2010

REFERENCE

1938

Austrian-born actress **HEDY LAMARR** makes her American film debut in 1938 in *Algiers*. Her nude performance in the 1933 German movie *Ecstasy* caught censors' attention worldwide and led to the movie being banned in the U.S. She escapes Nazi Europe and is signed to a Hollywood contract at MGM in 1937. She appears as Delilah in Cecil B. DeMille's 1949 epic *Samson and Delilah* which is Paramount Pictures' most profitable movie to that date. Her patented invention of a "Secret Communication System" is incorporated today in wireless communication technology. She has been inducted into the National Inventors Hall of Fame.

Singer and actress **ALICE FAYE,** who debuts in films in 1934, is famously cast as the lead in 1938 in *Alexander's Ragtime Band,* one of the most successful musicals of the 1930s.

During her almost forty-year film career, actress **BARBARA STANWYCK** is nominated for four Best Actress Oscars. The first, in 1938, is for *Stella Dallas*. She is nominated again in 1942 for *Ball of Fire*, in 1945 for *Double Indemnity* and in 1949 for *Sorry, Wrong Number*. In 1982, Stanwyck receives an Honorary Award "for superlative creativity and unique contribution to the art of screen acting."

In 1938, the *Los Angeles Times* asks actress **HEDDA HOPPER** to write a gossip column, *Hedda Hopper's Hollywood*. She writes until her death and is famously known for her feud with another gossip columnist, Louella Parsons (see 1914).

A silent film actress who makes the transition to talkies, **ALICE BRADY** wins a Best Supporting Actress Oscar in 1938 for her performance in *In Old Chicago*.

Writer and actress **OLIVE COOPER** has many writing credits from the mid-1930s through 1950, including many Westerns. In 1938, she writes the story and the screenplay for *Cocoanut Grove*.

Helen Thurston and Lou Costello

Stuntwoman **HELEN THURSTON** debuts as a stunt double for Katharine Hepburn (see 1934) in *Bringing Up Baby*. Over the course of her thirty-year career, Thurston stunt doubles for many of the leading ladies of the day.

Primarily a writer of Westerns, in 1938, **PATRICIA HARPER** writes the original story for *Western Jamboree*.

A screenwriter in the 1930s and 1940s, **KATHRYN SCOLA** writes the screenplay for *Alexander's Ragtime Band* in 1938.

Screenwriter **HAGAR WILDE** writes the screenplay for the 1938 movie *Bringing Up Baby*, starring Katharine Hepburn (see 1934). Another of her important screenplays is for the 1949 movie *I Was a Male War Bride*.

Author and screenwriter **DOROTHY PARKER** has a long career in the entertainment industry. She is nominated for two Oscars—the first in 1938 is for Best Writing, Screenplay for *A Star is Born*. The second, in 1948, is for Best Writing, Original Story for *Smash-Up: The Story of a Woman*. Prior to her time in Hollywood, Parker writes for *Vanity Fair* and then *The New Yorker* and is a founding member of the Algonquin Round Table. The Round Table includes writers, actors and critics who meet daily for lunch at the Algonquin Hotel. Their table talk often makes its way into their newspaper articles. Known for her wit and often biting satire, Parker once said of Katharine Hepburn (see 1934), "She runs the gamut of emotions from A to B." Parker has been featured on a U.S. postage stamp.

> **I hate writing, I love having written.**
>
> —DOROTHY PARKER

1939

The movie cameras used to film *Gone with the Wind* have lenses made with **KATHARINE BLODGETT'S** non-reflective glass or so-called invisible glass. Blodgett receives her patent for non-reflective glass in 1938, while working for General Electric. Within a short period of time, all projectors and cameras in the filmmaking industry use her invisible glass as do World War II periscopes and spy cameras in airplanes. She is inducted posthumously into the National Inventors Hall of Fame in 2007 in recognition of her technical contributions.

The color supervisor for Technicolor feature films made at MGM between 1934 and 1939, editor **BLANCHE SEWELL** starts her career under the tutelage of Viola Lawrence (see 1958). One of the films she edits in 1939 is *The Wizard of Oz*.

Novelist and screenwriter **LENORE COFFEE** is nominated for the 1939 Best Writing, Screenplay Oscar for *Four Daughters*. *Street of Chance*, for which she is credited as a writer, is nominated for the Best Writing, Achievement Oscar in 1931. Her forty-year film career spans silent films and talkies. From her autobiography: "I was in one of my interminable waits to see [Irving] Thalberg, when his secretary told me they were having a very heated conference about a script which needed work; when the door opened I heard one of the men say, 'Why don't you put Coffee on this? She's free now.' Whereupon Irving replied, 'For Christ's sake, don't give me a writer with any ideas! She'll have them and I'll *listen* to them and we just haven't time!' Backhanded praise, but it amused me."

Olympic medal-winning ice skater **SONJA HENIE** acts in movies and choreographs her own ice skating routines. She is a top movie moneymaker in 1938 and appears on the cover of *Time* magazine in 1939.

Stuntwoman **BETTY DANKO** stunt doubles for the Wicked Witch of the West in the filming of the 1939 version of *The Wizard of Oz*.

Actress and stuntwoman **LILA FINN** is also an athlete who wins a silver medal in volleyball in the 1959 Pan American Games at the age of 50. Her movie industry career spans sixty years with more than 100 films, including *Gone with the Wind* in which she doubles for Vivien Leigh (see 1940) in some stunts. Finn serves as the founding president of the Stuntwomen's Association of Motion Pictures and helps found the Screen Actors Guild.

Scene from
The Little Princess

FLORENCE RYERSON writes the screenplay for the 1939 movie *The Wizard of Oz*.

A screenwriter for over thirty years, **ETHEL HILL** writes the screenplay for *The Little Princess* starring Shirley Temple (see 1935). She is also a racehorse owner and is known for wearing jodhpurs and other riding gear to work.

In 1939, at age 17, actress **DEANNA DURBIN** receives an Academy Juvenile Award along with Mickey Rooney "for their significant contribution in bringing to the screen the spirit and personification of youth, and as juvenile players setting a high standard of ability and achievement." A bigger attraction than Shirley Temple, at one point in her career Durbin sings in musicals but retires from movies in 1948.

An actress known for her red hair, **MAUREEN O'HARA** appears in the 1939 film *The Hunchback of Notre Dame*, early in her career. She works in the industry for more than thirty years and becomes known as the "Queen of Technicolor." In 2014, she receives an Honorary Academy Award recognizing "one of Hollywood's brightest stars, whose inspiring performances glowed with passion, warmth and strength."

Actress **CLAIRE TREVOR** debuts in film in 1933 and has the leading role in the 1939 Western *Stagecoach*. She wins a Best Supporting Actress Oscar in 1949 for *Key Largo* and receives two more nominations in the same category in 1938 and 1955 for *Dead End* and *The High and The Mighty*, respectively.

A stage actress who makes her film debut in 1915, **MARY BOLAND** returns to the stage after appearing in a few movies. Much more successful in her second foray into the film industry beginning in 1931, she often plays the motherly type and is remembered for her role in *The Women* (1939). She stays in the film industry twenty-five years.

FAY BAINTER makes her movie debut in 1934. She wins the Best Supporting Actress Oscar in 1939 for *Jezebel*. She is also nominated in 1939 for the Best Actress Oscar for *White Banners*. Her long film career includes another Oscar nomination in 1962 for Best Supporting Actress for her role in *The Children's Hour*.

Famous for portraying Glinda the Good Witch of the North in the 1939 *The Wizard of Oz* **BILLIE BURKE** receives a Best Supporting Actress Oscar nomination in that year for *Merrily We Live*.

Horsewoman **HAZEL HASH WARP** serves as a stunt double for Vivien Leigh (see 1940) in the horse riding scenes and falls down the steps for her in *Gone with the Wind*. Warp says of the fall "I was black and blue for a while. But I know how to fall. The director said I spoiled them because I knew what to do." Leigh insisted that Warp also be her stunt double in *Wuthering Heights*, Leigh's next movie: "Leigh told them that she wanted [Warp] or she wouldn't work." Of her time as a stuntwoman in Hollywood, Warp says, "I never will forget it. I liked it, everything about it. I just liked my work."

Screenwriter **ELEANORE GRIFFIN** shares the 1939 Best Writing, Original Story Oscar for *Boys Town*. She works for almost thirty years in Hollywood.

Screenwriter **ELIZABETH HILL** shares the 1939 Best Writing, Screenplay Oscar nomination for *The Citadel*.

KAY VAN RIPER writes the screenplay for the 1939 movie *Babes in Arms*, one of MGM's well-known musicals.

1939

Technicolor director for almost 400 movies from 1934 to 1949, **NATALIE KALMUS** oversees the color for the 1939 movies *The Wizard of Oz* and *Gone with the Wind*. Married to Technicolor founder Herbert T. Kalmus, she puts together a package that makes "color" an acceptable risk for the Hollywood studios. She says, "My role was playing ringmaster to the rainbow." And, "If you are properly devoted toward a career of any sort, you won't have to seek advice about it. No one is going to be able to stop you however hard they try."

THE BIG FUN AND MUSIC FILM SENSATION!

Mickey ROONEY • Judy GARLAND

BABES IN ARMS

CHARLES WINNINGER • GUY KIBBEE • JUNE PREISSER
GRACE HAYES • BETTY JAYNES • DOUGLAS McPHAIL
RAND BROOKS • LENI LYNN • JOHN SHEFFIELD
Directed by BUSBY BERKELEY
Produced by ARTHUR FREED

HUNDREDS IN BIG CAST!

Judy Garland in *The Wizard of Oz*

1940s

HOLLYWOOD'S
GOLDEN AGE

The age of classic cinema, the 1940s are considered Hollywood's Golden Age. Stars, such as Betty Grable and Lauren Bacall, manifested glamour and mystique. Advances in film technology grew significantly.

The Oscars opened this decade with a bang, awarding *Gone with the Wind* eight Academy Awards, including Best Picture. Vivien Leigh won her Oscar for Best Actress. Hattie McDaniel became the first African American to be nominated for, and win, an Oscar: Best Supporting Actress. Judy Garland landed an Academy Juvenile Award for her performance as Dorothy in *The Wizard of Oz*. Both of these films showed the promise of Technicolor, with audiences loving it.

During World War II, however, studios saved money by making many films in black-and-white. Popular black-and-white films included *Mrs. Miniver*, which won Best Picture and the Best Actress Oscar for Greer Garson. Beloved holiday films were made in this decade: *It's a Wonderful Life* (1946) with Donna Reed and *Miracle on 34th Street* (1947) starring a young Natalie Wood.

Audiences wanted and got variety in stories and characters. Women screenwriters worked hard filling this demand, earning Academy Award nominations and winning Oscars. Two women won Academy Awards for editing during the 1940s, another strong place for women at this time.

An Academy Award for costume designers was established in 1948, recognizing the significant contribution this field made to the production of films. Two categories would exist for many years—one for films in color and one for films in black-and-white. In 1949, Edith Head received an Oscar nomination for *The Emperor Waltz*, the first of her thirty-five nominations, including eight wins, making her both the most honored costume designer and woman in Academy Award history. Also in 1949, Carmen Dillon was the first woman to win a shared Oscar for Best Art Direction (Black-and-White) for *Hamlet*.

Ida Lupino began directing films during this decade and became the second female member to join the Director's Guild of America, after Dorothy Arzner. And the door to studio management was cracked open when Virginia Van Upp was made Executive Producer at Columbia Pictures in 1945.

Hollywood flourished during the 1940s, an era of magic and prestige.

VIVIEN LEIGH wins her first Best Actress Oscar for *Gone with the Wind* in 1940. She will win again in 1952 for *A Streetcar Named Desire*.

BETTY GRABLE stars in *Down Argentine Way*, her first major Hollywood film. In the top ten box office star category for a record-setting twelve years, she is the highest salaried American woman in 1946 and 1947.

Singer and actress **JUDY GARLAND** receives a Juvenile Academy Award for her performance as Dorothy in *The Wizard of Oz*. The citation reads "for her outstanding performance as a screen juvenile during the past year." She receives a Best Actress Oscar nomination in 1955 and a Best Supporting Actress Oscar nomination in 1962. She has been featured on a U.S. postage stamp.

1940

Animator, director and experimental filmmaker **MARY ELLEN BUTE** makes visual music films. *Tarantella* is released in 1940 and is stored by the Library of Congress in the National Film Registry (see 1988).

> "For years I have tried to find a method for controlling a source of light to produce images in rhythm. It was particularly while I listened to music that I felt an overwhelming urge to translate my reactions and ideas into a visual form that would have the ordered sequence of music. I worked towards simulating this continuity in my paintings. Painting was not flexible enough and too confined within its frame."

—MARY ELLEN BUTE

Italian-born storyboard artist **BIANCA MAJOLIE** who becomes the first female storyboard artist at Walt Disney Productions in 1935, writes the story for what becomes the Nutcracker Suite segment in the 1940 movie *Fantasia*. One of her stories, which becomes *Elmer the Elephant*, teaches the animators at Disney an important lesson, *"We could not have made any of the feature films without learning this important lesson: Pathos gives comedy the heart and warmth that keeps it from becoming brittle."*

Writer **MILDRED CRAM** shares the 1940 Best Writing, Original Story Oscar nomination for *Love Affair*.

While employed at Walt Disney, writer **SYLVIA MOBERLY-HOLLAND** works on story development for the 1940 movie *Fantasia*.

Editor **DOROTHY SPENCER** begins her career as a cutter in 1929. She is nominated for four Best Film Editing Oscars, her first in 1940 for *Stagecoach*. Her other nominations are for *Decision Before Dawn* (1952), *Cleopatra* (1964), and *Earthquake* (1975).

> Besides patience, I think you have to be dedicated to become a film editor. That's always been more important to me than anything else. I guess my whole life has been made up of wanting to do the best I could. I enjoy editing, and I think that's necessary, because editing is not a watching-the-clock job. I've been on pictures where I never even knew it was lunchtime, or time to go home. You get so involved in what you're doing, in the challenge of creating—because I think cutting is very creative.

—DOROTHY SPENCER

HATTIE McDANIEL is the first African American to win an Oscar. The Best Supporting Actress award comes in 1940, for her role as Mammy in *Gone with the Wind*. She and the other African-American actors from *Gone with the Wind* are prohibited from attending the film's premiere in 1939 due to the segregation in force at that time in Atlanta, Georgia. She has been featured on a U.S. postage stamp.

Actress **DOROTHY LAMOUR** performs in the entertainment industry for fifty years. She is best remembered for co-starring in the *Road to . . .* series of movies with Bob Hope and Bing Crosby. In 1940, Lamour appears in the first of those movies, the *Road to Singapore*.

1941

1941 The U.S. enters World War II. The war will provide unprecedented employment opportunities for millions of American women. These women, personified by Rosie the Riveter, provide much of the labor to produce the materials necessary for World War II.

A descendent of Harriet Beecher Stowe—who wrote *Uncle Tom's Cabin*, **ELIZABETH BEECHER** writes Westerns for the film industry in the early 1940s. Her first is *Underground Rustlers*, a movie released in 1941.

Actress, director and producer **IDA LUPINO** appears in *High Sierra* in 1941 opposite Humphrey Bogart. She turns to directing, "I had to do something to fill up my time," after being suspended from acting for objecting to decisions made by studio executives. She is the only woman in the 1950s who both directs and produces films and the only woman director within the Hollywood studio system. In 1950, she becomes the Director's Guild of America's second female director member. After directing many action movies, her ability to direct a love story is questioned and she says, "You don't tell a man. You suggest to them. 'Let's try something crazy here. That is, if it's comfortable for you, love.' I'd say, 'Darlings, Mother has a problem. I'd love to do this. Can you do it? It sounds kooky, I know. But can you do this [lit'l ol thang] for Mother?' And they do it—they just go and do it. I loved being called Mother." In 1972, she says "I'd love to see more women working as directors and producers. Today it's almost impossible to do it unless you are an actress or writer with power. . . . I wouldn't hesitate right this minute to hire a talented woman if the subject matter were right."

" I wouldn't hesitate right this minute to hire a talented woman if the subject matter were right. "
—IDA LUPINO

A silent film actress who makes the transition to talkies, **MARJORIE RAMBEAU** is nominated for two Oscars for Best Supporting Actress. She is nominated for the first Oscar in 1941 for *Primrose Path* and the second in 1954 for *Torch Song*. The Reuben Sandwich is developed for her when she visits Reuben's Restaurant and Delicatessen in New York City.

Screenwriter **BELLA SPEWACK** and her husband, Sam Spewack, are a writing team for theater and film. In 1941, they are nominated for a Best Writing, Original Story Oscar for *My Favorite Wife*.

Film editor **ANNE BAUCHENS** edits her first film for Cecil B. DeMille in 1915 and her last in 1956. She wins the 1941 Best Film Editing Oscar for *North West Mounted Police*. Her three other film editing Oscar nominations are for *Cleopatra* (1935), *The Greatest Show on Earth* (1953), and *The Ten Commandments* (1957). She is nicknamed "Trojan Annie" as she often works eighteen-hour days and demonstrates tremendous stamina.

1941

————— 1941 —————

Actress **JANE DARWELL** receives a Best Supporting Actress Oscar for her role as the matriarch of the Joad family in *The Grapes of Wrath*. She is also remembered for her role as Bird Woman in *Mary Poppins*.

Screenwriter **ALMA REVILLE** writes many of the scripts for her husband Alfred Hitchcock's movies, including *Suspicion* in 1941. Reville and Joan Harrison (see 1941) collaborate on the script for the movie.

Considered the most accomplished rider to perform in Westerns, stuntwoman **EVELYN FINLEY** performs stunts for almost fifty years. In 1941, she is the stunt double for Gale Storm in *Jesse James at Bay*.

> "Now I work with Mr. DeMille very closely from the very inception of the story to the final finish of a picture. To me, each DeMille production is a chapter in hard work and concentration that completes itself when it comes to a close. I am busy, thoroughly busy, throughout. My hours are long, from eight to eight. When I'm not actually editing, I'm on the set observing. Mr. DeMille likes me to be there to get the feel of the scenes and to understand what he wants when I work on them."

—ANNE BAUCHENS

Actress, dancer and singer **GINGER ROGERS** wins the Best Actress Oscar in 1941 for *Kitty Foyle*. She is named a WAMPAS Baby Star (see 1922) in 1932. Known for her dance movies with Fred Astaire in the 1930s, it was said, "Sure he (Astaire) was great, but don't forget that Ginger Rogers did everything he did . . . backwards and in high heels."

1941

> Some day they will have to admit that a woman can function successfully as an executive, too.
>
> —JOAN HARRISON

Screenwriter and producer **JOAN HARRISON** is one of the three female major producers in Hollywood during the 1940s—with Virginia Van Upp (see 1934) and Harriet Parsons (see 1948). A trusted assistant to Alfred Hitchcock (his "valuable idea woman"), she is nominated for two Oscars in 1941—Best Writing, Screenplay for *Rebecca* and Best Writing, Original Screenplay for *Foreign Correspondent*. In 1943, she becomes a producer at Universal Studios. In 1944, after she starts producing, she says about the management, "The objection comes from higher up, the front office. They—those ultimate 'they' who have the say-so on such decisions—simply do not want to give a woman authority. That's their objection. They recognize our capabilities, but it goes against the grain of the male ego to place a woman in a position of responsibility. . . . The front office attitude resents a woman in authority and it probably always will—they recognize women writers but prefer to keep us in prescribed grooves. Some day they will have to admit that a woman can function successfully as an executive, too."

Just after the onset of World War II, the United Service Organizations (USO) is founded to enhance military morale and build support at home for the military. More than 400,000 performances are put on for the troops from 1941 to 1947. Many of the Hollywood personalities portrayed in this book and active in the industry at this time perform.

1942 The first woman to receive screen credit as an animator at The Walt Disney Studios. **RETTA SCOTT** starts in the story department and later transitions to animation. She animates the "dog pack" chase scene in *Bambi* (released in 1942). She would later contribute to *Fantasia*, *Dumbo* and "The Wind in the Willows" segment of the *Adventures of Ichabod and Mr. Toad,* among others. Later, Scott provides storybook illustrations for Disney publications. In 2000, posthumously, Retta Scott is named a Disney Legend.

© Disney

"Chinatown" watercolor by Retta Scott

An actress who makes the transition from silent films to talkies, **MARY ASTOR** has a career over four decades. Named a WAMPAS Baby Star (see 1922) in 1926, in 1942, she wins the Oscar for Best Supporting Actress for her work in *The Great Lie.*

In 1942, actress **JOAN FONTAINE,** sister of Olivia de Havilland (see 1947), wins a Best Actress Oscar for *Suspicion.* Over the course of her career, she receives two other Best Actress nominations—*Rebecca* (1941) and *The Constant Nymph* (1944).

Playwright and screenwriter **LILLIAN HELLMAN** is nominated for two Oscars, the first in 1942. That year, she receives the nomination for *The Little Foxes* in the category of Best Writing, Screenplay. In 1944, she receives another nomination in the category of Best Writing, Original Screenplay for *North Star.*

1942

An editor originally hired by D.W. Griffith, **IRENE MORRA** works in the industry for almost forty years. She shows Margaret Booth (see 1936) how to "cut." In 1942, she edits the *Road to Morocco*, one of seven comedy films in the *Road to...* series starring Bing Crosby, Bob Hope and Dorothy Lamour (see 1940).

A writer of Westerns during the 1930s and 1940s, **LUCI WARD** writes the original story and the screenplay for the 1942 movie *The Lone Star Vigilantes*.

Screenwriter **GLADYS ATWATER** writes a number of Westerns during her twenty-year film career. In 1942, she writes the original story for the movie *In Old California*, starring John Wayne.

1943
Set decorator **FAY BABCOCK** receives the first of her two Oscar nominations for Best Art Direction (Black-and-White), Interior Decoration in 1943 for *The Talk of the Town*.

Actress **AGNES MOOREHEAD** who begins her long, successful entertainment career in 1929, receives her first of four Oscar nominations for Best Supporting Actress in *The Magnificent Ambersons*. Her subsequent Oscar nominations are for *Mrs. Parkington* (1945), *Johnny Belinda* (1949), and *Hush... Hush, Sweet Charlotte* (1965).

Set decorator **JULIA HERON** is nominated for her first Oscar in 1942. The category is Best Art Direction (Black-and-White), Interior Decoration and the movie is *That Hamilton Woman*. Her additional nominations in related categories are in 1943 for *Jungle Book*, 1945 for *Casanova Brown* and in 1960 for *The Big Fisherman*. In 1961, she shares the Best Art Direction (Color), Set Decoration Oscar for *Spartacus*.

Set of *That Hamilton Woman*, from left: Sara Allgood, Vivien Leigh

1942-3

One of America's top-ten box office draws from 1942 to 1946, **GREER GARSON** wins the Best Actress Oscar in 1943 for *Mrs. Miniver*. Over her career, she receives six other Best Actress nominations.

Teresa Wright (left) and Greer Garson in *Mrs. Miniver*

1943

British novelist and screenwriter **CLAUDINE WEST** moves to Hollywood and writes many British-themed scripts. In 1943, she shares the Best Writing, Screenplay Oscar for *Mrs. Miniver*. She is also nominated that year in the same category for *Random Harvest*. In 1940, she is nominated for the Best Writing, Screenplay Oscar for *Goodbye, Mr. Chips*.

GLADYS CARLEY works for Oscar-winning film editor Anne Bauchens (see 1941) and edits the 1943 film *Mardi Gras*.

A sex symbol in the 1940s and 1950s, actress **JANE RUSSELL** makes her first film in 1943, *The Outlaw*.

Veda Ann Borg and Madame Sul-Te-Wan
in *Revenge of the Zombies*

In an entertainment career spanning five decades and bridging the silent film era and talkies, **MADAME SUL-TE-WAN** pioneers for African Americans in the movie industry. Appearing in both *The Birth of a Nation* (1915) and *Intolerance* (1916), Sul-Te-Wan is the first African American to sign a movie contract. During her long career, she works with the prominent stars of the day. In 1943, she appears in *Revenge of the Zombies*.

Actress **ROSALIND RUSSELL,** who makes her screen debut in 1934, receives the first of her four Best Actress Oscar nominations in 1943 for *My Sister Eileen*. Russell receives the Jean Hersholt Humanitarian Award (see 1956) from the Academy in 1973.

1943

1944 LAUREN BACALL

makes her film debut opposite Humphrey Bogart in *To Have and Have Not*. Considered one of the greatest film stars by the American Film Institute (see 1999), she is nominated for a Best Supporting Actress Oscar for *The Mirror Has Two Faces* in 1997. She wins an Honorary Academy Award in 2009 "in recognition of her central place in the Golden Age of motion pictures."

JENNIFER JONES wins the Best Actress Oscar in 1944 for *The Song of Bernadette*. She is nominated for Best Actress four more times.

Singer, dancer and actress **BETTY HUTTON** appears in *The Miracle of Morgan's Creek* in 1944, which leads her to stardom. Hutton makes her last Hollywood movie in 1957.

Greek actress **KATINA PAXINOU** wins a Best Supporting Actress Oscar in 1944 for her Hollywood film debut *For Whom the Bell Tolls*. She appears in a few more Hollywood films before returning to Europe and Greece and pursuing a stage career. She is considered the greatest Greek actress of the twentieth century.

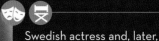

1944-5

Swedish actress and, later, director **MAI ZETTERLING** bursts into public awareness with her performance in *Torment* in 1944. In the early 1960s, she says, "As an actress, I had been horrified many times by directors who weren't careful with their jobs, people with vast reputations who never even bothered to do their homework.... Little by little, I began to realize that making films was what I wanted to do." Said of her, "*she admits ... she hates the manners men have when reacting to female aggressiveness. Zetterling pooh-poohs the notion that a woman loses her sensuality because she is in command.*"

" There are many things I feel haven't been aired on the screen, haven't been looked at from a woman's viewpoint. So naturally I make films about women. "

—MAI ZETTERLING

1945 With the end of World War II, most of the more than six million women who entered the workforce during the war are forced out of traditionally male jobs.

Award-winning actress **MARGARET O'BRIEN** begins her film career at age four. In 1945, she wins the Academy Juvenile Award for *Meet Me in St. Louis* with the citation "outstanding child actress of 1944." Her career continues for seven decades.

Margaret O'Brien (left) with Judy Garland

A screenwriter with more than sixty credits, **GLADYS LEHMAN** is nominated for the 1945 Best Writing, Original Screenplay Oscar for *Two Girls and a Sailor*. In 1933, she is one of the founders of the Screen Writers Guild. Lehman helps found the Motion Picture Relief Fund (see 1921).

A screenwriter for twenty years, **ELIZABETH REINHARDT** shares the 1945 Best Writing, Screenplay Oscar nomination for *Laura*. In 1999, the National Film Registry (see 1988) at the Library of Congress selects *Laura* for preservation.

Primarily a stage actress, **ETHEL BARRYMORE** debuts in films in 1914. Over her forty-year film career, Barrymore wins the Best Supporting Actress Oscar in 1945 for *None But the Lonely Heart* and receives three additional Best Supporting Actress nominations.

The "Cowgirl of the Typewriter," one of the few women writing Western screenplays in Hollywood during the 1940s and early 1950s, **FRANCES KAVANAUGH** writes the screenplay for the 1945 movie *Song of Old Wyoming*. With over thirty film credits, she is inducted into the Cowgirl Hall of Fame and Museum in 2014.

The recipient of three Oscars and nominee for four more, actress **INGRID BERGMAN** receives her first Academy Award for Best Actress in a Leading Role in 1945, for her performance in *Gaslight*. She is considered to be in the upper echelons of movie talent by the American Film Institute (see 1999.)

Charles Boyer and
Ingrid Bergman
in *Gaslight*

A film editor with more than 60 film credits, **BARBARA McLEAN** spends her career at 20th Century Fox. McLean wins the Best Film Editing Oscar in 1945 for *Wilson*. She garners six additional Oscar nominations in the same category—the first in 1936 and the last in 1951.

> " Why do *you* think that the film editors who are women, who have been in it since I've been in it, are the best in the business? Why? Because you had to be good or you wouldn't get there. "
>
> —BARBARA McLEAN

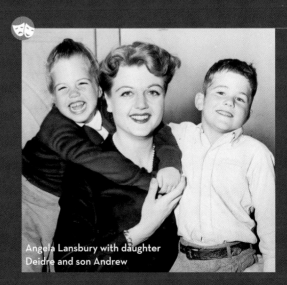

Angela Lansbury with daughter Deidre and son Andrew

During her over seventy-year career, **ANGELA LANSBURY** has received three Best Supporting Actress Oscars. The first is in 1945 for *Gaslight*. The others are for *The Picture of Dorian Gray* (1946) and *The Manchurian Candidate* (1963). Recognizing her career longevity and substance, she is presented with an Honorary Academy Award in 2014: "To Angela Lansbury, an entertainment icon who has created some of cinema's most memorable characters, inspiring generations of actors."

PEGGY ANN GARNER wins the 1946 Academy Juvenile Award "For the outstanding actress of 1945." In that year, as a teenager, she performs in *A Tree Grows in Brooklyn* as well as *Junior Miss*.

Ranked by the American Film Institute (see 1999) as #10 on its greatest female stars of classic Hollywood cinema, **JOAN CRAWFORD** receives the 1946 Best Actress Oscar for *Mildred Pierce*. She had been named a WAMPAS Baby Star (see 1922) in 1926.

One of the top movie stars of the 1940s, **RITA HAYWORTH** is nicknamed "The Love Goddess." Her film career lasts almost four decades. One of the top 25 greatest movie actresses of all time as rated by the American Film Institute (see 1999), in 1946, she stars in *Gilda*.

1946

1946

Composer and librettist **ANN RONELL** is nominated for Best Music, Original Song as well as Best Music, Scoring of a Dramatic or Comedy Picture for the movie *Story of G.I. Joe.*

Actress **AVA GARDNER'S** breakout performance is in the 1946 movie *The Killers.* In 1954, she is nominated for a Best Actress Oscar for *Mogambo.*

Screenwriter **TESS SLESINGER** is nominated for the 1946 Best Writing, Screenplay Oscar for *A Tree Grows in Brooklyn.*

Disney artist Mary Blair working in Brazil with company founder Walt Disney

Artist and animator **MARY BLAIR** is the background and color stylist for the 1946 animated movie *Song of the South*. She also works on *Peter Pan*, *Cinderella* and *Alice in Wonderland*. Blair receives the Winsor McCay award (see 1972) in 1996.

Novelist and screenwriter **LEIGH BRACKETT** writes the screenplay for the 1946 movie *The Big Sleep*. Often writing in the science fiction genre, she is credited with the screenplay for *Star Wars: Episode V—The Empire Strikes Back*. She is the first woman shortlisted for science fiction's Hugo Award. The story of how Hawks hired her for *The Big Sleep* is Hollywood legend.

> " Hawks liked my dialogue and called my agent. He was somewhat shaken when he discovered that it was Miss and not Mister Brackett, but he rallied bravely and signed me on anyway, for which I have always been extremely grateful. "

—LEIGH BRACKETT

Elizabeth Taylor
(left) and
Anne Revere in
National Velvet

1947 Screenwriter **CATHERINE TURNEY** is a contract worker for Warner Brothers, one of the first women writers to be hired in such a fashion. She writes the screenplay for the 1947 movie *The Man I Love*. She says, "One of the reasons that they hired me is that the men were off at the war, and they had all these big female stars. The stars had to have roles that served them well. They themselves wanted something in which they weren't just sitting around being a simpering nobody."

A direct descendent of American Revolutionary hero Paul Revere, actress **ANNE REVERE** blends a stage and film career. She debuts on film in 1934 and is nominated for three Best Supporting Actress Oscars, winning one. Her win is in 1946 for *National Velvet*. Her other nominations are in 1944 for *The Song of Bernadette* and in 1948 for *Gentleman's Agreement*. Her movie career has a twenty-year hiatus due to her affiliation with the Communist Party during the 1950s and her subsequent blacklisting. She returns to the movies in 1970.

Set decorator **MILDRED GRIFFITHS** shares a Best Art Direction—Interior Decoration, Color Oscar nomination for the movie *National Velvet* which stars Elizabeth Taylor (see 1961).

Tyrone Power (left) and Anne Baxter in
The Razor's Edge

Actress **ANNE BAXTER** wins the 1947 Oscar for Best Actress in a Supporting Role for *The Razor's Edge*. The granddaughter of architect Frank Lloyd Wright, she performs in the film industry for forty years. She is nominated for the 1951 Best Actress Oscar for her performance in *All About Eve*.

The House Un-American Activities Committee (HUAC) is established by the U.S. House of Representatives in 1938 to find Americans with communist ties. In 1947, the HUAC holds nine days of hearings targeting the Hollywood film industry and looking for individuals and movies that are deemed to support communist propaganda. Eventually, more than 300 artists, including directors, actors, and screenwriters are blacklisted (or boycotted) by the studios. Few individuals are able to rebuild their careers after they are blacklisted.

1946-7

Actress **OLIVIA DE HAVILLAND** wins her first Best Actress Oscar in 1947 for *To Each His Own*. She appears in the blockbuster *Gone with the Wind* and is nominated for the 1940 Best Actress in a Supporting Role Oscar for that performance. de Havilland wins her second Best Actress Oscar in 1950 for *The Heiress*. Her other Oscar nominations are for Best Actress for *Hold Back the Dawn* (1942) and *The Snake Pit* (1949). One of the leading movie stars during what is termed the Golden Age of Hollywood, de Havilland is the sister of Joan Fontaine (see 1942).

Sally Benson and director Mervyn LeRoy consult over set sketches for *Little Women*

From left: Muriel Box, Anne Crawford and Michael Medwin on the set of *Street Corner*

Screenwriter **SALLY BENSON** is nominated for the 1947 Best Writing, Screenplay Oscar for *Anna and the King of Siam*.

Director, producer and screenwriter **MURIEL BOX** shares the 1947 Best Writing, Original Screenplay Oscar for *The Seventh Veil*.

An accomplished horsewoman who began trick riding at age 14, stunt-woman **POLLY BURSON** performs stunts for many Westerns. In the 1947 movie *The Perils of Pauline*, she stunt-doubles for Betty Hutton (see 1944).

In 1947, experimental filmmaker, director and writer **MAYA DEREN** becomes the first filmmaker to receive a Guggenheim Fellowship for creative work in motion pictures. The American Film Institute establishes the Maya Deren Award in 1986 which is presented to independent filmmakers. The award is given from 1986 to 1996.

> " I make my pictures for what Hollywood spends on lipstick. "

Celeste Holm and Gregory Peck in
Gentleman's Agreement

1948 Stage actress **CELESTE HOLM,**

who makes her film debut in 1946, wins the Best Supporting Actress Oscar in 1948 for *Gentleman's Agreement*. She is nominated twice more for the same Academy Award: in 1950 for *Come to the Stable* and in 1951 for *All About Eve*.

1948

Katherine Dunham preforms in island costume on stage during Shore Excursion dance.

"The matriarch and queen mother of black dance," choreographer, dancer and actress **KATHERINE DUNHAM** choreographs and acts in the 1948 movie *Casbah*. She has been featured on a U.S. postage stamp and is the recipient of the National Medal of Arts and the Kennedy Center Honors.

A stuntwoman for more than twenty years, **SHARON LUCAS** is the stunt double for Jane Russell in the 1948 movie *The Paleface*.

Editor **MONICA COLLINGWOOD** is nominated for the 1948 Best Film Editing Oscar for *The Bishop's Wife*. She later edits the *Lassie* series and Lassie's television movies.

1949
Cinematographer, writer and producer **JANICE LOEB** is nominated for the Best Documentary, Feature Oscar for *The Quiet One*. In 1950, she shares the nomination for the Best Writing, Story and Screenplay Oscar for the same movie with her sister-in-law Helen Levitt (see 1950).

German-born writer **IRMA VON CUBE** shares the 1949 Best Writing, Screenplay Oscar nomination for *Johnny Belinda*.

> Stella Adler was much more than a teacher of acting. Through her work she imparts the most valuable kind of information—how to discover the nature of our own emotional mechanics and therefore those of others. She never lent herself to vulgar exploitations, as some other well-known so-called 'methods' of acting have done. As a result, her contributions to the theatrical culture have remained largely unknown, unrecognized and unappreciated.
>
> —MARLON BRANDO

Dame of the Order of the British Empire, actress **JEAN SIMMONS** is nominated for a Best Supporting Actress Oscar in 1949 for *Hamlet*. Her second Oscar nomination, this time for Best Actress, comes in 1970 for *The Happy Ending*. Simmons is primarily a film actress who starts in British movies and appears primarily in Hollywood films from the 1950s through the end of her career in 2009.

An actress and a Sennett Bathing Beauty (see 1915) in the early days of her career, **IRENE LENTZ** (known simply as Irene) opens a dress shop and later turns to costume designing. She serves as head costume designer at MGM. In 1949, she is nominated for the Best Costume Design, Black-and-White Oscar for *B.F.'s Daughter*. She is nominated for the Best Costume Design, Color Oscar in 1961 for *Midnight Lace*.

Actress **JANE WYMAN** makes her film debut in 1932. Nominated four times for the Best Actress Oscar, she wins in 1949 for *Johnny Belinda*. She marries future president Ronald Reagan in 1940, a marriage that lasts until 1949.

1949

Actress and acting teacher **STELLA ADLER** founds the Stella Adler Studio of Acting in 1949. One of her most famous students is Marlon Brando—she also teaches Elizabeth Taylor (see 1961) and Judy Garland (see 1940), among many others.

Author and screenwriter **VERA CASPARY** has a fifty-year film writing career. In 1949, she adapts the screenplay for *A Letter to Three Wives*.

A stage, television and film actress, **BARBARA BEL GEDDES** wins the 1949 Best Supporting Actress Oscar for *I Remember Mama*.

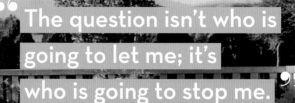

> " The question isn't who is going to let me; it's who is going to stop me. "

—AYN RAND

paraphrase from *The Fountainhead*

1949

Russian-born American author **AYN RAND** is best known as the novelist who wrote *The Fountainhead* and *Atlas Shrugged*. She writes the screenplay for the movie version of *The Fountainhead*, released in 1949.

Freelance costume designer **DOROTHY JEAKINS** shares her first Oscar in 1949—the Best Costume Design, Color Oscar for *Joan of Arc*. She wins two more and is nominated an additional nine times. Her other wins are Best Costume Design, Color for *Samson and Delilah* (1951—shared), and Best Costume Design, Black-and-White for *The Night of the Iguana* (1965).

Stage and film costume designer **BARBARA KARINSKA,** referred to as Karinska, shares the Best Costume Design, Color Oscar for *Joan of Arc*. In 1953, she is nominated for the Best Costume Design, Color for *Hans Christian Andersen*.

Ingrid Bergman
in *Joan of Arc*

British art director **CARMEN DILLON** enjoys a forty-year career in the film industry, during which she wins one shared Oscar and is nominated for another. The win comes in 1949 for Best Art Direction (Black-and-White), Set Decoration for the movie *Hamlet*. The nomination is in 1947 in the category of Best Art Direction (Color), Interior Decoration for the movie *The Chronicle History of King Henry the Fifth with His Battell Fought at Agincourt in France.*

An Olympic-caliber swimmer before she becomes an actress, **ESTHER WILLIAMS** is featured in films termed *aquamusicals*, which feature synchronized swimming and diving. One of these aquamusicals is the 1949 *Neptune's Daughter*. In 1952, Williams stars in a biographical movie about Annette Kellerman (see 1916) titled *Million Dollar Mermaid* and is branded the "Million Dollar Mermaid" herself.

1949

Audrey Hepburn

1950s

THE BREAKUP OF THE STUDIO SYSTEM

Societal trends significantly affected the movie industry following World War II and into the 1950s. Men returned from war, which forced many women out of the workforce. Families moved to the expanding suburbs and expected to find services there. They turned their attention to television and attendance declined at movie theaters located near city centers. Drive-in theaters became the rage, but suburban multiplexes wouldn't show up for another decade or more.

Under new trust-busting laws, studios were no longer allowed to own their own theaters. The studio system began to break up. The many individuals required to put a movie together were no longer under contract, but were instead hired on a project-by-project basis. This may have resulted in greater creativity and opportunities for actors to negotiate higher salaries, but it also meant significantly less job security. The women who were screenwriters and film editors lost ground. Even fewer women held decision-making roles in this new system.

Hollywood producers looked to television to help their bottom lines, with many major studios, such as Disney and Warner Brothers Pictures, becoming increasingly involved throughout the decade. One notable television "first" occurred in March 1953 when the Academy Awards were broadcast, receiving the largest audience in television's short history.

Although there were fewer female screenwriters, some of the most memorable films of the decade were written by women, sometimes with nods from The Academy. In directing, Ida Lupino's continued work was a bright spot in a decade with few remarkable projects from women. But women did receive Oscar nominations in the field of editing, with Adrienne Fazan winning the Oscar for *Gigi* in 1959. The costume designers flourished, with Oscar nominations going to women in every year of the decade and some Oscar wins along the way.

A milestone was reached when Dorothy Dandridge became the first actress of African-American descent to earn an Academy Award nomination for Best Actress for her performance in *Carmen Jones*.

This decade was also known for McCarthyism, Senator Joseph McCarthy's war on communism, which led to many Hollywood figures being "blacklisted" or boycotted. This stigma forced many out of the industry—some for years, some forever.

With the growth of television and the suburbs and the changes in the studio system, the movie industry was in a very different place by the end of the decade than it had been at the beginning.

The first woman to hold a major ambassadorial post abroad and the recipient of the Presidential Medal of Freedom, **CLARE BOOTHE LUCE** also writes plays and screenplays. In 1950, she is nominated for the Best Writing, Story Oscar for *Come to the Stable*. Luce has been inducted into the National Women's Hall of Fame.

Cinematographer and writer **HELEN LEVITT** shares the 1950 nomination for Best Writing, Story and Screenplay Oscar for *The Quiet One* with her sister-in-law Janice Loeb (see 1949).

Voice actress **LUCILLE BLISS** is known as the "Girl with the Thousand Voices." Her first character is the evil stepsister Anastasia in the 1950 animated movie *Cinderella*. She works in film and television for over 50 years.

⊢ 1 9 5 0 ⊣

First gaining national recognition for her role in the 1950 movie *The Jackie Robinson Story*, actress **RUBY DEE** is nominated for an Oscar for Best Supporting Actress in 2008 for *American Gangster*.

Costume designer **LEAH RHODES'S** thirty-year career includes the 1950 Best Costume Design, Color Oscar (shared) for *Adventures of Don Juan*.

In her film debut, **MERCEDES McCAMBRIDGE** wins the Best Supporting Actress Oscar in 1950 for *All the King's Men*. She is nominated a second time for *Giant* in 1957.

Costume designer extraordinaire **EDITH HEAD** wins eight Oscars for her work and is nominated another twenty-seven times. Over her more than six decades in the business, she becomes a household name in America, designs costumes for every major talent, and is personally close with most of them. Her designs become worldwide fashion. Her Oscar wins (in Color and in Black-and-White, some shared) are: *The Heiress* (1950), *Samson and Delilah* (1951), *All About Eve* (1951), *A Place in the Sun* (1952), *Roman Holiday* (1954), *Sabrina* (1955), *The Facts of Life* (1961), *The Sting* (1974).

> Dearie . . . You don't want to be a designer. The producers wouldn't like it. They all like to work with men.
>
> —EDITH HEAD

Singer and actress **ETHEL WATERS** is the second African American woman to be nominated for an Oscar—the first being Hattie McDaniel (see 1940). She is nominated for a Best Supporting Actress Oscar in 1950 for *Pinky*. Waters has been featured on a U.S. postage stamp.

1950

DEBORAH KERR receives the first of her six Best Actress Oscar nominations for *From Here to Eternity*. In 1994, she receives an honorary Oscar as "an artist of impeccable grace and beauty, a dedicated actress whose motion picture career has always stood for perfection, discipline and elegance."

Costume designer **MARJORIE BEST** shares the 1950 Best Costume Design, Color Oscar for *Adventures of Don Juan*. She receives three more nominations, for *Giant* (1957), *Sunrise at Campobello* (1961) and *The Greatest Story Ever Told* (1966).

Writer **VIRGINIA KELLOGG** is nominated for the 1950 Best Writing, Motion Picture Story Oscar for *White Heat*. In 1951, she shares the nomination for the Best Writing, Story and Screenplay Oscar for *Caged*.

Stuntwoman **LUCILLE HOUSE** is the stunt double for Maureen O'Hara (see 1939) in the 1950 movie *Tripoli*.

Elizabeth Taylor, in a dress by Marjorie Best

Voice actress **JUNE FORAY** has over 300 credits during her amazing 80-year long career. She is the voice of Lucifer in the 1950 movie *Cinderella*. She voices many familiar characters including Rocky the Flying Squirrel, establishes the Annie Award (see 1972) in animation and is the driving force for the institution of the Best Animated Feature Oscar. Said of her, "June Foray is not the female Mel Blanc. Mel Blanc was the male June Foray."

1951

Nominated six times for Best Supporting Actress, **THELMA RITTER** receives her first Oscar nomination in 1951 for *All About Eve*. Over the course of her more than forty-year career, she wins a Tony and is remembered for her portrayals of working-class women and her strong New York accent.

Bette Davis and Thelma Ritter in *All About Eve*

Primarily a rodeo performer and an inductee into the Pro Rodeo Hall of Fame and The National Cowboy Hall of Fame, stuntwoman **EDITH HAPPY (CONNELLY)** appears in the 1951 movie *Westward the Women*. Her daughter Bonnie Happy (see 1985) and her daughter-in-law Marguerite Happy (see 1991) are also stuntwomen.

CZENZI ORMONDE writes the screenplay for Alfred Hitchcock's 1951 thriller *Strangers on a Train*.

Screenwriter **EDNA ANHALT**, in partnership with her husband, Edward Anhalt, is nominated for two Best Writing, Motion Picture Story Oscars. The first, in 1951, is for *Panic in the Streets*. The second, in 1953, is for *The Sniper*.

JUDY HOLLIDAY reprises her successful Broadway role for the film *Born Yesterday* and wins the Best Actress Oscar in 1951.

Primarily a stage actress, **JOSEPHINE HULL** wins a Best Supporting Actress Oscar in 1951 for *Harvey*, in a role she had originally played on stage.

Over her forty-year career, costume designer **GWEN WAKELING** is a favorite of Cecil B. DeMille. In 1951, she shares the Best Costume Design, Color Oscar for *Samson and Delilah*.

Loretta Young, in a gown by Gwen Wakeling

Hedy Lamarr in
Samson And Delilah

Costume designer **ELOIS JENSSEN** shares her first Oscar in 1951 for Best Costume Design, Color for *Samson and Delilah*. She is nominated for Best Costume Design in 1983 for *TRON*. She spends two years as the costume designer for the television sitcom starring Lucille Ball (see 1937), *I Love Lucy*.

Called "Woman of a Thousand Faces," actress **ELEANOR PARKER** is nominated for three Best Actress Oscars. The first, in 1951, is for *Caged*. Her subsequent nominations are for *Detective Story* (1952) and *Interrupted Melody* (1956).

1952 Costume designer **IRENE SHARAFF** works across the fields of performing arts (theater, opera, dance and film), is nominated for fifteen Oscars and wins five. Her first win is in 1952 for Best Costume Design, Color for *An American in Paris*. Her subsequent Oscars include *The King and I* (1957), *West Side Story* (1962), *Cleopatra* (1964) and *Who's Afraid of Virginia Woolf?* (1967). The Theatre Development Fund Irene Sharaff Awards are established in 1993 to honor a member of the costume design community. Irene Sharaff receives the inaugural award. Subsequent award recipients are expected to embody the qualities of excellence that Sharaff demonstrated: a keen sense of color, a feeling for material and texture, an eye for shape and form, and a sure command of the craft.

> " . . . you can acquire chic and elegance, but style itself is a rare thing. "
> —IRENE SHARAFF

Kim Hunter and Marlon Brando
in *A Streetcar Named Desire*

An accomplished horsewoman before entering the movie industry, **MAY BOSS** performs her first stunts in 1957 in the movie *The Story of Will Rogers*. She doubles for many well-known actresses over her forty-year career including Sandra Dee (see 1957), Rita Hayworth (see 1946) and Doris Day (see 1960).

KIM HUNTER reprises the role of Stella Kowalski, whom she had played in the original Broadway production of *A Streetcar Named Desire,* for the movie. She wins the Best Supporting Actress Oscar in 1952 for that role.

1953 Stuntwoman **DONNA HALL** grows up in a rodeo family and performs stunts for forty years. She performs her first stunt at age eight. An accomplished horsewoman, she executes difficult maneuvers including transfers to stagecoaches, trains and wagons, as well as transfers between teams. In 1953, she is the stunt double for Doris Day (see 1960) in *Calamity Jane!* She is mentored by Polly Burson (see 1947). Hall is a founding member of the Stuntwomen's Association of Motion Pictures.

An animator for 45 years, **PHYLLIS CRAIG** begins her career as a painter for the 1953 movie *Peter Pan*. She works on *Sleeping Beauty* and *101 Dalmatians* early in her career. In 1993, she is the first color key artist to win the Annie Award (see 1972). Women in Animation, of which she is a founding member, establishes the Phyllis Craig Scholarship after her death. The scholarship is awarded to women in animation pursuing education.

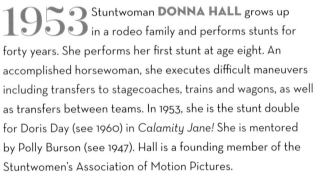

From author and screenwriter Mollie Gregory, "Are stunts important? They are more than that. They are fundamental to the mystery, excitement and thrills provided by action movies, and stuntwomen help create that experience."

Although primarily a theater actress, **SHIRLEY BOOTH** wins the Academy Award for Best Actress in 1953 for her role as Lola Delaney in *Come Back, Little Sheba* for which she had also won a Tony Award on Broadway.

An Austrian novelist and screenwriter, **GINA KAUS** moves to the U.S. with the outbreak of World War II. The 1953 movie that she adapts, *The Robe*, wins two Oscars and is nominated for three more, including Best Picture.

Actress **GLORIA GRAHAME,** who makes her film debut in 1944, later appears in the 1946 movie *It's a Wonderful Life*. In 1948, she is nominated for the Best Supporting Actress Oscar for *Crossfire*. In 1953, she wins that Oscar for *The Bad and The Beautiful*.

A costume designer with more than 100 film credits, **HELEN ROSE** wins her first Oscar in 1953 for Best Costume Design, Black-and-White for *The Bad and the Beautiful*. Rose wins another Oscar in the same category in 1956 for *I'll Cry Tomorrow*. She garners eight more Oscar nominations, some for the black-and-white costume design category, and others for color.

1953

1954

For six decades, screenplay writer, lyricist and librettist **BETTY COMDEN** collaborates with Adolph Green on successful musical movies. Their two Oscar nominations are both for Best Writing, Original Screenplay, the first in 1954 for *The Band Wagon* and the second in 1956 for *It's Always Fair Weather*. They collaborate on many well-known movies including *Singin' in the Rain, On the Town* and *Bells are Ringing*.

Screenwriter and songwriter **HELEN DEUTSCH** is nominated in 1954 for the Best Writing, Screenplay Oscar for *Lili*. She also provides the lyrics for a song in the movie.

Betty Comden and Adolph Green

An award-wining photographer, director, writer and editor, **RUTH ORKIN** shares the 1954 Best Writing, Motion Picture Story Oscar nomination for *Little Fugitive*. *Little Fugitive* has been added to the National Film Registry (see 1988) at the Library of Congress.

Composer and lyricist **SYLVIA FINE** is nominated for her first Best Music, Original Song Oscar in 1954. This shared nomination is for the song "The Moon Is Blue" from the movie of the same name. She is nominated again in 1960 for the same category for her song "The Five Pennies" from the movie of the same title. Her husband is actor Danny Kaye.

DONNA REED receives the Best Supporting Actress Oscar in 1954 for *From Here to Eternity*. She is also well-remembered for the 1946 film *It's a Wonderful Life*.

James Stewart and Donna Reed in *It's a Wonderful Life*

Ranked as the third-greatest female movie star in Golden Age Hollywood by the American Film Institute (see 1999), British-born actress **AUDREY HEPBURN** wins the Best Actress Oscar in 1954 for *Roman Holiday*. She receives four additional nominations for the Best Actress Oscar for *Sabrina* (1955), *The Nun's Story* (1960), *Breakfast at Tiffany's* (1962) and *Wait Until Dark* (1968). She receives the Jean Hersholt Humanitarian Award (see 1956) in 1993. Hepburn has been featured on a U.S. postage stamp and was awarded the Presidential Medal of Freedom for her work as a UNICEF Goodwill Ambassador.

1955

Actress **EVA MARIE SAINT**, whose entertainment career spans seven decades, wins the Best Supporting Actress Oscar for *On the Waterfront*.

Screenwriter **MARY LOOS** writes the screenplay for the 1955 movie *Gentlemen Marry Brunettes* from the novel written by her aunt Anita Loos (see 1912).

Screenwriter **DOROTHY KINGSLEY** works in radio before moving to films. She is nominated for the 1955 Best Writing, Screenplay Oscar for *Seven Brides for Seven Brothers*.

Rosa Parks refuses to give up her seat on a Montgomery, Alabama, bus, starting a year-long boycott that eventually scores a major victory for the Civil Rights Movement.

Actress **KIM NOVAK** who signs her first film contract in 1954, becomes a critically acclaimed actress in 1955 with *Picnic*. She also becomes a top moneymaker.

GRACE KELLY wins the Best Actress Oscar in 1955 for *The Country Girl*. The year before, she had been nominated for Best Supporting Actress for *Mogambo*. She has been featured on a U.S. postage stamp.

The first African-American actress to be nominated for the Best Actress Oscar, **DOROTHY DANDRIDGE** earns that distinction in 1955 for her performance in *Carmen Jones*. She performs in movies for almost thirty years, but racism and the associated dearth of parts open for her limit her film choices.

1955

NATALIE WOOD, who debuts in film at the age of four in 1943, and comes to public attention a few years later when she appears in *Miracle on 34th Street*, receives her first of three Oscar nominations in 1956 for Best Supporting Actress in *Rebel Without a Cause*. Her two Best Actress nominations are in 1962 for *Splendor in the Grass* and in 1964 for *Love with the Proper Stranger*. Her film career is cut short by her tragic death.

One of the highest paid screenwriters during the 1930s, **SONYA LEVIEN** sells her first script in 1919. She successfully transitions from silent films to talkies and in 1956 shares the Best Writing, Story and Screenplay Oscar for *Interrupted Melody*. Her previous nomination is in 1934 for Best Writing, Adaptation, for *State Fair*.

ANNA MAGNANI receives the Best Actress Oscar in 1956 for *The Rose Tattoo*. She is nominated again for a Best Actress Oscar in 1958 for *Wild Is the Wind*.

1956

Writer, producer and director **NANCY HAMILTON** wins the 1956 Best Documentary, Feature Oscar for *The Unconquered: Helen*, (*Helen Keller in Her Story*), the first woman to win this award.

A Tony-winning stage actress before embarking on a film career, **JO VAN FLEET** wins the Best Supporting Actress Oscar in 1956 for *East of Eden*.

For fifty years, soprano **MARNI NIXON** ghost sings for many actresses, although that information is hidden from the public and sometimes from the actresses as well. A sample of her work includes *The King and I* (1956—Deborah Kerr), *West Side Story* (1961—Natalie Wood and Rita Moreno), and *My Fair Lady* (1964—Audrey Hepburn).

> " A woman has as good a chance as a man to become a successful screenwriter. Her sex creates no awkwardness or difficulty. She has always been a familiar figure in the screen ranks. "
>
> —SONYA LEVIEN

 Screenwriter **ISOBEL LENNART** receives two Oscar nominations for her screenplays. The first, in 1956, is for Best Writing, Screenplay for *Love Me or Leave Me*. The second, in 1961, is for *The Sundowners*.

Editor **ALMA MacRORIE** is nominated for the 1956 Best Film Editing Oscar for *The Bridges at Toko-Ri*.

The Jean Hersholt Humanitarian Award is instituted by the Academy of Motion Pictures Arts and Sciences in 1956 in honor of Danish actor Jean Hersholt who begins his American film career in 1915. Hersholt serves as president of the Motion Picture Relief Fund for 18 years and as Academy president. He is a renowned philanthropist. The award is given to an "individual in the motion picture industry whose humanitarian efforts have brought credit to the industry." It is awarded for the first time in 1957.

Female recipients to date include:

Martha Raye – 1969

Rosalind Russell – 1973

Audrey Hepburn – 1993

Elizabeth Taylor – 1993

Sherry Lansing – 2007

Oprah Winfrey – 2012

Angelina Jolie – 2014

Debbie Reynolds – 2016

1957 Experimental filmmaker, director, cinematographer and actress **MARIE MENKEN** directs *Glimpse of the Garden*. This movie has been selected for preservation by the National Film Registry (see 1988) at the Library of Congress.

DOROTHY MALONE wins the Best Supporting Actress Oscar in 1957 for *Written on the Wind*. Her entertainment career lasts for more than fifty years.

In 1957, actress **SANDRA DEE** makes her first movie, *Until They Sail*, for which she wins a Golden Globe Award in 1958. By 1959, she is a household name due to her appearances in *Gidget* and *Imitation of Life*.

A close confidante of Walt Disney, **HAZEL GEORGE** often writes songs using the name of Gil George (Gilman was her maiden name). She writes lyrics and songs for some classic movies including the 1957 movie *Old Yeller* and the 1959 movie *The Shaggy Dog*.

1958 The first Asian-American woman to win an acting Academy Award, actress **MIYOSHI UMEKI** wins the Best Supporting Actress Oscar in 1958 for *Sayonara*.

A very early cutter at Vitagraph Studios, **VIOLA LAWRENCE** (pictured left) edits her first film in 1912, and spends much of her career at Columbia Pictures, where she is promoted to supervising editor. Lawrence is nominated for two shared Best Film Editing Oscars, the first in 1958 for *Pal Joey* and the second in 1960 for *Pepe*. She says, "Quite naturally, I'm on the woman's side in my profession. I don't think there are enough women cutters.... If you ask me, women have more heart and feeling than men in this work.... Now, listen to my masculine contemporaries yell when they hear this!"

1958

JOANNE WOODWARD wins the 1958 Best Actress Oscar for *The Three Faces of Eve*. She will receive three more Oscar nominations over her more than fifty-year career.

Nominated for a Best Actress Oscar in 1958 for *Peyton Place*, **LANA TURNER** has a fifty-year career. Debuting in 1937, Turner is a pin-up girl, an ingénue, a femme fatale, and a serious dramatic actress.

1959 Singer and actress **PEARL BAILEY** appears in the film *Porgy and Bess*.

SUSAN HAYWARD receives the Best Actress Oscar in 1959 for *I Want to Live!* She had previously been nominated for the same award four times. Hayward's film career lasts thirty-five years.

Primarily a stage actress, Dame Commander of the Order of the British Empire **WENDY HILLER** wins the Best Supporting Actress Oscar in 1959 for *Separate Tables*. Her two other Oscar nominations are for Best Actress for *Pygmalion* in 1939 and for Best Supporting Actress in 1967 for *A Man for All Seasons*.

In her almost forty-year editing career, **ADRIENNE FAZAN** wins one Best Film Editing Oscar and is nominated for another. Her win comes in 1959 for *Gigi*. Her first nomination is in 1952 for *An American in Paris*. Of her Oscar, she says "It was simply another indication of a job well done."

> "We selected Adrienne because of her reputation. . . She had an indomitable spirit. She refused to give in. I loved working with her."
>
> —GEORGE SEATON

Already a Tony-winning stage actress, **MAUREEN STAPLETON** is nominated for her first Best Supporting Actress Oscar for her film debut in 1959 *Lonelyhearts*. She is nominated twice more before she wins the Best Supporting Actress Oscar in 1982 for *Reds*.

One of the most popular sex symbols of the 1950s, actress **MARILYN MONROE** signs her first movie contract in 1946. After her appearance in the 1950 movie *All About Eve*, 20th Century Fox signs her to a seven-year contract. Her performances in *Niagara* and *Gentlemen Prefer Blondes*, both in 1953, launch her as a sex symbol. Wanting to be more, Monroe enrolls in acting school. In 1959, she appears in *Some Like It Hot*. Her last movie, *The Misfits* (1961), is also co-star Clark Gable's last movie. Both die suddenly before they can make another film; she of a barbiturate overdose, he of a heart attack. Marilyn Monroe has been featured on a U.S. postage stamp.

Screenwriter and producer **FAY KANIN** serves as President of the Academy of Motion Picture Arts and Sciences from 1979 to 1983. In 1959, she is nominated for the Best Writing, Story and Screenplay—Written Directly for the Screen Oscar for *Teacher's Pet*. She says, "I don't believe there is such a thing as 'a woman's story.' I resent it when men say that emotions are the precinct of women. The men I like best are the ones who show their emotions. Both sexes lose out when we are categorized this way."

On producing she says, "I insist on co-producing now [mid-1980s]. It allows me the close collaboration I enjoy. As a writer, I think it's better for the movie."

Peter Glenville talks to acting group, Fay Kanin seated left

Julie Andrews

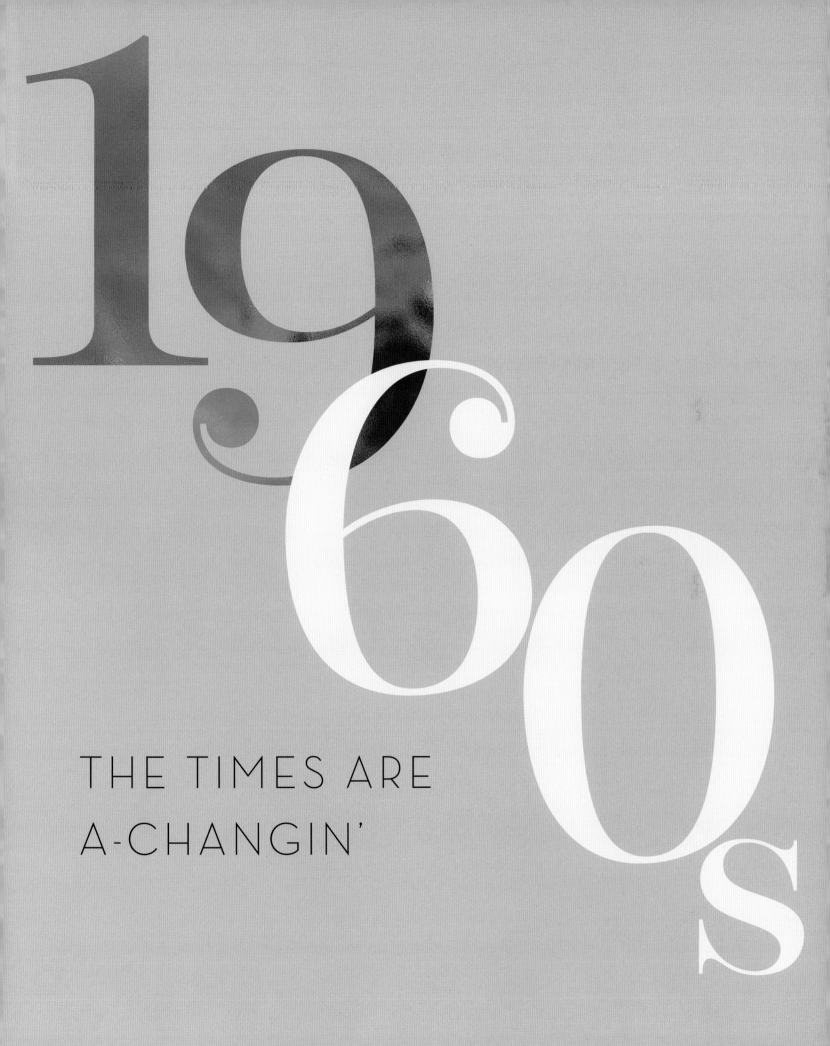

1960s

THE TIMES ARE A-CHANGIN'

The movie industry was not immune to the sexual revolution, the Vietnam War, the women's movement and other forces at play during the 1960s. Many films in this decade, such as *The Graduate* and *Guess Who's Coming to Dinner,* tried to stay relevant to the issues of the day. But big musicals made a splash as well. Many won Best Picture awards, but only a few provided vehicles for actresses to win Oscars. Of note is the tie for the Best Actress Oscar in 1969 between Barbra Streisand's musical comedy *Funny Girl* and Katharine Hepburn's drama, *A Lion in Winter.*

A new phenomenon was on the rise. The purchasing power of teenagers grew in this decade, particularly that of teenage girls. A new category of films opened up as Hollywood welcomed this new market. The result was that young stars, such as Sandra Dee, Ann-Margret and Tuesday Weld, emerged as "teen queens." They lightheartedly talked about make-up and dating and still covered serious issues in their films.

The film industry had financial difficulties in this decade. Movie audiences declined, in part due to the dominance of television. American film companies began to diversify with records or television production. Although there were many women who attained star status and brought in big bucks at the box office for their films, these women did not have influence or power within the movie industry itself.

Women continued as screenwriters, but fewer in number than in previous decades. None of the women who were nominated for Academy Awards for writing in this decade took home the Oscar. Some women film editors, who were also decreasing in numbers, received Oscar nominations in this decade, with only one win—to Anne V. Coates for *Lawrence of Arabia* in 1963.

Women, however, thrived in set decoration, art direction and costume design, perhaps because sewing and the arts fall under the category of "women's work." In costume design, Edith Head continued her string of Oscar nominations and wins. Many more women were recognized and gained influence in this area as well, with multiple women being nominated in every year of the 1960s.

The cultural turmoil of the 1960s set the stage for the struggle to come as women strove to regain their power, in the film industry and throughout society.

Costume designer **ALICE DAVIS** is hired by Walt Disney to design the costumes for the 1960 film *Toby Tyler*. She works with Mary Blair (see 1946) to design the costumes for Walt Disney's "It's a Small World" exhibit at the 1964/1965 World's Fair. She is named a Disney Legend in 2004.

Actress **JUANITA MOORE** is the third African American to be nominated in the Best Supporting Actress category. That nomination comes in 1960 for her performance in *Imitation of Life*.

SIMONE SIGNORET wins the 1960 Best Actress Oscar for *Room at the Top*. The first French actress to receive an Oscar, she is nominated again in 1966 for *Ship of Fools*. Signoret is considered one of the greatest French film stars.

⊢ 1 9 6 0 ⊣

1960

Nominated four times for either Best Actress or Best Supporting Actress, **SHELLEY WINTERS** wins her first Oscar (Best Supporting Actress) in 1960 for *The Diary of Anne Frank*. Her second Best Supporting Actress win is in 1966 for *A Patch of Blue*. Her film career lasts more than five decades.

A top moneymaker in Hollywood, singer and actress **DORIS DAY** is nominated for a Best Actress Oscar for *Pillow Talk*.

A set decorator with more than 100 credits, **RUBY LEVITT** is nominated for four shared Oscars in the category of Best Art Direction. The movies for which she is nominated are *Pillow Talk* (1960), *The Sound of Music* (1966), *The Andromeda Strain* (1972) and *Chinatown* (1975).

> " Initially I was worried about having problems with male crews, but then I found that those who don't like working with a woman simply don't join up. Pretty soon we begin functioning as people, not as members of different sexes. "
>
> —SHIRLEY CLARKE

Director, editor and producer **SHIRLEY CLARKE** is nominated for the Best Live Action, Short Subject Oscar in 1960 for *Skyscraper*. In 1963, she directs *Robert Frost: A Lover's Quarrel with the World*. She says, "I was never 'underground.' I was never 'Hollywood.' There was no group I was part of. I always hoped there was a niche I could fit into, but I never did.

"I chose independent filmmaking rather than studio filmmaking because I didn't want the studios to decide what people should see. I never thought about how hard it was to be an independent. My problem was to learn how to make films. I have never wanted to make a film that wasn't, for me, learning the next thing I wanted to find out about.

"I hope that as women make films they will start to say something that is meaningful to women in an entirely different way. And I don't mean about how women have babies—but with the sensitivity of someone who has looked with double vision, as women have had to, as black people have had to. They will give us greater understanding, not of men but of humanity, expressed much more broadly than we've been allowed to see."

Women's roles change dramatically during the 1960s. They are in the mainstream, in roles formerly male-only, as primary economic providers and in positions of public authority. Women constitute 38 percent of the workforce in 1960.

The first birth control pill is approved for sale in the United States.

Director and producer **MADELINE ANDERSON** completes *Integration Report One*, a film about the civil rights movement in the 1950s. She is also known for her 1970 film *I Am Somebody*, one of the first documentaries directed and produced by an African-American woman.

Costume designer **ELIZABETH HAFFENDEN** wins her first Best Costume Design, Color Oscar in 1960 for *Ben-Hur*. Her second Oscar in the same category comes in 1967 for *A Man for All Seasons* (shared).

Actress Carol Marsh (right) models a dress by Elizabeth Haffenden

1961 British actress **HAYLEY MILLS** wins the 1961 Academy Juvenile Award "for *Pollyanna*, the most outstanding juvenile performance during 1960." In 1961, she stars as twins in Disney's *The Parent Trap* and is named a Disney Legend in 1998.

Film critic and writer **RUTH WATERBURY** begins covering the movie industry in the 1920s. She serves as editor at *Photoplay* and *Silver Screen* magazines and at one point is an assistant to Louella Parsons (see 1914). Five-time president of the Hollywood Women's Press Club, her 1961 biography of Elizabeth Taylor is titled *Elizabeth Taylor: Her Life, Her Loves, Her Future*.

Nominated for two Academy Awards over the course of her career, actress, singer and dancer **ANN-MARGRET** debuts in 1961 in *Pocketful of Miracles* with Bette Davis (see 1936).

After starring in the musicals *Oklahoma!* (1955) and *Carousel* (1956), **SHIRLEY JONES** (named for Shirley Temple (see 1935)) wins the Best Supporting Actress Oscar in 1961 for *Elmer Gentry*.

JANET LEIGH is nominated for the Best Supporting Actress Oscar for *Psycho*. Leigh is discovered by Norma Shearer (see 1930), leading to a screen test at MGM. She makes more than 50 movies over her career.

Called one of the greatest female screen legends by the American Film Institute (see 1999), **ELIZABETH TAYLOR** makes her screen debut as a child actress in 1942 for *There's One Born Every Minute*. Known for her violet eyes and her great beauty, Taylor has a breakthrough role while still a teenager in the 1944 movie *National Velvet*. Making the transition to adult roles, she wins two Oscars over her career and is nominated for three more. Taylor wins her first Best Actress Oscar in 1961 for *BUtterfield 8*. Her second Best Actress Oscar is in 1967 for *Who's Afraid of Virginia Woolf?* She is also well-known for her jewelry collection, her romances and marriages—she is married eight times to seven men. She receives the Jean Hersholt Humanitarian Award (see 1956) in 1993.

LORRAINE HANSBERRY writes the screenplay for the film version of *A Raisin in the Sun*, the play she had originally written. She has been inducted into the National Women's Hall of Fame.

1962 **PIPER LAURIE** receives her first of three Academy Award nominations in 1962 for Best Actress in *The Hustler*. She will receive two Best Supporting Actress nominations—in 1977 for *Carrie* and in 1987 for *Children of a Lesser God*.

Dory and André Previn

Una Merkel (left) and Geraldine Page in *Summer and Smoke*

Lyricist, singer and songwriter **DORY PREVIN** is nominated three times for the Best Music, Original Song Oscar. The first two times are with her then husband, André Previn—in 1961 for the song "Faraway Part of Town" from the movie *Pepe* and in 1963 for the "Song from Two for the Seesaw (Second Chance)" from the movie *Two for the Seesaw*. Her third shared nomination is in 1970 for the song "Come Saturday Morning" from the movie *The Sterile Cuckoo*.

Actress **UNA MERKEL** begins her forty-year film career as a stand-in for Lillian Gish (see 1912) in the 1928 movie *The Wind*. In 1962, she is nominated for a Best Supporting Actress Oscar for *Summer and Smoke*.

SOPHIA LOREN is the first actress to win an Oscar for a film in a foreign language. She wins the Best Actress Oscar in 1962 for *Two Women*. She is nominated again for Best Actress in 1965 for *Marriage Italian Style*. Loren receives an Honorary Oscar in 1991 "For a career rich with memorable performances that has added permanent luster to our art form." Her entertainment career has spanned six decades.

1962

One of the handful of artists to have won an Oscar, Grammy, Emmy and Tony—and the first Latina to do so, actress, singer, and dancer **RITA MORENO** wins the Best Supporting Actress Oscar in 1962 for *West Side Story*. A recipient of the Presidential Medal of Freedom, Moreno is still active today, her career having spanned more than six decades. "Ha, ha. I showed them. I didn't make another movie for seven years after winning the Oscar. . . . Before *West Side Story*, I was always offered the stereotypical Latina roles. The Conchitas and Lolitas in Westerns. I was always barefoot. It was humiliating, embarrassing stuff. But I did it because there was nothing else. After *West Side Story*, it was pretty much the same thing—A lot of gang stories."

Rita Moreno (front, center)
in *West Side Story*

1963 Animator, director, producer, and writer **FAITH HUBLEY** and her husband, John Hubley, found Storyboard Studios and collaborate on short films. In 1960, the short she produces (and her husband directs), *Moonbird*, wins the Best Short Subject, Cartoons Oscar for him. She and her husband win two Oscars and are nominated for four more. The wins are in the category of Best Short Subject, Cartoons for *The Hole* (1963) and *A Herb Alpert & the Tijuana Brass Double Feature* (1967). She is a recipient of the Winsor McCay Award (see 1972) in 1975.

Over her sixty-year career, editor **ANNE V. COATES** is nominated for five Best Film Editing Oscars and awarded the Academy's Lifetime Achievement Award (in 2017). She wins the 1963 Oscar for *Lawrence of Arabia*. Her other nominations are for *Becket* (1965), *The Elephant Man* (1981), *In the Line of Fire* (1994), and *Out of Sight* (1999). The Lifetime Achievement Award citation reads: "In her more than 60 years as a film editor, she has worked side by side with many leading directors on an impressive range of films." She says, "In a way, I've never looked at myself as a woman in the business. I've just looked at myself as an editor. I mean, I'm sure I've been turned down because I'm a woman, but then other times I've been used because they wanted a woman editor."

1963

Costume designer **NORMA KOCH** wins the 1963 Best Costume Design, Black-and-White for *What Ever Happened to Baby Jane?* In 1965, she is nominated in the same category for *Hush…Hush, Sweet Charlotte*. In 1973, she is nominated for Best Costume Design for *Lady Sings the Blues* (with screenplay by Suzanne De Passe—see 1973).

> **"You have the courage of your convictions. When you're editing you have to make thousands of decisions every day and if you dither over them all the time, you'll never get anything done."**
>
> —ANNE V. COATES

During her forty-year Hollywood career, costume designer **MARY WILLS** becomes known as "the fabulous Miss Wills" due to her clothing designs. Her first job is as a sketch artist for *Gone with the Wind*. She wins the Best Costume Design, Color Oscar in 1963 for *The Wonderful World of the Brothers Grimm*. The first of her six other Oscar nominations is in 1953 and the last is in 1977.

Costume sketch by Mary Wills for Bette Davis as Queen Elizabeth in *The Virgin Queen*

1963

In 1963, **ANNE BANCROFT** wins the Best Actress Oscar for her portrayal of Anne Sullivan Macy in *The Miracle Worker*. She receives four more Oscar nominations for Best Actress over a fifty-year career.

Actress **PATTY DUKE** wins the Best Supporting Actress Oscar for her role as Helen Keller in *The Miracle Worker* in 1963. She serves as president of the Screen Actors Guild from 1985 to 1988.

First a gymnast, stuntwoman **PAULA DELL** trailblazes for stuntwomen in the film industry in the 1960s. Her first movie, *Son of Flubber*, is in 1963. A particularly memorable stunt is her being shot out of a cannon as Carol Channing's (see 1968) stunt double in *Thoroughly Modern Millie*. Dell is one of the founders of the Stuntwomen's Association of Motion Pictures in 1967. At the time of her death in 2017, a working stuntwoman said, "Any working stuntwoman today partly owes their career to her."

1964
Screenwriter and producer **HARRIET FRANK JR.** receives her first Oscar nomination in 1964 for Best Writing, Screenplay Based on Material from Another Medium for *Hud*. In 1980, she is nominated in the same category for *Norma Rae*.

A Dame Commander of the Order of the British Empire, character actress **MARGARET RUTHERFORD** wins the Best Supporting Actress Oscar in 1964 for *The V.I.P.s*. Known as a stage actress, Rutherford nevertheless appears in more than forty films.

A renowned British stage actress, **EDITH EVANS** also appears in films during the silent film era and, later, in talkies. She receives three Oscar acting nominations—*Tom Jones* (1964—Supporting Role), *The Chalk Garden* (1965—Supporting Role) and *The Whisperers* (1968—Leading Role).

A British costume designer and production designer on the stage and on film for thirty years, **JOCELYN HERBERT** shares the 1964 Best Art Direction (Color), Set Decoration Oscar for *Tom Jones*.

PHOEBE EPHRON shares a 1964 nomination for the Best Writing, Screenplay Based on Material from Another Medium for *Captain Newman, M.D.* with her husband and collaborator, Henry Ephron. Phoebe is the mother of Nora Ephron (see 1984) and Delia Ephron (see 1998).

The Civil Rights Act of 1964, prohibiting segregation in public facilities, government and employment, is enacted.

Movie and Tony-winning stage actress **PATRICIA NEAL** wins the Best Actress Oscar in 1964 for *Hud* and will receive a second nomination in 1969 for *The Subject Was Roses*, after her recovery from a stroke.

Elizabeth Taylor in *Cleopatra*

Costume designer **RENIÉ** wins the 1964 Best Costume Design, Color Oscar for *Cleopatra*. Her first nomination is in 1952 in the category of Best Costume Design, Black-and-White for *The Model and the Marriage Broker*. In 1954, she is nominated in this same category for *The President's Lady*. Her 1960 nomination in the category of Best Costume Design, Color is for *The Big Fisherman*. Her longevity is demonstrated by her final nomination in 1979 in the category of Best Costume Design for *Caravan*.

1965 The first woman to be awarded the Directors Guild of America Fellowship, producer, director and writer **STEPHANIE ROTHMAN** produces the 1965 movie *Beach Ball*. In 1979, she says, "It isn't up to men . . . And men have to realize it's all right to be what they want, even if the role is traditionally female. I wish the women's liberation movement could be followed by a men's liberation movement. . . I want my films to be judged on their own merits. But at the same time, I feel that calling attention to the fact that I am a woman might suggest to other women that they too could become directors. It might make the possibility of accomplishing this seem a little less bleak. When I left film school [in 1965] I found the fact that at least one woman, Shirley Clarke, was actively working in a field otherwise monopolized by men, was a source of reassurance to me that I might be able to do it too."

> " A great deal of the problem women have today is that they don't demand change. If you don't complain, no one knows you have a complaint. What roles women will play in the future depends on what women expect and want to happen to them. "
>
> —STEPHANIE ROTHMAN

Russian-born French actress **LILA KEDROVA** wins a Best Supporting Actress Oscar for her first English film, *Zorba the Greek*, in 1965. She specializes in playing eccentric or loony characters throughout much of the rest of her career.

Film critic for the *New Yorker* magazine from 1968-1991, **PAULINE KAEL** collects her earlier movie reviews in the surprise bestselling 1965 book *I Lost It at the Movies*.

British singer, dancer and actress **JULIE ANDREWS** wins a Best Actress Oscar for her film debut role as *Mary Poppins* in the movie of that name. During her career, she receives two more Best Actress nominations—in 1966 for *The Sound of Music* and in 1983 for *Victor/Victoria.* Honored as a Dame Commander of the Order of the British Empire, she has been involved with the film industry for five decades.

DEBBIE REYNOLDS is nominated for the Best Actress Oscar in 1965 for the *Unsinkable Molly Brown.* In 2016, she receives the Jean Hersholt Humanitarian Award (see 1956). Over her more than five decades in the entertainment business, she also earns Emmy and Tony nominations. She is the mother of actress Carrie Fisher (see 1977).

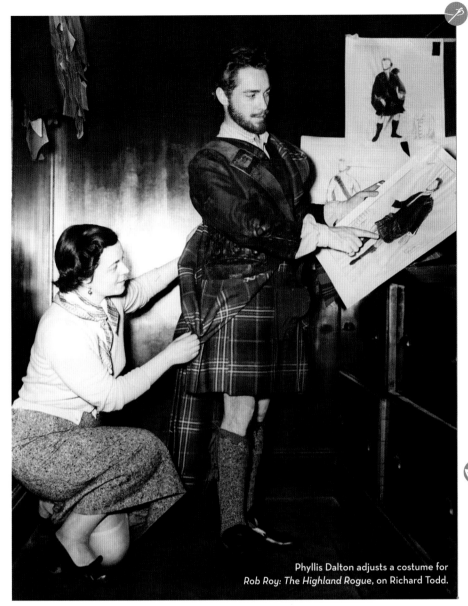

Phyllis Dalton adjusts a costume for
Rob Roy: The Highland Rogue, on Richard Todd.

1966 Costume designer **PHYLLIS DALTON** wins her first Oscar in 1966 for Best Costume Design, Color for *Doctor Zhivago*. Her second Oscar comes in 1990 for Best Costume Design for *Henry V*. She receives a nomination in 1969 for Best Costume Design for *Oliver!*

JULIE CHRISTIE wins the Best Actress Oscar in 1966 for *Darling*. She is nominated three additional times in the Best Actress category, for *McCabe & Mrs. Miller* (1972), *Afterglow* (1998) and *Away from Her* (2008).

The National Organization for Women (NOW) is founded with the goal of bringing about equality for all women, eliminating discrimination, securing reproductive rights and ending all forms of violence against women.

1966

In 1966, **RONA BARRETT** begins broadcasting Hollywood gossip on KABC-TV, a Los Angeles television station. She develops television specials, publishes magazines on Hollywood happenings, makes cameo appearances in movies and writes an autobiography.

1966

Costume designer **JULIE HARRIS** wins the 1966 Best Costume Design, Black-and-White Oscar for *Darling*. She works on two Beatles movies (*A Hard Day's Night* and *Help!*) as well as James Bond movies.

1967 President Lyndon Baines Johnson signs Executive Order 11375, which requires that affirmative action be taken on behalf of women and minorities in hiring.

A stuntwoman for 45 years and among the highest paid, **JULIE ANN JOHNSON** is one of the first woman stunt coordinators. Johnson is a founding member of the Stuntwomen's Association of Motion Pictures and co-founder of the Society of Professional Stuntwomen. In 1967, she performs stunts for *Doctor Doolittle*. Said of her, "Julie is one of the bravest women I have ever known, and there is no doubt that her courage and determination have helped make Hollywood a better and safer place to live and work. Today's stuntwomen, and future generations to come, owe her a debt of gratitude."

> **Once a stuntwoman, always a stuntwoman.**
>
> —JULIE ANN JOHNSON

Primarily a stage actress, **SANDY DENNIS** wins the Best Supporting Actress Oscar in 1967 for *Who's Afraid of Virginia Woolf?*

The Stuntwomen's Association of Motion Pictures is established.

Susannah York in *A Man For All Seasons*

Costume designer **JOAN BRIDGE** wins the 1967 Best Costume Design, Color Oscar for *A Man for All Seasons*.

1967-8

LYNN REDGRAVE receives her first Oscar nomination in 1967 for Best Actress in a Leading Role for *Georgy Girl*. She is nominated again in 1999 for Best Actress in a Supporting Role for *Gods and Monsters*. She is the sister of Vanessa Redgrave (see 1978).

Costume designer **THEADORA VAN RUNKLE** receives three Oscar nominations over her thirty-year career. The first, in 1968, is for *Bonnie and Clyde*. Her two other nominations are for *The Godfather: Part II* (1975) and *Peggy Sue Got Married* (1987). She receives the Costume Designer Guild's Lifetime Achievement Award in 2002.

Left to right: Gene Hackman, Estelle Parsons, Warren Beatty, Faye Dunaway and Michael J. Pollard in *Bonnie and Clyde*

1968 A theater, film and television actress, **ESTELLE PARSONS** (pictured second from left) wins a Best Supporting Actress Oscar in 1968 for *Bonnie and Clyde*. Her second nomination in the same category is the following year for her work in *Rachel, Rachel*.

CAROL CHANNING is nominated for Best Supporting Actress for *Thoroughly Modern Millie* in 1968. Her acting career will span more than five decades.

Actress **KATHARINE ROSS** is nominated for a Best Supporting Actress Oscar in 1968 for *The Graduate*.

Groundbreaking African-American actress, **BEAH RICHARDS** is nominated for a Best Supporting Actress Oscar in 1968 for *Guess Who's Coming to Dinner*. Over her fifty-year career in the entertainment business, she is also nominated for a Tony and wins two Emmys.

1968-9

1969 Considered one of the best stuntwomen who has ever lived, **JEANNIE EPPER** is from a stunt family (including Stephanie Epper—see 1970—and Eurlyne Epper—see 1983) and has more than 150 credits. In 1969, she performs stunts for *Hello Dolly!* She is probably best known for being Lynda Carter's stunt double for the television series *Wonder Woman*. Epper is a charter member of the Stuntwomen's Association of Motion Pictures (see 1967).

Jeannie Epper and screenwriter Carl Foreman, on location for *Mackenna's Gold*

Nicknamed "The Big Mouth," comedic actress **MARTHA RAYE** has a fifty-year career in the movies, on television and on the stage. In 1969, she receives the Jean Hersholt Humanitarian Award (see 1956) from the Academy for her volunteer efforts and service to the troops.

Actress and screenwriter **RUTH GORDON** wins her first Oscar on her fifth nomination—the 1969 Best Supporting Actress Oscar for *Rosemary's Baby*. Active in the entertainment field for seventy years, Gordon's other nominations are in both acting and writing. She says, "Pan me, don't give me the part, publish everybody's book but this one and I will still make it! Why? Because I believe I will. If you believe, it means you've got imagination . . . you don't face facts. What can stop you?

"And on that awful day when someone says, 'you're not pretty, you're no good,' think of me and don't give up!" Glenn Close (see 1983) says, "She had a great gift for living in the moment and it kept her ageless."

Lyricist and songwriter **MARILYN BERGMAN** and her husband Alan Bergman are perennial Oscar competitors for almost thirty years. Over that time, this powerhouse team wins three Oscars and is nominated for ten more. Their first win is in 1969 for Best Music, Original Song for the song "The Windmills of Your Mind" from the movie *The Thomas Crown Affair*. They win in 1974 in the same category for the song "The Way We Were" from the movie of the same title. Their 1994 Oscar, shared with Michel Legrand, is for Best Music, Original Song Score and Its Adaptation or Best Adaptation Score for the movie *Yentl*.

A stuntwoman who at one point doubles for Barbara Stanwyck (see 1938), **STEVIE MYERS** becomes an animal trainer for animal actors that perform in movies, commercials and on television. She owns the horse used by John Wayne in the 1969 movie *True Grit*.

Editor **EVE NEWMAN** is nominated for two Best Film Editing Oscars. The first, in 1969, is for *Wild in the Streets*. The second, in 1977, is for *Two-Minute Warning*.

Singer, writer, director, producer and actress **BARBRA STREISAND** wins the Best Actress Oscar in 1969 for *Funny Girl*. She wins her second Oscar in 1977 for Best Music, Original Song. For her 1983 movie, *Yentl*, she is the first person to direct, produce, co-author, star and sing in a major motion picture. Her additional Oscar nominations are for Best Picture, Best Actress and Best Music, Original Song. She is one of the small group of people who have won an Oscar, Grammy, Emmy and Tony. One of the most successful individuals in the entertainment business, Streisand has also won a Peabody and been honored with the Kennedy Center Honors and the Presidential Medal of Freedom. Discussing the fact that she was not nominated for Best Director for *Yentl*, she says, "It was strange. I didn't mind it for one reason: It really showed the sexism. I thought by not being nominated, I put a spotlight on the issue. I thought, 'Wow. This is so transparent.'" About her decision to be behind the camera, she says, "I didn't know it was a glass ceiling. I just thought, they don't believe in a woman's capacity to handle finances or to be the businessman. Years ago, I was told, 'You want control? A woman wants control? That's crazy!'"

> Speaking for myself, I have a deep commitment to making films about positive transformation and the unlimited potential for human growth.
>
> —BARBRA STREISAND

1969

Canadian dancer and choreographer **ONNA WHITE** (right) receives an Honorary Oscar in 1969 "For her outstanding choreography achievement for *Oliver!*"

Lucille Ball (left) and Onna White

Carrie Fisher

1970s

STARTING A COMEBACK

During this decade, women began making slow progress toward the goal of gender parity in the movie industry, paralleling a wider trend of women moving into the workforce. Emulating their sisters from the early days of the industry, women began finding ways to move their desired projects forward by multitasking. Whether they formed their own production companies or became their own screenwriters or cinematographers, they were able to direct and act in their own films.

More women were hired as screenwriters and demonstrated their success in writing stories for all audiences. This was especially true for Nancy Dowd's hockey film, *Slap Shot*, which she followed with a shared Oscar win in 1979 for *Coming Home*. Women writers were represented in nine of the ten Academy Award seasons in this decade.

Female editors let their voices be heard, becoming more influential and acknowledged by The Academy. Dede Allen, who edited Dowd's *Slap Shot*, was one of the most successful female editors, becoming the first to demand and receive a percentage of a film's profits. Margaret Booth's lifetime of editing was recognized by The Academy in 1978 with an Honorary Award for her years of outstanding work.

Although women film producers had been common in the early days of cinema, one broke a glass ceiling in this decade. In 1974, Julia Phillips became the first female producer to receive an Oscar for Best Picture, sharing the win for *The Sting*. She shared another nomination in 1977 for *Taxi Driver*.

A truly significant breakthrough occurred in this decade, when Lina Wertmuller became the first woman nominated for Best Director. Her film was *Seven Beauties* and the year was 1977. She received a second nomination that year for Best Screenplay Written Directly for the Screen for the same movie.

Although Virginia Van Upp had reached the level of production executive in the 1940s, it was not until this decade that a few women were studio executives again.

After decades of inequality, women in Hollywood once again began an upward climb.

Editor **FRANÇOISE BONNOT** wins the 1970 Best Film Editing Oscar for *Z*. She edits Julie Taymor's (see 2003) films starting in 1997.

Dame Commander of the Order of the British Empire **MAGGIE SMITH,** one of the most revered actresses of all time, wins her first Best Actress Oscar in 1970 for *The Prime of Miss Jean Brodie*. She wins the Best Actress Oscar again in 1979 for *California Suite* and will receive four additional nominations.

DYAN CANNON is the first Oscar-nominated actress to be nominated in the Best Short Film, Live Action category—in 1977 for *Number One*. She directs, produces, writes, edits, composes the music for and acts in this film. Her first Best Supporting Actress Oscar nomination is in 1970 for *Bob & Carol & Ted & Alice*. Her second is in 1979 for *Heaven Can Wait*.

1970

Costume designer **MARGARET FURSE** wins the 1970 Best Costume Design Oscar for *Anne of a Thousand Days*. She receives five more Oscar nominations for *The Mudlark* (1952), *Becket* (1965), *The Lion in Winter* (1969), *Scrooge* (1971) and *Mary, Queen of Scots* (1972). In honor of her accomplishments as a British citizen, the National Portrait Gallery in London, England houses a painting of her.

Genevieve Bujold as Anne Boleyn
in *Anne of the Thousand Days*

GOLDIE HAWN wins the Best Actress in a Supporting Role Oscar for *Cactus Flower*. She will be nominated for Best Actress in 1981 for *Private Benjamin*. Hawn has been producing movies since 1980.

As stated by Lillian Gish (see 1912): "In the early days of film many of the scenarists were women. Frances Marion wrote most of Mary Pickford's films. June Mathis wrote Valentino's stories and Anita Loos wrote for Douglas Fairbanks. Nowadays [early 1970s] the pictures are run by men and they are made for men and they seem to defile human relationships. But it was not always so. D.W. Griffith felt that if women didn't like a movie it would be a failure; if they liked it, it would become a success. Have the women in the audience been forgotten? If this is so, I think that is more a struggle between business and art in movies than between masculine and feminine."

1971 A frequent collaborator with Clint Eastwood, screenwriter **JO HEIMS** writes the screenplay and the story for the 1971 movie *Play Misty for Me*.

As Head of Casting at Warner Brothers studio, **NESSA HYAMS** casts *Summer of '42* in 1971. She later serves as the Vice President of West Coast Production for Columbia Pictures.

One of the founding members of the Stuntwomen's Association of Motion Pictures, stuntwoman **REGINA PARTON** performs stunts in movies for more than twenty years including the 1971 movie *Dirty Harry*.

Screenwriter **CAROLE EASTMAN** writes the scripts for four of Jack Nicholson's films including *Five Easy Pieces* for which she is nominated for a Best Screenplay Oscar in 1971.

Arthur Miller, Barbara Loden and Jason Robards Jr.

Actress **BARBARA LODEN** writes, directs and stars in the 1970 movie *Wanda*.

The sister of Jeannie Epper (see 1969) and aunt of Eurlyne Epper (see 1983), **STEPHANIE EPPER** is from a stunt family. Epper begins her career as a stunt double on the television show *My Friend Flicka*. Her movie career extends for thirty years and she performs stunts in the 1970 movie *Little Big Man*. She is a charter member of the Stuntwomen's Association of Motion Pictures (see 1967).

Producer **JOAN KELLER STERN** wins one Oscar and is nominated for a second in 1970, both for the movie *The Magic Machines*. Her nomination is for Best Documentary, Short Subject. She wins the Best Short Film, Live Action Oscar.

JANE ALEXANDER receives the first of her four acting Oscar nominations in 1971 for *The Great White Hope* (for Best Actress). An actress on the stage and on television as well as in movies, she serves as the Director of the National Endowment for the Arts.

Actress **ALI MacGRAW,** who comes to public attention in the 1969 film *Goodbye, Columbus,* receives a nomination for the Best Actress Oscar in 1971 for *Love Story.*

Jack Nicholson and Karen Black in *Five Easy Pieces*

GLENDA JACKSON wins the first of her two Best Actress Oscars in 1971 for *Women in Love.* Her second, in 1974, is for *A Touch of Class.* The actress, who later serves as a member of the English Parliament, receives two more nominations.

An actress with more than 200 film credits, as well as a screen-writer, **KAREN BLACK** receives a Best Supporting Actress Oscar nomination in 1971 for *Five Easy Pieces.*

1972

JANE FONDA wins her first Best Actress Oscar in 1972 for *Klute*. She wins again in 1979 for *Coming Home* and has received five other nominations. In 1985, she says. "I just wanted to be an actress—that's what I was trained for. No one told me I would end up having to negotiate and produce . . . but it's come to that. Now that I'm over forty-five, I find it's hard to get interesting roles, so I'm creating my own. With the decline of the studio system, which has its upside and its downside, it's up to actresses to develop their own projects. *Coming Home, China Syndrome, Nine to Five, On Golden Pond* and *Rollover* are all films we've created and developed—and it's been very rewarding."

> "Now that I'm over forty-five, I find it's hard to get interesting roles, so I'm creating my own."
> —JANE FONDA

Costume designer **YVONNE BLAKE** wins the 1972 Best Costume Design Oscar for *Nicholas and Alexandra*. She receives another nomination in the same category in 1976 for *The Four Musketeers*.

The Writers Guild of America establishes a women's committee to "provide the means of ending discrimination against women writers in the industry and to work to improve the image of women in film, television and radio, and to sponsor events designed to increase knowledge of the craft and the marketplace."

The Annie Award is established by the Los Angeles Branch of the International Animated Film Society to recognize excellence in film animation. June Foray (see 1950) originates the idea of awards in animation.

The Winsor McCay Award is established by the International Animated Film Society. It is given to individuals in recognition of lifetime or career contributions in animation and is named in honor of a pioneer in animation.

"There is no greater agony than bearing an untold story inside you."

—MAYA ANGELOU

1972

Writer and actress **MAYA ANGELOU** becomes the first African-American woman to have a screenplay produced when *Georgia, Georgia* is released in 1972. A member of the Director's Guild of America, she says "If you stick to your guns as a woman, you're stubborn. But if you stick to your guns as a man, you're persistent. And if you're black and female and six feet tall—PHEW!" Angelou has been inducted into the National Women's Hall of Fame.

Suzanne de Passe with cast of
The Jacksons: An American Dream

1973 Producer **MARTINA HUGUENOT** VAN DER **LINDEN** shares the 1973 Best Documentary, Short Subject Oscar for *This Tiny World*. She shares a nomination in 1963 for the Best Short Subject, Live Action Oscar for *Big City Blues*.

African-American producer, music and television executive, and screenwriter **SUZANNE DE PASSE,** is nominated for the 1973 Best Writing, Story and Screenplay Based on Factual Material Not Previously Published or Produced Oscar for *Lady Sings the Blues*.

CLORIS LEACHMAN wins the Best Supporting Actress Oscar in 1972 for *The Last Picture Show*.

> "No person in the United States shall, on the basis of sex, be excluded from participation in, or denied the benefits of, or be subject to discrimination under any education program or activity receiving federal assistance." Title IX, Education Amendments of 1972 to the Civil Rights Act of 1964.

LIV ULLMANN receives the first of her two Oscar nominations in the Best Actress category in 1973 for *The Emigrants*. Her second is in 1977 for *Face to Face*.

Character actress **EILEEN HECKART** is nominated for her first of two Best Supporting Actress Oscars in 1957 for *The Bad Seed*. She wins the Academy Award in 1973 for *Butterflies are Free*.

Writer, director and producer **SARAH KERNOCHAN** wins the first of her two Oscars in 1973. The first is for Best Documentary, Feature for *Marjoe*. The second, the 2002 Best Documentary, Short Subject is for *Thoth*.

Animator **ANN GUENTHER** began her career as an inker on *Sleeping Beauty*. In 1973, she works as a background artist for *Robin Hood*.

1973

Nominated for a Best Actress Oscar in 1973 for *Sounder*, **CICELY TYSON** has worked in the film industry for more than fifty years. Her stage and television work has led to Tony and Emmy awards.

Producer **ROSILYN HELLER** is appointed Vice President of Columbia Pictures in 1973, an early female studio executive. Her major films while at Columbia include *Taxi Driver*, *Julia*, *Close Encounters of the Third Kind*, and *The China Syndrome*.

Screenwriter **JAY PRESSON ALLEN** (pictured below right) is nominated for the Best Writing, Screenplay Based on Material from Another Medium Oscar in 1973 for *Cabaret*. She is nominated again in the same category in 1982 for *Prince of the City*. During her career, which begins when she writes *Marnie*, a 1964 Alfred Hitchcock movie, she is one of the few women making a living as a screenwriter. She also writes the screenplay for *Funny Lady* which stars Barbra Streisand (see 1969).

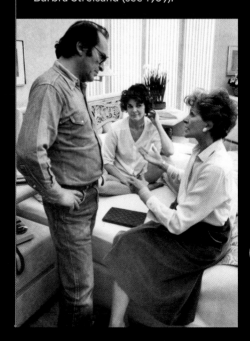

The daughter of actress Judy Garland (see 1940) **LIZA MINNELLI** wins the Best Actress Oscar in 1973 for *Cabaret*. Her previous Best Actress nomination is in 1970 for *The Sterile Cuckoo*.

1973-4

DIANA ROSS is nominated for the 1973 Best Actress Oscar for her performance in *Lady Sings the Blues*.

" I can understand why the men kept us out for such a long time. They wanted to keep this to themselves. It's great to have a big job. "

—MARCIA NASATIR

1974 In 1974, **MARCIA NASATIR** becomes the first female vice president at United Artists where she helps develop *The Big Chill, Carrie, Rocky* and *Coming Home*. Her story is told in the 2016 documentary, *A Classy Broad*. She says, "If I'd been born 20 years later, I would be head of a studio, which I would have liked. But I'm... happy to see other women carry the torch even further."

"They offered me the job of story editor but I wouldn't take the job unless it was a vice presidency. That would break the deal, I was told. After all, no women held those jobs. Women read, men do. But titles are imperative. Don't let anyone tell you different. I knew that no one would negotiate with me seriously unless I was vice president. I stood firm."

Film critic and author **MOLLY HASKELL** reviews movies for *The Village Voice*, *New York*, and *Vogue*. Her 1974 book (revised in 1987) is titled *From Reverence to Rape: The Treatment of Women in the Movies*.

The first female producer to win an Academy Award for Best Picture, **JULIA PHILLIPS** achieves that feat in 1974 for *The Sting*. She is nominated again for the Best Picture Oscar in 1977 for *Taxi Driver*.

Writer and producer **GLORIA KATZ** shares the 1974 Best Writing, Story and Screenplay Based on Factual Material or Material Not Previously Published or Produced Oscar nomination with her frequent collaborator George Lucas and her husband and collaborator Willard Huyck for the movie *American Graffiti*.

1974

Actress and comedienne **MADELINE KAHN** receives two Best Supporting Actress Oscar nominations in two consecutive years. The first is in 1974 for *Paper Moon* and the second is in 1975 for *Blazing Saddles*.

MARSHA MASON receives the first of her four Best Actress Oscar nominations in 1974 for *Cinderella Liberty*. She will be nominated in 1978 for *The Goodbye Girl*, in 1980 for *Chapter Two* and in 1982 for *Only When I Laugh*.

French writer and director **SUZANNE SCHIFFMAN,** who often works with director François Truffaut, shares a 1974 nomination with him for the Best Writing, Original Screenplay Oscar for the movie *Day for Night*.

HOLLYWOOD: *Her Story* 225

LINDA McCARTNEY shares the 1974 Best Music, Original Song Oscar nomination for the song "Live and Let Die" from the movie of the same name with her husband, former Beatle Paul McCartney.

Actress **PAM GRIER** stars in *Foxy Brown* in 1974. She is considered one of the greatest female action stars in the history of film.

An inker for Walt Disney Studios, **GRACE GODINO** works on *The Nine Lives of Fritz the Cat* in 1974. A Renaissance woman, she also is a stand-in for Rita Hayworth (see 1946) in *Gilda* (1946) and *The Lives of Carmen* (1948).

Tatum O'Neal in *Paper Moon*

The youngest person to win an Academy Award, **TATUM O'NEAL** achieves that feat at ten years old and receives the Best Supporting Actress Oscar for *Paper Moon*.

SIEW-HWA BEH founds a new magazine, *Women in Film*.

1974

1975

Screenwriter, director, producer, and actress **JOAN TEWKESBURY** writes the screenplay for *Nashville*, which is nominated for an Academy Award for Best Picture. On the topic of female sensibility, she says, "I hate the idea of a woman's view point; . . . a viewpoint is a viewpoint is a viewpoint. It's colored by more things than just what sex you are. It's colored by where you grew up, who you spend time with, who you loved, and whether that was good or rotten."

Producer, singer and songwriter **JUDY COLLINS** (pictured) shares the 1995 Oscar nomination for Best Documentary, Feature with director, producer and writer **JILL GODMILOW** for *Antonia: A Portrait of a Woman*. Godmilow is the recipient of a Guggenheim Fellowship. This film has been selected for the National Film Registry (see 1988) at the Library of Congress.

DIANE LADD has received three Best Supporting Actress Oscar nominations over her almost seventy-year entertainment career. The first, in 1975, is for *Alice Doesn't Live Here Anymore*.

Composer and conductor **ANGELA MORLEY** is nominated for two shared Oscars. Believed to be the first transgendered person to be so nominated, the nominations are in 1975 for Best Original Song Score for the movie *The Little Prince* and in 1978 for Best Original Song Score for the movie *The Slipper and the Rose: The Story of Cinderella*.

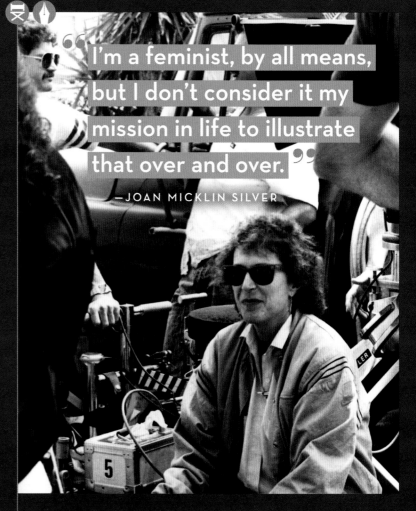

> I'm a feminist, by all means, but I don't consider it my mission in life to illustrate that over and over.

—JOAN MICKLIN SILVER

1975

Stuntwoman **KITTY O'NEIL** performs stunts for the 1975 movie *Airplane*. She becomes deaf as an infant, learns to swim and dive and becomes a stuntwoman at the urging of her boyfriend, later husband. She is the first woman member of Stunts Unlimited. A movie of her story is released in 1979 starring Stockard Channing titled *Silent Victory: The Kitty O'Neil Story*. O'Neil performs many of the stunts for the movie.

Director and writer **JOAN MICKLIN SILVER** is best known for her 1975 film *Hester Street*, for which Carol Kane is nominated for a Best Actress Oscar, and the 1988 film *Crossing Delancey*. In 1980, she says, "I'm a feminist, by all means, but I don't consider it my mission in life to illustrate that over and over. I want to tell all sorts of stories. I don't think I would ever make a film against my political beliefs—a sexist film. On the other hand, I don't think it's my duty to show powerful women, or women triumphing against all odds, unless that happens to be the particular story I want to tell."

Costume designer **THEONI ALDREDGE** wins her first Best Costume Design Oscar in 1975 for *The Great Gatsby*. Her designs for that film are adapted for a clothing line that is sold in Bloomingdale's. She was previously nominated twice for Best Costume Design, Black-and-White—in 1961 for *Pote tin Kyriaki* and in 1963 for *Phaedra*. She says, "What you do is enhance it, because the costumes are there to serve a producer's vision, a director's viewpoint and, most importantly, an actor's comfort. To me, good design is design you're not aware of."

The Steadicam is invented isolating the camera operator's movement and allowing smooth shots even over irregular surfaces. The inventor, Garrett Brown, later receives an Academy Award of Merit for his invention.

Actress **TALIA SHIRE** is known for her roles in the Godfather and Rocky movies. She receives a Best Supporting Actress Oscar nomination for *The Godfather: Part II* in 1975 and a Best Actress Oscar nomination for *Rocky* in 1977.

GENA ROWLANDS receives two nominations as Best Actress in a Leading Role for *A Woman Under the Influence* (1975) and *Gloria* (1981). In 2016 she receives an Honorary Oscar "in recognition of her unique screen performances."

DIAHANN CARROLL is nominated for a Best Actress Oscar in 1975 for *Claudine*.

Actress and stuntwoman **SUSAN BACKLINIE** has the distinction of being the first shark victim in the 1975 movie *Jaws*.

ELLEN BURSTYN wins a Best Actress Oscar in 1975 for *Alice Doesn't Live Here Anymore*. She has five additional Oscar nominations. The nominations span three decades, with her first in 1972 for *The Last Picture Show*, and her most recent in 2001 for *Requiem for a Dream*.

1976

After making a name for herself on television through the program *Rowan & Martin's Laugh-In*, **LILY TOMLIN** begins her film career. She is nominated for Best Supporting Actress in 1976 for *Nashville*, in her first film performance. Actress and comedienne Tomlin continues to combine a stage, television and film career for more than fifty years. During that time, she wins Emmy and Tony awards, a Grammy and the Screen Actors Guild Lifetime Achievement Award.

Dolly Parton (left), Lily Tomlin and Jane Fonda

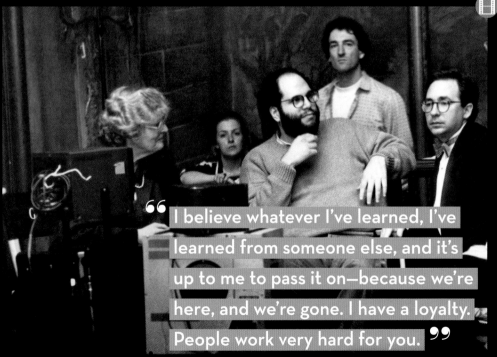

Over her six-decade film editing career, **DEDE ALLEN** is nominated for three Oscars, each in the category of Best Film Editing—*Dog Day Afternoon* (1976), *Reds* (1982) and *Wonder Boys* (2001). One of the first film editors to negotiate a cut of the film's profits, Allen has three films on the Motion Picture Editors Guild's 75 best edited films of all time: *Bonnie and Clyde*, *Dog Day Afternoon* and *Reds*.

> " I believe whatever I've learned, I've learned from someone else, and it's up to me to pass it on—because we're here, and we're gone. I have a loyalty. People work very hard for you. "
>
> —DEDE ALLEN

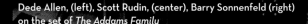

Dede Allen, (left), Scott Rudin, (center), Barry Sonnenfeld (right) on the set of *The Addams Family*

Costume designer **MILENA CANONERO** wins her first of four Oscars in 1976. The 1976 Best Costume Design Oscar is awarded for *Barry Lyndon*. Her other Oscar wins are for *Chariots of Fire* (1982), *Marie Antoinette* (2007) and *The Grand Budapest Hotel* (2015). She has five additional nominations.

LOUISE FLETCHER wins the Best Actress Oscar in 1976 for her portrayal of Nurse Ratched in *One Flew Over the Cuckoo's Nest*.

JOAN DIDION writes the screenplay for the 1976 movie *A Star is Born*.

" **We tell ourselves stories in order to live.** "

—JOAN DIDION

Actress, director and producer **LEE GRANT** wins the Best Supporting Actress Oscar for *Shampoo* in 1976. She is nominated for the same award on three other occasions, the first in 1952 for *Detective Story*. For twelve years (until 1964), she is not allowed to act in films because she is blacklisted.

> I've always felt that I was an outsider, and that was the right place for me to be, and I'm happy in that place . . . I've always taken enormous chances with my career in losing everything. I did lose everything. When I was blacklisted . . . it was a very mixed feeling. On the one hand I was hurt and destroyed. On the other hand, it was an enormous feeling of freedom.

—LEE GRANT

Editor **LYNZEE KLINGMAN** is nominated for the 1976 Best Film Editing Oscar for *One Flew Over the Cuckoo's Nest*.

Stuntwoman **LESLIE HOFFMAN** becomes a union member in 1976. She performs stunts in the 1984 movie *A Nightmare on Elm Street*. In 1981, she is the first stuntwoman elected to the Board of Directors of the Screen Actors Guild.

Editor **VERNA FIELDS** is known as "Mother Cutter" to directors Peter Bogdanovich, George Lucas and Steven Spielberg. With the commercial success of films she edits, including *What's Up, Doc?*, *American Graffiti* and *Jaws*, Fields becomes Vice President for Feature Production at Universal Studios. Her first Best Film Editing Oscar nomination is in 1974 for *American Graffiti*. She wins the Oscar in that category in 1976 for *Jaws*. She says, "I'm enormously proud of a lot of pictures I've done. By God, I saved the picture, and I've been given credit for it. I don't think my creative input has ever been denied by the fact that the director has complete control." For *Jaws*, she reports "I was the liaison with the studio for Steven [Spielberg]. When there was thought of ditching the picture because the shark wasn't working, I told them, 'Keep doing it, even if you need to use miniatures.'"

Stuntwoman **MARY PETERS (SCANNELL)** performs stunts for over thirty years. Her first movie, in 1976, is *Carrie*.

 With more than 100 credits during her forty-year stunt career, **GLORY FIORAMONTI** performs stunts in *Rocky* and *Carrie* in 1976.

 Actress and producer **CLAIRE WILBUR** wins an Oscar in 1976 for Best Documentary, Short Subject for *The End of the Game*. In 1977, she is nominated for a Best Short Film, Live Action Oscar for *Nightlife*. As an actress, she is best known for her role as Elvira in the off-Broadway play and movie *Score*, the only cast member from the stage production in the film.

 Screenwriter **GLADYS HILL** shares the 1976 Best Writing, Screenplay Adapted from Other Material Oscar nomination with John Huston for *The Man Who Would Be King*. She serves as his assistant for twenty years.

 Costume designer **ULLA-BRITT SÖDERLUND** wins the 1976 Best Costume Design Oscar for *Barry Lyndon*.

 # 1977
Lyricists **CAROL CONNORS** and **AYN ROBBINS** receive the first of two Oscar nominations, both in the category of Best Music, Original Song, for "Gonna Fly Now" from *Rocky*. The second shared nomination is in 1978 for the song "Someone's Waiting for You" from *The Rescuers*.

Animator, director and producer **CAROLINE LEAF** is nominated for the 1977 Best Short Film, Animated for *The Street*. Celebrated for her long service to the National Film Board of Canada, Leaf creates new animation techniques including sand animation and paint-on-glass. In 2017, Leaf receives a Winsor McCay Lifetime Achievement Award (see 1972) for her career contributions to animation.

A film writer and director in Monaco, **DANIÈLE THOMPSON** shares the 1977 Best Writing, Screenplay Written Directly for the Screen Oscar Nomination for *Cousin Cousine*.

1976-7

In 1977, director and writer **LINA WERTMULLER** becomes the first woman to be nominated for the Best Director Oscar for *Pasqualino Settebellezze (Seven Beauties)*. She is also nominated for a second Oscar for the movie, Best Writing, Screenplay Written Directly for the Screen.

What would make me really sad would be the realization that my success is due to being a woman.

—LINA WERTMULLER

Actress **FAYE DUNAWAY** wins the Best Actress Oscar for *Network* in 1977. Her previous two nominations in the same category were for *Bonnie & Clyde* and *Chinatown*.

Carrie Fisher and
Mark Hamill while
filming *Star Wars*

The daughter of Debbie Reynolds (see 1965), **CARRIE FISHER** will always be remembered by the movie-going public as Princess Leia in the Star Wars movies, the first one of which, *Star Wars: Episode IV—A New Hope*, is released in 1977.

BEATRICE STRAIGHT wins the Best Supporting Actress Oscar in 1977 for *Network*. At just over five minutes long, hers is the shortest performance to ever win this award.

Director, producer and writer **LYNNE LITTMAN** wins the 1977 Best Documentary, Short Subject for *Number Our Days*. Her moving image collection is held at the Academy Film Archive.

Producer and writer **BARBARA MYERHOFF** writes and helps produce the Oscar-winning short subject documentary *Number Our Days* (see 1977—Lynne Littman).

Director and producer **BARBARA KOPPLE** wins two Best Documentary, Feature Oscars. The first, in 1977, is for *Harlan County, U.S.A.* The second, in 1991, is for *American Dream*.

Producer **SUZANNE BAKER** becomes the first Australian woman to win an Academy Award when she wins the 1977 Best Short Film, Animated Oscar for *Leisure*.

During the course of her twenty-year career as a stuntwoman, **JEAN COULTER** performs stunts in movies and television including the 1977 movie *Airport '77*.

1978 One of the first African-American female animators, **BRENDA BANKS** is the key animator in 1978 for *Lord of the Rings*. She works in animation for more than twenty-five years.

Animator **RUTH KISSANE** works in the industry for thirty years and creates many Peanuts television specials during that time. In 1978, she is the animator for *Watership Down*.

Film editor **MARCIA LUCAS** shares the 1978 Best Film Editing Oscar for *Star Wars*. Her previous shared nomination is in the same category in 1974 for *American Graffiti*. She meets George Lucas while he is attending film school and they are married from 1969 to 1983.

VANESSA REDGRAVE wins the Best Supporting Actress Oscar in 1978 for *Julia*. Nominated another five times as either Best Actress or Best Supporting Actress, Redgrave also wins a Tony Award and is a Dame Commander of the Order of the British Empire. She is the sister of Lynn Redgrave (see 1967).

Actress, director and producer **DIANE KEATON** wins an Oscar for Best Actress for *Annie Hall*. She receives three more nominations for Best Actress— *Reds* (1982), *Marvin's Room* (1997) and *Something's Gotta Give* (2004).

Stuntwoman **EVELYNE CUFFEE** performs stunts for the 1978 movie *Hooper*. Her stunts include riding motorcycles, high falls, riding horses and swimming. She is the first woman in the Black Stuntmen's Association (founded in 1967).

> " I feel the stunt group had an impact on the entire industry. Without us, the other doors wouldn't have opened. "
>
> —EVELYNE CUFFEE

A producer who spends the vast majority of her career with the Canadian National Film Board, **BEVERLY SHAFFER** shares the 1978 Best Short Film, Live Action Oscar for *I'll Find a Way* with editor and producer **YUKI YOSHIDA**.

Called the Godmother of the American independent film movement, **JULIA REICHERT** has been nominated for three Academy Awards. Her film *Growing Up Female*, recently selected for inclusion in the National Film Registry (see 1988), is regarded as the first feature documentary of the modern women's movement. Her first shared Oscar nomination in 1978 is for Best Documentary, Feature for *Union Maids*. She shares a nomination in the same category in 1984 for *Seeing Red*. Her 2010 shared nomination is in the category of Best Documentary, Short Subject titled *The Last Truck: Closing of a GM Plant*.

Screenwriter, actress and director **ELAINE MAY** is nominated for her first Oscar for Best Writing, Screenplay Based on Material from Another Medium for *Heaven Can Wait*. She will be nominated a second time for Best Writing, Screenplay Based on Material Previously Produced or Published for *Primary Colors* in 1999. She says. "There's always some idiot who'll come up to you and say, 'You're a great gal, you think exactly like a man!' For Chrissake, I always thought intelligence was neuter."

She also says, "I tell you when you direct, you do anything. You beg, you shout, you discuss, you say nothing, you kid. . . But you really do anything. I'm not a pro as a director. I'm a pro at thinking about movies. I'm a pro at talking about them. You ask me anything about a movie and I can answer you in movie language; budget, schedule, gross, net distribution . . . and that's most of it, you know. If you can do that you can get hired anytime."

1978

1979

Director and writer **CLAUDIA WEILL** wins an international Oscar (The David di Donatello) for her first work as a director, *Girlfriends*. Film historian Ally Acker says of *Girlfriends*, "... Weill breaks a long, unaccepted taboo on the big screen with *Girlfriends*, a film that finally makes women's personal relationships an important enough topic to merit a big screen feature. Maybe everything was possible. Maybe the tide in the culture for women really was turning."

The first black woman to attend the film school at the University of Southern California, **FRANCES E. WILLIAMS** is an activist in addition to being an actress. She serves on the boards of the Screen Actors Guild, Actors' Lab and Actors Equity. In 1979, forty years after she appears in her first movie, Williams has a role in *The Jerk* with Steve Martin.

The President of Documentary and Family Programming for HBO and Cinemax, producer **SHEILA NEVINS** joins HBO in 1979. Documentaries produced during her tenure have garnered twenty-six Academy Awards. The Directors Guild of America honored her in 2011 for her "unwavering commitment to documentary filmmakers and the advancement of the documentary genre."

Six women Directors Guild of America (DGA) directors spearhead a class action suit challenging race and gender discrimination in the U.S. film and television industry. In 1985, women direct 0.5% of the top films put out by the major studios.

Costume designer and production designer **PATRICIA NORRIS** is nominated for six Costume Design Oscars over her forty-five year career. They are for *Days of Heaven* (1979), *The Elephant Man* (1981), *Victor, Victoria* (1983), *2010* (1985), *Sunset* (1989), and *12 Years a Slave* (2014). She is the only person to have received Lifetime Achievement Awards from both the Costume Designers Guild and the Art Directors Guild.

 Screenwriter **NANCY DOWD** is most known for the movies *Slap Shot* and *Coming Home*. She shares the 1979 Best Writing, Screenplay Written Directly for the Screen Oscar for *Coming Home*.

Animator, producer and writer **EUNICE MACAULAY** wins a Best Short Film, Animated Oscar in 1979 for *Special Delivery*. She is nominated again in the same category in 1988 for *George and Rosemary*.

JILL CLAYBURGH receives her first nomination for a Best Actress Oscar in 1979 for *An Unmarried Woman*. She receives her second in 1980 for *Starting Over*.

Specializing in jumps and falls from tall buildings, stuntwoman **JADIE DAVID** often stunt doubles for Pam Grier (see 1974). In 1979, she performs in the movie *Time After Time*. She says, "Your mind has to overcome your body. If I'm standing on a building and I have to do a high fall, every part  of my brain says, "Don't do this." But then they say "Action!" and my body goes into autopilot. You override something that's not natural for human beings."

Producer, editor and cinematographer **JACQUELINE PHILLIPS SHEDD** wins the 1979 Best Documentary, Short Subject Oscar for *The Flight of the Gossamer Condor*.

 Screenwriter **JEANNE ROSENBERG** writes the screenplay for the 1979 movie *The Black Stallion*. In 1991, she writes the screenplay for *White Fang*.

Oprah Winfrey

1980s

WOMEN MANAGE THEIR FUTURES

A significant event for women occurred in 1980 when Sherry Lansing became President of 20th Century Fox. Following in Lansing's footsteps, some women were hired by major studios to fill positions with considerable decision-making power.

Women continued multitasking in order to make the films that interested them. Barbra Streisand co-wrote, directed, produced and starred in *Yentl* (1983). Gale Anne Hurd co-wrote and produced *The Terminator* (1984). It was just the beginning for them both.

The decade delivered a slew of memorable performances from actresses. Musicals in this decade were all but absent, but Grammy-winner Cher found her way into an acting career, taking home the Academy Award for Best Actress for her role in *Moonstruck* in 1988. Meryl Streep has received a record-setting 21 Oscar nominations, including three Oscar wins, in her career. Seven of her nominations occurred in this decade, including her first two Oscar wins—1980 for *Kramer vs. Kramer* (Best Supporting Actress) and 1983 for *Sophie's Choice* (Best Actress).

Women received Oscar nominations in nine of the ten years of this decade for Best Film Editing with some Oscar wins, being trusted to edit films of all types. Two women won Oscars for editing films that also won the Best Picture Oscar—Claire Simpson for *Platoon* in 1987 and Gabrielle Cristiani for *The Last Emperor* in 1988. Women were nominated in six of the ten years in this decade for the Best Picture Oscar. Oscar nominations and wins for women also picked up in the Best Documentary categories—Feature and Short Subject.

Women showed that they could write stories on any type of subject matter, earning Academy Award nominations for their screenplays, too. Nora Ephron found her niche with romantic comedies. Ruth Prawer Jhabvala won the writing Oscar for Best Screenplay Based on Material from Another Medium for *A Room with a View* in 1987.

Also for *A Room with a View*, Jenny Beavan received the Oscar for Best Costume Design. Women working on costume design continued to be successful in this decade, with nominations every year and some Oscar wins as well. Suzanne M. Benson became the first woman to be nominated in the Best Effects, Visual Effects category and took home the Oscar for *Aliens* in 1987.

But although some women directors had box office success, The Academy did not honor a woman in this decade with a Best Director nomination.

Women were moving forward in the movie business, but there was still a long way to go.

Novelist **DIANE JOHNSON** co-writes the screenplay for the 1980 movie *The Shining*.

The "Divine Miss M," singer, comedienne and actress **BETTE MIDLER** is nominated for her first Best Actress Oscar in 1980 for *The Rose*. Her second nomination is in 1992 for *For the Boys*.

PATRICIA RESNICK writes the screenplay for the 1980 movie *9 to 5*, starring Jane Fonda (see 1972), Lily Tomlin (see 1976) and Dolly Parton (see 1981).

—| 1 9 8 0 |—

1980

A stuntwoman with more than 100 credits over her forty-year career, **SANDRA LEE GIMPEL** performs stunts in the 1980 movie *Airplane!*

SALLY FIELD wins the first of her two Best Actress Oscars in 1980 for *Norma Rae*. She will win again in 1985 for *Places in the Heart*.

Actress and stuntwoman **SHARON SCHAFFER** performs stunts for the 1980 movie *The Blues Brothers*.

TANYA SANDOVAL RUSSEL performs stunts for the 1980 movie *The Blues Brothers*. She is the first Latina stuntwoman, opening doors for many others, and the founder of the United Stuntwomen's Association.

 Over her more than thirty-year career, stuntwoman **JANET BRADY** performs in more than 100 movies including *The Blues Brothers* in 1980. She doubles for Sally Field (see 1980) in both *Smokey and the Bandit* movies (1977 and 1980).

 A camerawoman for twenty-five years, **MADELYN MOST** is the second assistant camera for the 1980 movie *Star Wars: Episode V—The Empire Strikes Back*.

 A stuntwoman for twenty years, **GLYNN RUBIN** is the stunt coordinator for the 1980 movie *Private Benjamin*.

The most nominated actress in Academy Award history (twenty-one times), **MERYL STREEP,** debuts in *Julia* in 1977. Her first Oscar win is in 1980 for Best Supporting Actress in *Kramer vs. Kramer*. Her other Oscars include Best Actress for *Sophie's Choice* (1983) and the 2012 Oscar in the same category for *The Iron Lady* (2012). She says, "I speak out about women because I am one. I see inequities and disparity in pay at the very top of our industry and at the bottom. And I see it in every industry and across cultures... I don't think about "empowering women"— it's about enhancing humanity." In a tribute to Streep, Nora Ephron (see 1984) says "I highly recommend having Meryl Streep play you.... She plays all of us better than we play ourselves. Although it's a little depressing knowing that if you want to audition to play yourself you would lose out to her. Some days, when I'm having a bad day, I call up Meryl and she'll come and she'll step in for me. She's so good, people don't really notice. I call her at the end of the day and find out how I did, and inevitably it's one of the best days I've ever had."

In 1980, writer, director and editor **KATHLEEN COLLINS** becomes the first African-American woman to produce and release a full-length feature film with *The Cruz Brothers and Miss Malloy*. She is credited with blazing the trail that enabled Julie Dash (see 1991) to find commercial distribution.

> " I don't spend a lot of time worrying about how I am perceived by other people. . . . The artist must be fundamentally honest. What you should get is his or her soul. If you get anything else, they have cheated themselves first, and they have cheated you second. "

—KATHLEEN COLLINS

1980

In 1980, after serving as executive story editor at MGM and senior vice president of production at Columbia, **SHERRY LANSING** becomes the first woman president at the helm of a major studio in Hollywood history (20th Century Fox) at the age of 35. In 1988, she shares a nomination for the Best Picture Oscar for *Fatal Attraction*. From 1992–2005, Lansing serves as Chairman and CEO of Paramount Pictures. In 2007, she receives the Jean Hersholt Humanitarian Award for her work in cancer research. In 2017, Lansing is inducted into the National Women's Hall of Fame. She says, "I've never thought that my failures had anything to do with me being a woman. If you have the passion, and the conviction and you really believe in something, eventually you will get it done.

"When I got my first acting job, I walked on the set and I looked around and I said, I don't want to be an actress. What everyone else is doing is so much more interesting. There were script supervisors and directors and cameramen that seemed to be having a lot more fun than I was. They seemed to be using their minds and their emotions in a way I was comfortable with . . . Besides, I was a terrible actress."

Producer **SARAH PILLSBURY** wins the 1980 Best Short Film, Live Action Oscar for *Board and Care*. Her feature films include *Desperately Seeking Susan* and *The River's Edge*.

Stuntwoman and horsewoman **SAMMY THURMAN (BRACKENBURY)** performs stunts for *The Blues Brothers* in 1980. Thurman is inducted into the Rodeo Hall of Fame in 2012.

Set decorator **LINDA DESCENNA** has been nominated for five shared Oscars all in the category of Best Art Direction. The first, in 1980, is for *Star Trek: The Motion Picture*. Her subsequent nominations are for *Blade Runner* (1983), *The Color Purple* (1986), *Rain Man* (1989) and *Toys* (1993).

Producer **PAULA WEINSTEIN** becomes president of production for United Artists. One of the movies she produces is the *Fabulous Baker Boys, in 1989*.

1981
In her third film after her discovery by Jack Nicholson in the reception room at Paramount Pictures' New York offices, **MARY STEENBURGEN** wins the 1981 Best Supporting Actress Oscar for *Melvin and Howard*.

A film critic and contributing writer at the *Austin Chronicle*, **MARJORIE BAUMGARTEN** is the newspaper's film reviewer for twenty-five years.

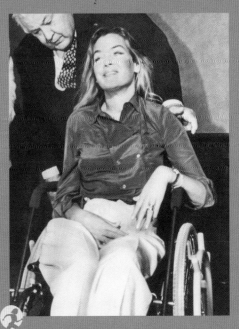

Singer and songwriter **LESLEY GORE** is nominated for an Oscar for Best Music, Original Song for "Out Here on My Own" from the movie *Fame*.

SISSY SPACEK, who receives the first of her six Best Actress nominations in 1977 for *Carrie*, wins in 1981 for *The Coal Miner's Daughter* for which she is also nominated for a Grammy.

Stuntwoman **HEIDI VON BELTZ** is paralyzed performing a stunt during *The Cannonball Run* in 1981. Her lawsuit leads to new safety guidelines during movie production.

1981

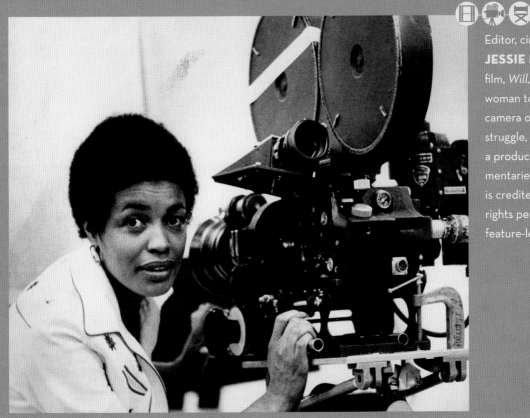

Editor, cinematographer and director **JESSIE MAPLE** releases a feature-length film, *Will*, in 1981. The first African-American woman to be admitted to the New York camera operators union after a long legal struggle, Maple and her husband found a production company to produce documentaries. With the release of *Will*, Maple is credited with being the first post-civil rights period African American to direct a feature-length film.

Film editor **THELMA SCHOONMAKER** works for Martin Scorsese for more than forty years. During that time, she garners three Oscar wins for Best Film Editing and four additional nominations. The wins come for *Raging Bull* (1981), *The Aviator* (2005), and *The Departed* (2007). She says, "From the very first moment I worked with Marty, I think he realized I was someone who would do what was right for his films, and major egos would not be a problem. . . . He gradually over the years began to appreciate that and rely on that much more, and, as I became more experienced, he was able to rely on my judgment much more. . . . When we work together, it's just the most amazing time. We talk about everything in the editing room, in addition to the editing we're doing. It's a very rich collaboration. Wonderful. I'm a very lucky person."

" I like the creativity of it. You have tremendous control in editing. You're not dealing with a big set and hundreds of actors and huge crews, and you're not forced to make decisions under pressure and not get what you want and have to settle for something else. " —THELMA SCHOONMAKER

1981

Screenwriter and director **JANE WAGNER** writes a number of the movies in which her partner, and later wife, Lily Tomlin (see 1976) appears. Wagner writes the 1981 movie *The Incredible Shrinking Woman.*

John Travolta, Jane Wagner and Lily Tomlin while filming *Moment by Moment*

DOLLY PARTON is nominated for her first Best Original Song Oscar in 1981, for "Nine to Five" in the movie of the same name. She receives her second nomination in 2006 for "Travelin' Thru" in the movie *Transamerica*. Parton wins multiple Grammys and is nominated for an Emmy as well.

> " The way I see it, if you want the rainbow, you gotta put up with the rain. "

—DOLLY PARTON

1981

An actress known for her roles in television sitcoms, **MARY TYLER MOORE** appears in film as well and is nominated in 1981 for the Best Actress Oscar for *Ordinary People*.

1982 Cinematographer **BRIANNE MURPHY** becomes the first director of photography at a major Hollywood studio. In 1982, she wins an Academy Award of Merit for the concept, design and manufacture of the MISI (Mitchell Insert Systems, Inc.) camera insert car and process trailer. This is a specially designed car with many safety features that protect the technicians who are shooting close-ups of moving cars during action sequences. A trailblazer, in 1980 she is the first woman invited to join the American Society of Cinematographers (ASC), where she will remain the only woman member for fifteen years. A founder of Women in Film, Murphy is also a founding member of Behind the Lens, an organization for women who work as film technicians. She says, "Whenever I would try to get into the union, I was told they weren't taking women into camera.

". . . I certainly did aspire to ASC membership. It's the highest honor that anyone can get in the professional cinematographer's ladder."

> " There were no film schools, no role models. The secrets of the trade were passed down from generation to generation and, let's face it, from father to son. We've come a long way, but we must continue to reach out to women and know that the road less traveled is worth the effort. "
>
> —BRIANNE MURPHY

Director, producer, animator and writer **AYOKA CHENZIRA** is an early African-American female animator and the first African American to earn a Ph.D. in Digital Media Arts from Georgia Tech. She is probably best known for her 1982 film *Hair Piece: A Film for Nappyheaded People*.

> " I'm not much into digestive cinema where you sit down and digest your dinner. I want people to be on their feet testifying. "
>
> —AYOKA CHENZIRA

1982

"The camera crew by its nature presents a special situation for a camerawoman. This crew is hierarchical, with specifically defined responsibilities for each member, limiting parameters, mutually exclusive roles. The camera crew consists of: the director of photography, or cinematographer, who is responsible for the overall 'look' of the film and the lighting; the camera operator who actually operates the camera; the first assistant, in charge of equipment, who pulls focus and 'zooms' during shots; and the second assistant, who loads film, slates, marks feet and generally assists the first assistant. A camera crew is an entity which is supposed to work together as a unit; but it is definitely not a team of equals. There is a distinct stratification, status, rank, whatever you choose to call it, and professional jealousy often not far below the surface. 'Moving up' to a higher classification is difficult, not encouraged, governed by almost byzantine rules . . . Male crew members have had their ideas about "women's place" reinforced by their experiences, by the long-standing tradition of all-male crews. Most are not used to dealing with women on the set, let alone recognizing them as equals, peers, colleagues."

—ALEXIS KRASILOVSKY

Stuntwoman **RITA EGLESTON** (pictured right) performs in *TRON* and *Blade Runner*, two movies released in 1982. She is the regular stunt double for Lindsay Wagner (pictured left) as the *Bionic Woman* on television.

Director, writer and producer **AMY HECKERLING** directs the 1982 movie *Fast Times at Ridgemont High*. In 1995, Heckerling writes and directs *Clueless*.

Dionne Warwick and
Luther Vandross (front),
Burt Bacharach and
Carole Bayer Sager (rear)

During her career, composer **CAROLE BAYER SAGER** shares one Oscar win and has five additional shared nominations, all in the category of Best Music, Original Song. Her shared win in 1982 is for the Best Music, Original Song Oscar for the song "Arthur's Theme (Best That You Can Do)" from the movie *Arthur*.

 Stuntwoman **PAULA MOODY** performs stunts for *Star Trek II: The Wrath of Kahn*. A disabling injury that she sustains on set in 1991, is one of the drivers for the establishment of The Stuntwomen's Foundation (founded by Anne Ellis—see 1987) to provide funds for stuntwomen unable to work due to injuries.

 Director and producer **SHELLEY LEVINSON** wins the 1982 Best Short Film, Live Action Oscar for *Violet*.

 Stuntwoman **CINDY FOLKERSON** works in the industry for twenty years. In 1982, she performs stunts for *Poltergeist*.

A stuntwoman with a more than thirty-year career, **EURLYNE EPPER** performs stunts in the 1993 movie *Scarface*. She is from a family of stunt performers that includes Jeannie Epper (see 1969) and Stephanie Epper (see 1970).

Co-founder of Amblin Entertainment, and one of the most successful producers in Hollywood, **KATHLEEN KENNEDY** has been nominated for eight Best Picture Oscars. The first of those nominations comes in 1983 and is for *E.T. the Extra-Terrestrial*.

JESSICA LANGE wins her first Oscar in 1983 for Best Supporting Actress in *Tootsie*. She is nominated in that same year for Best Actress for *Frances* (the first performer in forty years to receive two nominations in the same year). She wins the Best Actress Oscar in 1995 for *Blue Sky*.

1983

Screenwriter, producer and director **NANCY MEYERS** shares the 1983 Best Writing, Screenplay Written Directly for the Screen Oscar nomination for *Private Benjamin*. She has several big-screen successes in addition to *Private Benjamin* including *The Parent Trap* (1998), *Something's Gotta Give* (2003) and *The Intern* (2015). Regarding *Private Benjamin*, Goldie Hawn (see 1970) says the film was "a big deal because women at the time weren't usually put in lead roles without a strong male counterpart." Diane Keaton (see 1977) says about Meyers, "She's a pioneer with regard to representing older women. She's the only one delivering the fantasy for women over 55."

Stuntwoman **VICTORIA VANDERKLOOT** stunt doubles for Jennifer Beals in the 1983 movie *Flashdance*.

Producer **CHRISTINE OESTREICHER** wins the 1983 Best Short Film, Live Action Oscar for *A Shocking Accident*. This is her second nomination in two years in the same category—the movie nominated for the 1982 Oscar is *Couples and Robbers*.

An Irish makeup artist, **MICHÈLE BURKE** wins shared Oscars for Best Makeup in 1983 for *Quest for Fire* and 1993 for *Bram Stoker's Dracula*. Her nominations are *The Clan of the Cave Bear* (1987), *Cyrano de Bergerac* (1991), *Austin Powers: The Spy Who Shagged Me* (2000) and *The Cell* (2001).

A makeup artist for forty years, **SARAH MONZANI** shares the 1983 Best Makeup Oscar for the movie *Quest for Fire*.

Former president of the Motion Picture Editors Guild, editor **CAROL LITTLETON** receives an Oscar nomination in 1983 for Best Film Editing for *E.T. the Extra-Terrestrial*.

> " I feel like I am carrying on a long tradition of women editors. But I don't feel like a pioneer. I feel like the pioneering has gone on through those like Margaret Booth and Dede Allen who have more or less revolutionized the whole notion of film editing. "
>
> —CAROL LITTLETON

1983

Screenwriter and producer **MELISSA MATHISON** is nominated for the 1983 Best Writing, Screenplay Written Directly for the Screen Oscar for *E.T. the Extra-Terrestrial*.

Melissa Mathison at home in Los Angeles with her then husband, Harrison Ford (right), and Steven Spielberg

Editor, director and writer **TERRE NASH** wins the 1983 Best Documentary, Short Subject Oscar for *If You Love This Planet*.

Singer, songwriter and composer **BUFFY SAINT-MARIE** shares the 1983 Best Music, Original Song Oscar for the song "Up Where We Belong" from the movie *An Officer and a Gentleman*.

1983

Actress **GLENN CLOSE** is nominated for her first Best Supporting Actress Oscar for her role in *The World According to Garp*, which she had performed on Broadway before acting in the film. Over her four decades in the film industry, she is nominated five more times for acting Oscars.

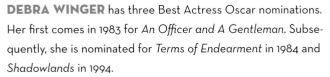

DEBRA WINGER has three Best Actress Oscar nominations. Her first comes in 1983 for *An Officer and A Gentleman*. Subsequently, she is nominated for *Terms of Endearment* in 1984 and *Shadowlands* in 1994.

1984 Canadian writer, director and producer **CYNTHIA SCOTT** wins the Best Documentary, Short Subject Oscar in 1984 for *Flamenco at 5:15*.

Screenwriter **ALICE ARLEN** shares the nomination for the 1984 Best Writing, Screenplay Written Directly for the Screen Oscar with Nora Ephron (see 1984) for *Silkwood*.

British set decorator **TESSA DAVIES** shares the 1984 Best Art Direction-Set Decoration Oscar nomination for *Yentl*.

Producer and production designer **POLLY PLATT** shares the 1984 Best Art Direction-Set Decoration Oscar nomination for *Terms of Endearment*. Said of her: "[Polly] couldn't walk into a gas station and get gas without mentoring somebody. Movies are a team sport, and she made teams function. She would assume a maternal role in terms of really being there. The film was everything, and ego just didn't exist."

> " If you want to be successful and you are a woman, you have to understand that there's all kinds of horrible stuff that comes with it, and you simply cannot do anything about it, but move on. "
>
> —NORA EPHRON

Writer, director and producer **NORA EPHRON** is nominated in 1984 for her first of three Oscars, all in the category Best Writing, Screenplay Written Directly for the Screen. In 1984, the nomination is for *Silkwood*. In 1990, the nomination is for *When Harry Met Sally* and in 1994, the nomination is for *Sleepless in Seattle*. Her last film is *Julie & Julia*. In 2013, The Tribeca Film Festival establishes the Nora Ephron Prize, given annually to inspire women writers and directors, in her honor. She is the daughter of Phoebe Ephron (see 1964) and the sister of Delia Ephron (see 1998). On the difficulty of getting films made, Ephron says: "I always think every movie should begin with a logo that says. . . "[Such and such studio] did everything in its power to keep from making this movie."

She also says, "Most directors, I have discovered, need to be convinced that the screenplay they're going to direct has something to do with them, and this is a tricky thing if you write screenplays where women have parts that are equal to or greater than the male part. . . . You look at a list of directors and it's all boys; it certainly was when I started as a screenwriter. So I thought, I'm just going to become a director and that'll make it easier."

Said by Susan Seidelman (see 1994) after Ephron died, "I learned a few things from Nora:

- That you could be a serious writer (and director) and walk into a creative meeting wearing a fur coat and a little black dress, with perfectly coifed hair and manicured nails and be taken very seriously.
- That you can age with style and grace and still be respected in an industry that worships youth.
- That you could be a hardworking filmmaker and still have the time and energy to be a devoted wife and mother.

I knew very few women in the film industry who were juggling work with a busy family life so I paid particular attention to the way Nora did it. I remember script meetings at her apartment . . . at which her young sons wandered in and out of the room casually and even joined in whatever conversation we were having without it being a big deal. This blending of work and family seemed natural and unpretentious."

Tom Hanks and Nora Ephron while filming *You've Got Mail*

66 [The film business] is a *very male* business. Vast portions of it . . . might as well be the United States Army in 1943. 99

—NORA EPHRON

1984

Screenwriter **BARBARA BENEDEK** shares the 1984 nomination for Best Writing, Screenplay Written Directly for the Screen for *The Big Chill*.

A stuntwoman since 1980, **MARIAN GREEN** performs stunts for the 1984 movie *The Terminator*. She has performed stunts in more than 100 movies including *Spider-Man: Homecoming* and *The Hunger Games: Mockinjay – Part 2*.

A stuntwoman with a thirty-year career, **DONNA KEEGAN** is also a director and producer. As a board member of the Screen Actors Guild, she served as National Chairperson for Stunts and Safety and served as an expert witness when death or injury occurred on the movie set. Early in her career, in 1984, Keegan performs stunts for *Indiana Jones and the Temple of Doom*.

Screenwriter and producer **GALE ANNE HURD** begins in the film industry as an executive assistant and, over time, becomes involved in production. After forming her own company, Pacific Western Productions, in 1982, she writes and produces the 1984 movie *The Terminator*. She also produces *Aliens* which wins two Oscars and is nominated for five more in 1987 and *The Abyss* which wins one Oscar is nominated for three others in 1990. Honored widely for her leadership in the film industry, in 2011 she becomes a governor of the Academy of Motion Picture Arts and Sciences. Her aunt is stuntwoman Jewell Jordan (Mason) (see 1937).

1984

Production designer **ANNA ASP** and art director **SUSANNE LINGHEIM** (both from Sweden) share the 1984 Best Art Direction, Set Decoration Oscar for the movie *Fanny and Alexander*.

A visual effects artist for more than thirty years, **LAUREL KLICK** works on *The Terminator* in 1984.

 KATHLEEN ROWELL writes the screenplay for the 1984 movie *Joy of Sex*.

 A film editor in the industry for more than forty years, **LISA FRUCHTMAN** wins the 1984 Best Film Editing Oscar for *The Right Stuff*. She is also nominated for the Best Film Editing Oscar for *Apocalypse Now* (1980) and *The Godfather: Part III* (1991).

 Actress and composer **IRENE CARA** shares the 1984 Best Music, Original Song Oscar for the song "Flashdance . . . What a Feeling" from the movie *Flashdance*. She acts and sings in the movie.

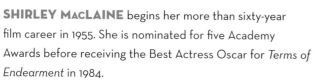 **SHIRLEY MacLAINE** begins her more than sixty-year film career in 1955. She is nominated for five Academy Awards before receiving the Best Actress Oscar for *Terms of Endearment* in 1984.

Producer **JANICE PLATT** wins the 1984 Best Short Film, Live Action Oscar for *Boys and Girls*. She is nominated in the same category in 1985 for *The Painted Door*.

Active in the film industry for forty years, actress **ALFRE WOODARD** is nominated for Best Supporting Actress in 1984 for *Cross Creek*.

Character actress **LINDA HUNT'S** performance as Billy Kwan (a man) in *The Year of Living Dangerously* is her breakout role and leads to her 1984 Oscar for Best Supporting Actress.

Robert Duvall, Shirley MacLaine, Linda Hunt and Jack Nicholson

A stuntwoman for more than 35 years, **KYM WASHINGTON LONGINO** has doubled for many actresses including Oprah Winfrey, Whoopi Goldberg and Halle Berry. In 1985, she performs stunts for the movie *The Color Purple*.

Production designer **PATRIZIA VON BRANDENSTEIN** shares the 1985 Best Art Direction-Set Decoration Oscar for *Amadeus*. She shares the nomination for the 1982 and 1988 Oscars in the same category for *Ragtime* and *The Untouchables*.

LEORA BARISH writes the screenplay for the 1985 movie *Desperately Seeking Susan*.

─┤ 1985 ├─

Nominated for Best Supporting Actress in 1985 for *Swing Shift*, **CHRISTINE LAHTI** wins an Oscar in 1996 for Best Live Action Short Film for *Lieberman in Love*, which she directed.

A Dame Commander of the Order of the British Empire who is primarily a stage actress, **PEGGY ASHCROFT** wins the 1985 Best Supporting Actress Oscar for *A Passage to India*.

Director and producer **NEEMA BARNETTE** has her directorial debut in 1985 with the movie *Sky Captain*. Later, she becomes the first African-American woman to get a deal with a major studio when she signs with Sony Pictures.

A specialist in underwater and mountaintop shots, camera operator **SUSAN WALSH** is first assistant camera for the 1985 movie *Silverado*.

Stuntwoman **MARY ALBEE** performs stunts during the filming of *Pee-wee's Big Adventure* in 1985.

During her twenty-year career as a stuntwoman, **SIMONE BOISSEREE** performs for many well-known movies, including the 1985 *Rambo: First Blood Part II*.

The first female sound editor to win an Oscar, **KAY ROSE** wins a Special Achievement Award in sound editing in 1985 for *The River*.

The first female stunt performer, the first stunt coordinator and the first female second unit director in Canada, **BETTY THOMAS QUEE** performs stunts in the 1985 movie *The Aviator*.

Editor **NENA DANEVIC** is nominated for the 1985 Best Film Editing Oscar for *Amadeus*.

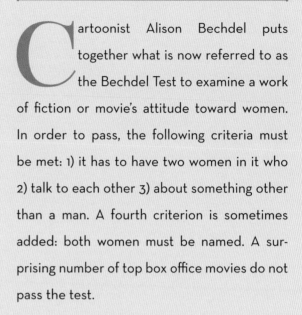

Cartoonist Alison Bechdel puts together what is now referred to as the Bechdel Test to examine a work of fiction or movie's attitude toward women. In order to pass, the following criteria must be met: 1) it has to have two women in it who 2) talk to each other 3) about something other than a man. A fourth criterion is sometimes added: both women must be named. A surprising number of top box office movies do not pass the test.

Director, producer and writer **MARJORIE HUNT** wins the 1985 Best Documentary, Short Subject Oscar for *The Stone Carvers*.

Producer **LAUREN SHULER DONNER** produces *Ladyhawke* and *St. Elmo's Fire* in 1985. She will later become well-known for the X-Men series, which grosses billions in box office receipts worldwide.

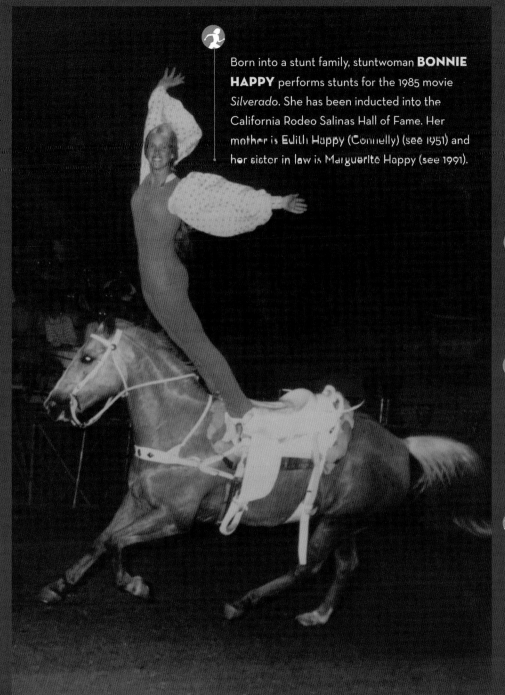

Born into a stunt family, stuntwoman **BONNIE HAPPY** performs stunts for the 1985 movie *Silverado*. She has been inducted into the California Rodeo Salinas Hall of Fame. Her mother is Edith Happy (Connelly) (see 1951) and her sister in law is Marguerite Happy (see 1991).

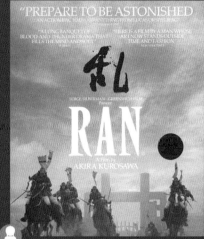

Japanese production designer **SHINOBU MURAKI** shares the 1986 Oscar nomination for Best Art Direction, Set Decoration for *Ran*.

Screenwriter **JANET ROACH** shares the 1986 Best Writing, Screenplay Based on Material from Another Medium Oscar nomination for *Prizzi's Honor*.

JO CARSON works for twenty-five years as a camera operator and in visual effects. Her movies include *Star Trek IV: The Voyage Home* in 1986. Carson serves as President of Behind the Lens, an association for professional camera women.

1986
Writer and producer **VICTORIA MUDD** and writer, director, editor and producer **MARIA FLORIO** share the 1986 Best Documentary, Feature Oscar for *Broken Rainbow*.

Novelist and screenwriter **PAMELA WALLACE** wins the 1986 Best Writing, Screenplay Written Directly for the Screen Oscar for *Witness*.

1985-6

Writer and director **JOYCE CHOPRA** is known for her first feature-length film, *Smooth Talk,* which wins awards at the 1986 Sundance Film Festival.

Argentinian screenwriter **AIDA BORTNIK** shares the 1986 Best Writing, Screenplay Written Directly for the Screen Oscar nomination for *La historia oficial.* A writer for more than forty years, Bortnik writes the screenplay for the first Argentinian film nominated for the Best Foreign Language Film Oscar (*The Truce,* 1975) and the first one to win in that same category (*La historia oficial,* 1986).

After seven nominations, **GERALDINE PAGE** wins a Best Actress Oscar in 1986 for *A Trip to Bountiful.* Her first nomination was in 1954 for Best Supporting Actress for *Hondo.* She has a forty-year entertainment career.

Costume designer **EMI WADA** wins the 1986 Best Costume Design Oscar for *Ran.*

The third generation of her family to win an Oscar, **ANJELICA HUSTON** receives hers in 1986 for Best Supporting Actress in *Prizzi's Honor*. Her father and grandfather had won before her. Huston later receives nominations in both the Best Actress and Best Supporting Actress categories.

In 1986, media mogul, actress, and producer **OPRAH WINFREY** is nominated for her first Oscar for Best Supporting Actress in the movie *The Color Purple*. Winfrey has received the Jean Hersholt Humanitarian Award and, as a producer, received another Oscar nomination for Best Picture for *Selma*. She has been inducted into the National Women's Hall of Fame.

Willard Pugh and Oprah Winfrey
The Color Purple

In 1986, director and producer **RANDA HAINES** directs *Children of a Lesser God* for which Marlee Matlin (see 1987) wins the Best Actress Oscar.

BARBARA DE FINA produces *The Color of Money* in 1986. The movie garners one Oscar win and three additional nominations. Paul Newman wins the Best Actor Oscar and the movie receives Oscar nominations for Best Actress in a Supporting Role; Best Art Direction, Set Decoration and Best Writing, Screenplay Based on Material from Another Medium.

Over the course of more than forty years in the film industry, Irish set decorator **JOSIE MacAVIN** is nominated for two shared Oscars and wins another all in the category of Best Art Direction, Set Decoration. Her shared win comes in 1986 for *Out of Africa*. Her previous nominations are for *Tom Jones* (1964), and for *The Spy Who Came in from the Cold* (1966).

1987

Producer and studio executive **DAWN STEEL** becomes President of Columbia Pictures in 1987. She entered the film industry in 1978 as Director of Merchandising and Licensing at Paramount Pictures, handling merchandise tie-ins for *Star Trek: The Motion Picture*. She rose through the ranks at Paramount before becoming the studio head at Columbia. One of the movies produced during her tenure at Columbia is *When Harry Met Sally*. Nora Ephron (see 1984) said of her, "Dawn certainly wasn't the first woman to become powerful in Hollywood, but she was the first woman to understand that part of her responsibility was to make sure that eventually there were lots of other powerful women. She hired women as executives, women as producers and directors, women as marketing people. The situation we have today, with a huge number of women in powerful positions, is largely because of Dawn Steel."

KATHLEEN TURNER is nominated for the Best Actress Oscar in 1987 for *When Peggy Sue Got Married.* Her breakout role is in the 1981 movie *Body Heat.*

A stuntwoman and stunt coordinator with more than 200 credits, **ALISON REID** performs stunts for *Adventures in Babysitting* in 1987. She later focuses on directing through her own production company.

Pro wrestler and stuntwoman **STEPHANIE FINOCHIO** (ring name Stephanie Trinity) is a stunt double in the 1987 movie *Anaconda.*

Editor **SUSAN E. MORSE** collaborates with Woody Allen for more than twenty years. During that time, she is nominated for the 1987 Best Film Editing Oscar for *Hannah and Her Sisters.*

1987

Canadian director, writer and producer **BRIGITTE BERMAN** wins the 1987 Best Documentary, Feature Oscar for *Artie Shaw: Time is All You've Got.*

Producer and writer **LESLIE DIXON,** the granddaughter of Depression-era photographer Dorothea Lange, writes the screenplay for the 1987 movie *Overboard.*

Producer and director **VIVIENNE VERDON-ROE** wins the Best Documentary, Short Subject Oscar in 1987 for *Women—for America, for the World.* She also received a nomination for the same Oscar category in 1984 for *In the Nuclear Shadow: What Can the Children Tell Us?*

MARLEE MATLIN wins the Best Actress Oscar for *Children of a Lesser God* in 1987. She is the only deaf actress to win this award to date.

Costume designer **JENNY BEAVAN** has a total of ten Best Costume Design Oscar nominations and two wins. Her wins are for *A Room with a View* (1987) and *Mad Max: Fury Road* (2016).

Costume designed by Jenny Beavan for *Ever After*

Songwriter **CYNTHIA WEIL** shares the 1987 Best Music, Original Song Oscar nomination for the song "Somewhere Out There" from the movie *An American Tail*. She is married to songwriter Barry Mann, with whom she shares the Oscar nomination. Together they have won Grammy awards.

Barry Mann and Cynthia Weil

Mentored by Dede Allen (see 1976), editor **CLAIRE SIMPSON** wins the 1987 Best Film Editing Oscar for *Platoon*. She is nominated again in 2006 for *The Constant Gardener*. She says, "Cutting rooms are only dark and gloomy places if you make them so. Hard work, educated taste, sharp instincts and a flair for the absurd have been essential to my career as an editor as well as important ingredients for my life. And never underestimate the value of good luck. I know many extraordinarily talented people who have not been lucky enough to win an Academy Award. Don't get me wrong, it was remarkably validating to win. But what really counts is to face every working day with the guts to be honest both with your director and with the material you're working with. If you can't do that, don't take the job."

> " **Hard work, educated taste, sharp instincts and a flair for the absurd have been essential to my career...** "

—CLAIRE SIMPSON

Claire Simpson and director Oliver Stone

1987

Visual effects artist **SUZANNE M. BENSON** is the first woman to win an Oscar in the Best Effects, Visual Effects category. That shared win comes in 1987 for *Aliens*.

In the film industry for over thirty years with more than 100 film credits, stuntwoman **ANNIE ELLIS** performs in the 1987 movie *Fatal Attraction*.

Belgian producer, screenwriter and animator **LINDA VAN TULDEN** shares the 1987 Best Short Film, Animated Oscar for *A Greek Tragedy*.

A stuntwoman with more than 150 credits, **DONNA EVANS** performs stunts in *Lethal Weapon* and the *Witches of Eastwick* in 1987.

Camerawoman **ALICIA CRAFT SEHRING** shoots for the 1987 movie *La Bamba*.

Author and screenwriter **RUTH PRAWER JHABVALA** wins her first of two Oscars in 1987 for Best Writing, Screenplay Based on Material from Another Medium for *A Room with a View*. She wins again in 1993 for Best Writing, Screenplay Based on Material Previously Produced or Published for *Howard's End*. Her third nomination is in 1994 for *The Remains of the Day*.

On the set of *Hannah and Her Sisters*

DIANNE WIEST wins the first of her two Best Supporting Actress Oscars in 1987 for *Hannah and Her Sisters* and her second Oscar in 1995 for *Bullets Over Broadway*, both Woody Allen movies. She is also nominated in 1990 for *Parenthood*.

Set decorator **CAROL JOFFE** shares the first of her two Oscar nominations in the category of Best Art Direction, Set Decoration in 1987 for *Hannah and Her Sisters*. She shares the second nomination in 1988 for *Radio Days*.

SIGOURNEY WEAVER earns her first Oscar nomination in 1987 for Best Actress in the movie *Aliens*. She has since been nominated both for Best Actress (*Gorillas in the Mist*, 1989) and Best Supporting Actress (*Working Girl*, 1989).

British set decorator **JOANNE WOOLLARD** shares her first Oscar nomination in 1988 for the movie *Hope and Glory* in the category of Best Art Direction, Set Decoration. Her second shared Oscar nomination (2014) is for the movie *Gravity* and is in the category Best Production Design.

Director and producer **DEBORAH DICKSON** has been nominated for three Oscars. The first, in 1988, is in the category Best Documentary, Short Subject for *Frances Steloff: Memoirs of a Bookseller*. Her other nominations are both shared and are in the category of Best Documentary, Feature: *Suzanne Farrell: Elusive Muse* (1997) and *LaLee's Kin: The Legacy of Cotton* (2002).

Screenwriter and director **MARY AGNES DONOGHUE** writes the screenplay for the 1988 movie *Beaches*.

1988

Producer and director **JANA SUE MEMEL** wins her first Best Short Film, Live Action Oscar in 1988 for *Ray's Male Heterosexual Dance Hall* and her second in 1996 for *Lieberman in Love*. She is also nominated in the same category in 1993 for *Contact* and in 1994 for *Partners*.

AMY HOLDEN JONES writes the screenplay for the 1988 movie *Mystic Pizza*. The cast includes Julia Roberts (see 2001) in her first major movie role.

Singer and actress **CHER** wins a Best Actress Oscar for her role in *Moonstruck* in 1988. She was previously nominated in 1984 for Best Supporting Actress for her role in *Silkwood*.

Producers and directors **PAMELA CONN** (pictured left) and **SUE MARX** (pictured right) win the Best Documentary, Short Subject Oscar for *Young at Heart*.

A stuntwoman active in the industry for more than thirty years, in 1988 **TRACY KEEHN DASHNAW** is the stunt double for Kim Basinger (see 1998) for *My Stepmother Is an Alien*.

Producer and director **AVIVA SLESIN** wins the 1988 Best Documentary, Feature Oscar for *The Ten-Year Lunch: The Wit and Legend of the Algonquin Round Table*. Author and screenwriter Dorothy Parker (see 1938) is one of the founders of the Algonquin Round Table and a central figure in the documentary.

The National Film Registry (NFR) is established to archive culturally, historically or aesthetically significant films. Films must be at least ten years old to be selected, and as many as twenty-five can be added each year. The NFR operates under the auspices of the National Film Preservation Board of the Library of Congress.

Italian film editor **GABRIELLA CRISTIANI** wins the 1988 Best Film Editing Oscar for *The Last Emperor*.

Actress **OLYMPIA DUKAKIS** wins an Academy Award for Best Actress in a Supporting Role for her role as Cher's (see 1988) mother in *Moonstruck*.

In 1988, actress, director and producer **PENNY MARSHALL** directs *Big*, the first film directed by a woman to gross more than $100 million at the box office. It is nominated for two Oscars including Best Actor and Best Writing, Screenplay Written Directly for the Screen. *Awakenings*, which she directs in 1990, is nominated for three Academy Awards, including Best Picture and Best Actor. She also directs the 1992 movie, *A League of Their Own*, starring Geena Davis (see 1989), Madonna and Rosie O'Donnell, among others.

" I have a strange combination of fearlessness and massive insecurity. "

—PENNY MARSHALL

1988

Named Songwriter of the Year for three consecutive years and having won a Grammy and an Emmy, songwriter **DIANE WARREN** receives nine Oscar nominations, all in the Best Music, Original Song category. Her first is a shared nomination in 1988 for the song "Nothing's Gonna Stop Us Now" from the movie *Mannequin*. Her most recent is in 2018 for the song "Stand Up for Something" from the movie *Marshall*.

Diane Warren (right) with recording artist Mya

Gloria Allred says, "Camerawomen are often in only token numbers... They fear asserting their rights to be free of sex discrimination because they fear being retaliated against by not getting a promotion, or by being demoted, or by being terminated, or by not getting another job, because they have stood up for themselves... It's only because of the women who were brave enough to file lawsuits that women ever won the opportunity to be behind the camera in the first place."

Director, producer, and cinematographer **CHRISTINE CHOY** is nominated for the 1989 Best Documentary, Feature Oscar for *Who Killed Vincent Chin?* She says, "So from then on [1976] I just began to make films, and most films I make deal with social change. Some people classify me as a 'political filmmaker'—and I'm not sure that's a correct label. I always get classified as either one category or another. It started with 'immigrant,' later on became 'Asian' later on became 'woman of color' 'minority.' "

1989 Writer and producer **ANNE SPIELBERG**, the sister of Steven Spielberg, shares the 1989 nomination for Best Writing, Screenplay Written Directly for the Screen Oscar for *Big*.

Michelle Pfeiffer and John Malkovich in *Dangerous Liaisons*

MICHELLE PFEIFFER receives her first Oscar nomination for Best Supporting Actress in *Dangerous Liaisons*. She receives best actress nominations in 1990 (*The Fabulous Baker Boys*) and 1993 (*Love Field*).

1989

Singer, songwriter and composer **CARLY SIMON** wins the 1989 Best Music, Original Song Oscar for the song "Let the River Run" from the movie *Working Girl*. She is the first artist to win the Oscar, Grammy and Golden Globe Award for a song that is written, composed and sung all by the same person.

A stuntwoman whose favorite stunt is doing full burns, **LINDA FETTERS HOWARD** performs stunts for *Star Trek V: The Final Frontier* in 1989. She serves as President of the Stuntwomen's Association of Motion Pictures in the mid-1990s.

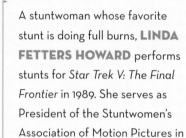

A makeup artist for thirty-five years, **BARI DREIBAND-BURMAN** shares a 1989 nomination for the Best Makeup Oscar for *Scrooged*.

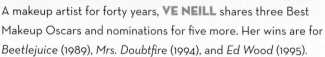

A makeup artist for forty years, **VE NEILL** shares three Best Makeup Oscars and nominations for five more. Her wins are for *Beetlejuice* (1989), *Mrs. Doubtfire* (1994), and *Ed Wood* (1995).

GEENA DAVIS wins a Best Supporting Actress Oscar for *The Accidental Tourist* in 1989. A women's rights activist and film producer, she establishes the Geena Davis Institute on Gender in Media, a research-based institution that works to change the image of women and girls in media.

1989

In 1989, writer, director and producer **EUZHAN PALCY** becomes the first African-American woman director whose film is produced by a major Hollywood studio. The movie, *A Dry White Season*, results in a Best Supporting Actor Oscar nomination for Marlon Brando, whom she convinces to appear in the movie. Palcy becomes the first African American to direct an actor to an Oscar nomination. She says, "I hate the idea that every time you talk about something like Vietnam, you have to have a white hero. But I want to scream to people who say this; they should write more, and they should join me and fight against those who have the money and the power to produce a movie."

She also says, "I want to talk about the black struggle in my movies. But that doesn't mean my movies are only for black people. It also doesn't mean I won't have white characters in my scripts. I just want human beings, without any color."

Actress, director and producer **JODIE FOSTER** wins her first Best Actress Oscar in 1989 for *The Accused*. Her second win in the same category comes in 1992 for *The Silence of the Lambs*. Foster's first Oscar nomination is in 1977 for *Taxi Driver* (Best Supporting Actress) when she is a teenager. She is nominated for Best Actress again in 1995 for *Nell*. In 1991, Foster directs *Little Man Tate*. She says, "The movies that I make as a filmmaker are about what I've lived, who I know and what I believe in. The movies that I make as an actress are usually about who I'm not, who I've never been and who I've always wondered I might have been. A very different process.... As an actress, I guess I have a certain style of filmmaking which is much more narrative driven, much more story driven and is about one singular person having a journey. The films that I'm attracted to at this point in my life as a director [she was 35] are about people and their interaction and how messy it is. And how there are just no easy solutions. I'm much more interested in the kind of ensemble, grey area—the more subtle area—of who people are to each other. I can't really explain why that is, that as a filmmaker I have such a different voice than I do as an actress."

> "I've always had this idea that I wanted movies to make people better not worse."
>
> —JODI FOSTER

1989

A writer of strong women's stories, **ANNA HAMILTON PHELAN** shares the 1989 Best Writing, Screenplay Based on Material from Another Medium Oscar nomination for *Gorillas in the Mist: The Story of Dian Fossey*. The star of that movie, Sigourney Weaver (see 1987) says to Phelan, "if you and other writers stop writing about female characters, then our daughters and granddaughters will have no female images on the screen to identify with at all."

Judi Dench

1990s

BOX OFFICE SUCCESSES AND OSCAR TRIUMPHS

Many films of the 1990s were expensive blockbusters with high budget special effects and high-priced stars, such as *Titanic* (1997), with twelve Oscar nominations, including nine wins. Smaller independent studios also produced successful films, such as *Shakespeare in Love* (1998), winning seven of its thirteen Oscar nominations.

Sherry Lansing returned from independent producing in 1992 to chair the Paramount Motion Picture Group. Arguably her biggest gamble and biggest win was *Forrest Gump* (1994). It became one of the top five most profitable films at that time, making more than $600 million worldwide. Winning four Academy Awards, it also gave producer Wendy Finerman a shared Oscar in the Best Picture category.

Penny Marshall became the first woman to direct a film that earned more than $100 million, *A League of Their Own* (1992). That record didn't stand for long. *Wayne's World* (1992) from Penelope Spheeris came close on its heels and grossed more than $120 million.

Laura Ziskin was an independent producer on the big money-making film, *Pretty Woman* (1990), which made worldwide revenues of more than $450 million, before she became the president of a movie division at 20th Century Fox in 1994. Kathleen Kennedy left Amblin and set up her own production division at Paramount. She helped to produce the high-grossing *Jurassic Park* in 1993, with worldwide box office revenues of more than $1 billion.

Fifty-one years after Hattie McDaniel's Best Supporting Actress Oscar (1940), Whoopi Goldberg became the second African-American woman to earn the Academy Award for Best Supporting Actress, for her role in *Ghost* (1991). In 1994, Jane Campion became the second woman to be nominated for the Best Director Oscar, for *The Piano*. Campion was also nominated for Best Screenplay Written Directly for the Screen with Campion taking home the Oscar.

This decade brought the first female Oscar nominations in the area of Best Sound Mixing to Anna Behlmer for *Braveheart* in 1996. The next three shared Oscar wins for women in the Best Picture category occurred in the 1990s—Lili Fini Zanuck for *Driving Miss Daisy* (1990), Wendy Finerman for *Forrest Gump* (1995) and Donna Gigliotti for *Shakespeare in Love* (1999).

All of these women were helping to focus the direction of the film industry.

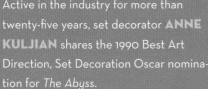

Active in the industry for more than twenty-five years, set decorator **ANNE KULJIAN** shares the 1990 Best Art Direction, Set Decoration Oscar nomination for *The Abyss*.

When director and producer **LILI FINI ZANUCK** wins the 1990 Best Picture Oscar for *Driving Miss Daisy*, she becomes only the second woman to receive an Academy Award for Best Picture. Her first film was the very successful *Cocoon* in 1985.

Producer and writer **LAURA ZISKIN** serves as executive producer for *Pretty Woman* in 1990 and produces *What About Bob?* in 1991.

⊢ 1990 ⊣

Cinematographer **ANETTE HAELLMIGK** is a camera operator for the 1990 movie *Total Recall*.

Camera operator **LIZ (ELIZABETH) ZIEGLER** is credited as the Steadicam (see 1975) operator for the 1990 movie *Ghost*.

A stuntwoman with more than 200 credits, **MELISSA STUBBS** performs stunts in the 1990 movie *Bird on a Wire*. She serves as a stunt coordinator/second unit director, with a specialty in fight choreography.

CAROLINE THOMPSON writes and produces the 1990 movie *Edward Scissorhands*.

Denise Di Novi tying up Geoff Stults while filming *Unforgettable*

Producer and director **DENISE DI NOVI** is the producer of the 1990 movie *Edward Scissorhands*.

Actress **MEG RYAN'S** breakout role is in *When Harry Met Sally* (written by Nora Ephron (see 1984)) for which she is nominated for a Golden Globe and other awards.

 JESSICA TANDY makes her movie debut in 1932 in British films, and her Hollywood debut in 1942. Over the course of her career, she appears in films periodically, alternating between movies and the stage. Her movie career revives in the mid-1980s and leads to her Oscar nomination. Tandy becomes the oldest woman to win an Oscar when she takes home the 1990 Best Actress Oscar for *Driving Miss Daisy*. She is eighty years old. Tandy is nominated for the Best Supporting Actress in 1992 for *Fried Green Tomatoes*. A veteran of the entertainment industry in a career that lasts for more than sixty years, Tandy wins Emmys and Tonys as well as an Oscar.

1990

*T*he *Los Angeles Times* runs a story with the headline "Women and Hollywood: It's Still a Lousy Relationship." At that time, according to a Screen Actors Guild report, men have 71% of all feature film acting roles, and women 29%. These statistics cause Meryl Streep (see 1980) to comment: "If the trend continues . . . by the year 2010 we may be eliminated from the movies altogether."

The first Irish actress to win an Academy Award, **BRENDA FRICKER** wins the Best Supporting Actress Oscar in 1990 for *My Left Foot: The Story of Christy Brown*.

A stuntwoman for more than thirty years, **CHRISTINE ANNE BAUR** performs stunts in the 1990 movie *Die Hard 2*.

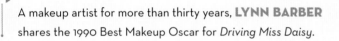

A makeup artist for more than thirty years, **LYNN BARBER** shares the 1990 Best Makeup Oscar for *Driving Miss Daisy*.

Camera operator **MICHELLE CRENSHAW** shoots *Home Alone* in 1990. She says, "I have been in the union since 1987. I came up the ranks. I was an intern, I was a loader, I was a first assistant, I am classified as a camera operator."

Hollywood Stuntwoman Hall of Fame Inductee and Reel Cowboy Silver Spur Honoree, **MARGUERITE HAPPY** comes from a rodeo family and marries into a stunt family. She begins stunt work in the movies in 1979 and in 1991 is one of the stunt doubles for Susan Sarandon as Louise in *Thelma & Louise*. Her mother-in-law is Edith Happy (Connelly) (see 1951) and her sister-in-law is Bonnie Happy (see 1985).

Costumes from 'La Bella Addormentata' by Franca Squarciapino

An Italian costume designer for theatre, opera and film, **FRANCA SQUARCIAPINO** wins the 1991 Best Costume Design Oscar for *Cyrano de Bergerac*.

1991 **ANNETTE BENING** has been nominated for four Oscars. The first is in 1991 as Best Supporting Actress for her role in *The Grifters*. Her other three nominations are for Best Actress.

Set decorator **LISA DEAN KAVANAUGH** shares the first of her two Oscar nominations in Best Art Direction, Set Decoration in 1991 for *Dances with Wolves*. Her second shared nomination is in 1999 for *Saving Private Ryan*.

Writer **LINDA WOOLVERTON** pens the screenplay for the 1991 animated version of *Beauty and the Beast*.

A motorcycle competitor who begins riding when she is six years old, stuntwoman **DEBBIE EVANS** is known for performing a headstand on the seat with the kickstand up. With over three hundred credits, Evans is considered one of the top stuntwomen in the movie industry. In 1991, she is the stunt double for Linda Hamilton in *Terminator 2*.

Stuntwoman **SONIA IZZOLENA** (Sonia Jo McDancer) performs in her first movie in 1991, *Naked Gun 2½: The Smell of Fear*.

─────────────── 1991 ───────────────

1991

The winner of a Best Supporting Actress Oscar in 1991 for her work in *Ghost*, **WHOOPI GOLDBERG** had also been nominated for a Best Actress Oscar for *The Color Purple* in 1986.

In 1987, **CECELIA HALL** is the first woman to be nominated for the Best Sound Effects Editing Oscar for *Top Gun*. In 1991, she wins the Best Sound Effects Editing Oscar for *The Hunt for Red October*. A Senior Vice President of Post Production Sound for Paramount Pictures, Hall becomes a professor of sound design.

Visual effects artist, director and writer **BETZY BROMBERG** provides optical supervision and film effects in 1991 for *Terminator 2*.

KATHY BATES wins an Oscar for Best Actress for *Misery* in 1991. She is nominated for two more Oscars and wins an Emmy.

In 1991, director, writer and producer **JULIE DASH** becomes the first African-American woman to have her full-length feature film released for national distribution. The film is *Daughters of the Dust*. It premieres at the Sundance Film Festival and is held in the National Film Registry (see 1988) at the Library of Congress.

Director, producer and writer **MARTHA COOLIDGE'S** film *Rambling Rose* is released. It earns two Oscar nominations—Best Actress for Laura Dern (see 1992) and Best Supporting Actress for Laura Dern's mother, Diane Ladd (see 1975). Coolidge serves as the first woman president of the Director's Guild of America (2002-2003). She says in 1990, "Ten years ago it would have made no difference [to have more women in decision-making positions]. But today, it would make a big difference. Women are changing. Women in power are changing. The relationships they can rely on, and their attitude toward the future has changed."

> A well-edited film is one where no one notices the editing because you've worked to make it invisible.
>
> —MARTHA COOLIDGE

1991-2

1992

A makeup artist for forty-five years, **CHRISTINA SMITH** shares Best Makeup Oscar nominations for *Hook* (1992) and *Schindler's List* (1994).

Sound effects editor **GLORIA BORDERS** shares the 1992 Best Effects, Sound Effects Editing Oscar for *Terminator 2: Judgment Day*. She shares a nomination in the same category in 1995 for *Forrest Gump*.

One of the very few African-American women in cinematography, camerawoman **SABRINA SIMMONS** serves as first assistant camera for the 1992 movie *White Men Can't Jump*. She says, "I think 1,800 people actually took the test [Camera Assistant Training Program]. They only took seven people, that time. . . . In the live action category, I was the only woman they took."

Writer, director and producer **PENELOPE SPHEERIS** directs the 1992 film *Wayne's World,* which became the highest grossing moneymaker of any film directed by a woman at that time.

MERCEDES RUEHL wins the Best Supporting Actress Oscar in 1992 for *The Fisher King.*

Director, screenwriter and producer **LESLIE HARRIS** is the first African-American woman to win a Special Jury Prize at the Sundance Film Festival. Her 1992 film *Just Another Girl on the I.R.T.* is distributed domestically and internationally by Miramax.

Director, producer and editor **ALLIE LIGHT** wins the 1992 Best Documentary, Feature Oscar for *In the Shadow of the Stars.*

Director, producer, editor and cinematographer **BARBARA HAMMER** is an avant-garde filmmaker considered to be one of the modern pioneers in lesbian film. Her first feature film, *Nitrate Kisses,* is released in 1992.

Director, writer and producer **DEBRA CHASNOFF** wins the 1992 Best Documentary, Short Subject Oscar for *Deadly Deception: General Electric, Nuclear Weapons and Our Environment.*

Set decorator **NANCY HAIGH** shares the 1992 Best Art Direction, Set Decoration Oscar for *Bugsy.* That is one of her two nominations in 1992. The other is in the same category for *Barton Fink.* Haigh has five additional shared Oscar nominations with the latest in 2017 for *Hail, Caesar!*

In the business for almost fifty years, Polish director and screenwriter **AGNIESZKA HOLLAND** is nominated for the 1992 Best Writing, Screenplay Based on Material Previously Produced or Published Oscar for *Europa Europa.* She has served as chair of the European Film Advisory Board.

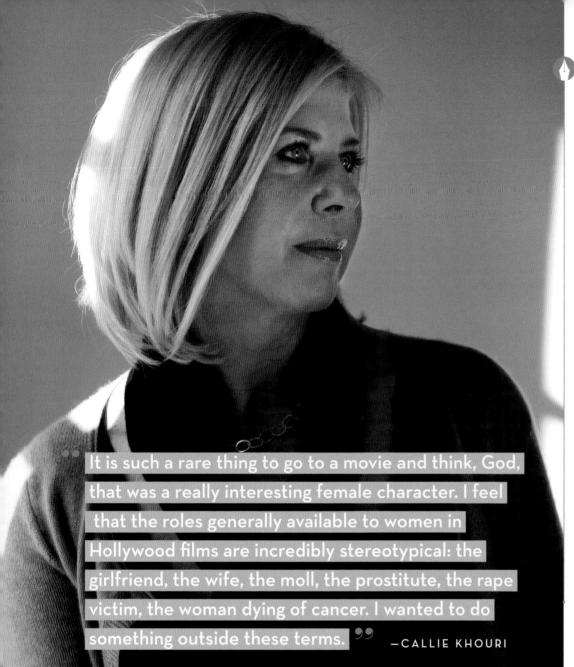

Writer, director and producer **CALLIE KHOURI** wins the Best Writing, Screenplay Written Directly for the Screen Oscar in 1992 for *Thelma & Louise* which she co-produces. About the reaction to the movie, she says "I think that people should not just look at my film but also at the way that it has been criticized to gauge the prevailing attitudes towards women in film at the moment. *Thelma & Louise* is not about feminists, it's about outlaws. We see plenty of movies of the genre with men. I don't see why it shakes everybody up to see it with women."

> It is such a rare thing to go to a movie and think, God, that was a really interesting female character. I feel that the roles generally available to women in Hollywood films are incredibly stereotypical: the girlfriend, the wife, the moll, the prostitute, the rape victim, the woman dying of cancer. I wanted to do something outside these terms. —CALLIE KHOURI

1992

Producer **LYNDA OBST** produces *This is My Life* in 1992. Over her more than twenty years in Hollywood, her films have garnered two Oscar wins and eleven additional Oscar nominations. She says, "Directing is the last frontier for women in the movie business. We are studio heads, we are producers and we are writers, but we are not directors in any numbers. The studios are certainly complicit, but I think there's some part of it that is women not saying: 'I want this job!' For a really long time, the powerful women in this town have been the nurturers of talent as opposed to the talent. And somehow, women haven't felt empowered to say, 'Give the money to me to make the movie.'"

Lynda Obst and Katie Holmes

Animator **SUE KROYER** works for Walt Disney Studios and others before forming Kroyer Films with her husband Bill Kroyer in 1987. They produce the film *Technological Threat,* which is nominated for the 1989 Best Short Film, Animated Oscar and the 1992 film *FernGully: The Last Rainforest.* They receive the June Foray Award (see 1995) in 2017.

Back row: Cicely Tyson, Mary Stuart Masterson, Mary Louise Parker; Front row: Kathy Bates, Fannie Flagg, Jessica Tandy

FANNIE FLAGG and **CAROL SOBIESKI** share the 1992 nomination for Best Writing, Screenplay Based on Material Previously Produced or Published Oscar for *Fried Green Tomatoes.*

1992

Wendy Tilby (left) and Amanda Forbis (right)

Canadian director, writer and animator **WENDY TILBY** is nominated for her first Best Short Film, Animated Oscar in 1992 for *Strings.* She shares her other two Oscar nominations in the same category with Amanda Forbis (see 2000) for *When the Day Breaks* (2000) and *Wild Life* (2012).

The daughter of Diane Ladd (see 1975), **LAURA DERN** debuts in one of Ladd's films in 1973, *White Lightning.* Nominated for two Oscars, Best Actress in 1992 for *Rambling Rose* and Best Supporting Actress in 2015 for *Wild,* Dern is still active after forty years in the entertainment business.

Lisa Henson with Elmo and puppeteer Kevin Clash

1993 Japanese costume designer **EIKO ISHIOKA** wins the 1993 Best Costume Design Oscar for *Dracula*. She is posthumously nominated in 2013 for Best Costume Design for *Mirror Mirror*.

Formerly an executive at Warner Brothers, producer **LISA HENSON** becomes president of Columbia Pictures in 1993—the youngest studio head at 33. While there, she oversees production of movies including *Little Women*, *Immortal Beloved*, and *Sense and Sensibility*. She is the daughter of Jim Henson, who created the Muppets.

Composer **LINDA THOMPSON** shares the 1993 nomination for the Best Music, Original Song Oscar for the song "I Have Nothing" from the movie *The Bodyguard*.

Director, producer and animator **JOAN GRATZ** wins the Best Short Film, Animated Oscar in 1993 for *Mona Lisa Descending a Staircase*. Gratz developed the animation technique called clay-painting.

Director and producer **GERARDINE WURZBURG** wins the 1993 Best Documentary, Short Subject Oscar for *Educating Peter*. She is nominated again in the same category in 2005 for *Autism Is a World*.

In 1993, **KRISTIN GLOVER** becomes the first woman known to operate an "A" camera, during the filming of *Hocus Pocus*.

> " I didn't go into camera work because I wanted to be a camera technician. It was because I have a strong, visual eye and I want to use it. "
>
> —KRISTIN GLOVER

Producer and director **BARBARA TRENT** wins the 1993 Best Documentary, Feature Oscar for *The Panama Deception*.

Stuntwoman **SONJA DAVIS** performs stunts in the 1993 movie *Heart and Souls*. In 1994, at age 32, she tragically dies during a stunt on a movie set.

Cinematographer and producer **JOEY FORSYTE** provides the cinematography for the 1993 film *Naked in New York*.

Czech animator and director **MICHAELA PAVLATOVA** is nominated in 1993 for Best Short Film, Animated Oscar for *Reci, reci, reci... (Words, Words, Words...)*.

On the set of *Howards End*

Production designer and Member of the Order of Australia **LUCIANA ARRIGHI** shares the 1993 Best Art Direction, Set Decoration Oscar for *Howards End*. She receives two additional shared Oscar nominations in the same category for *The Remains of the Day* (1994) and *Anna and the King* (2000).

MARISA TOMEI wins a Best Supporting Actress Oscar in 1993 for *My Cousin Vinny*. Her additional nominations in that category are in 2002 for *In the Bedroom* and 2009 for *The Wrestler*

1993

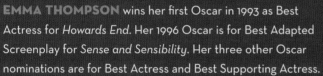 **EMMA THOMPSON** wins her first Oscar in 1993 as Best Actress for *Howards End*. Her 1996 Oscar is for Best Adapted Screenplay for *Sense and Sensibility*. Her three other Oscar nominations are for Best Actress and Best Supporting Actress.

Costume designer **RUTH E. CARTER** is nominated for two Best Costume Design Oscars—*Malcolm X* in 1993 and *Amistad* in 1998.

1994 One of the best selling artists in contemporary music, singer and songwriter **JANET JACKSON** is nominated for an Oscar for Best Music, Original Song for "Again" from the movie *Poetic Justice*.

Visual artist **PAMELA EASLEY** shares the 1994 nomination for the Best Effects, Visual Effects Oscar for the movie *Cliffhanger*.

Australian film editor **VERONIKA JENET** is nominated for the 1994 Best Film Editing Oscar for *The Piano*.

Author, director and film archivist **PEARL BOWSER** documents the early African-American film-makers helping to rediscover African-American filmmaker Oscar Michaeux. She serves as a commentator for and co-directs the 1994 documentary *Midnight Ramble*.

Makeup artist **YOLANDA TOUSSIENG** has shared two Oscars and been nominated for two more, all in the category of Best Makeup. Her two shared nominations are for *Master and Commander: The Far Side of the World* (2004) and *The Way Back* (2011). Toussieng has worked on more than 60 films during her more than thirty-five year career.

Producer and director **MARGARET LAZARUS** wins the Best Documentary, Short Subjects Oscar in 1994 for *Defending Our Lives*.

1994

Nicole Kidman in *Portrait of a Lady*

Australian costume designer **JANET PATTERSON** receives four Academy Award nominations over her thirty-year career, the first in 1994 for *The Piano*. Her subsequent nominations are for *The Portrait of a Lady* (1997), *Oscar and Lucinda* (1998), and *Bright Star* (2010).

ROSIE PEREZ is nominated for the Best Supporting Actress Oscar in 1994 for *Fearless*. Her breakout role is in *Do the Right Thing* in 1989, which she also choreographs.

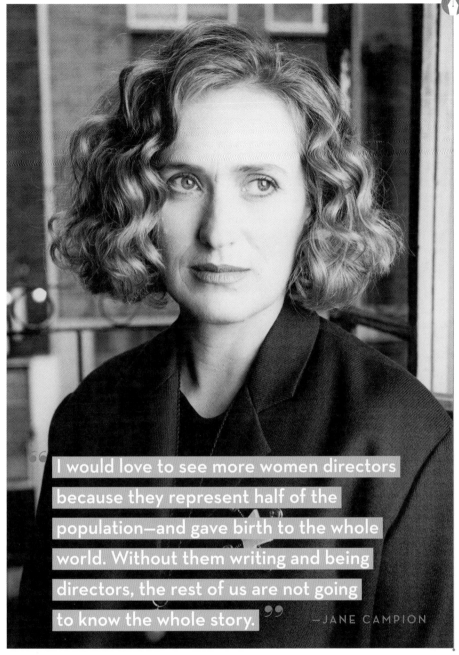

> I would love to see more women directors because they represent half of the population—and gave birth to the whole world. Without them writing and being directors, the rest of us are not going to know the whole story.
>
> —JANE CAMPION

Only the second woman in the history of the Academy Awards to be nominated for a Best Director Oscar (the first is Lina Wertmuller—see 1977), New Zealand writer, director and producer **JANE CAMPION** is nominated for that award in 1994 for *The Piano*. She receives an Oscar that year for the same movie under the category of Best Writing, Screenplay Written Directly for the Screen. Campion is the first female filmmaker to receive the Palme d'Or, the highest prize awarded at the Cannes Film Festival. Campion is a Dame Companion of The New Zealand Order of Merit. She says "The studio system is kind of an old boys' system and it's difficult for them to trust women to be capable." In 2009, she says, "I don't think the same support exists for women now. I think the 80s were a hard won era . . . but I think that's all gone now and I don't think that things are better at all anymore, as hard as it was then for women in general."

1994

Director, producer and writer **SUSAN RAYMOND** wins the 1994 Best Documentary, Feature Oscar for *I Am a Promise: The Children of Stanton Elementary School*. Her previous Oscar nomination in the same category is in 1992 for *Doing Time: Life Inside the Big House*.

Director and producer **SUSAN SEIDELMAN** is nominated in 1994 for the Best Short Film, Live Action Oscar for *The Dutch Master*. On her acceptance to the NYU film school, she says, "It was right after a lot of changes, after our battles had been fought for women. So in reaping some of the benefits of the women's movement at that time, I just assumed I could be a director. I never questioned that I couldn't, and as a result I was kind of ignorant. But I also think that ignorance is bliss. I wasn't aware how bad the statistics really were for women."

Polish costume designer **ANNA B. SHEPPARD** receives the first of her three Oscar nominations in Costume Design in 1994 for *Schindler's List*. Her subsequent nominations are for *The Pianist* (2003) and *Maleficent* (2015).

Polish set decorator **EWA BRAUN** shares the 1994 Best Art Direction, Set Decoration Oscar for *Schindler's List*. She has been working in the film industry since the late 1960s.

Hairstylist **JUDITH A. CORY** shares two Best Makeup Oscar nominations for *Schindler's List* (1994) and *Forrest Gump* (1995).

Ralph Fiennes (center left) and Liam Neeson (center) in *Schindler's List*

Director, writer and producer **GILLIAN ARMSTRONG** directs the 1994 movie version of *Little Women*.

At age eleven, New Zealand actress **ANNA PAQUIN** (pictured front) wins the Best Supporting Actress Oscar for *The Piano* directed by Jane Campion (see 1994).

HOLLY HUNTER wins the Best Actress Oscar in 1994 for *The Piano* in the same year that she is nominated for a Best Supporting Actress Oscar for *The Firm*. She has been nominated for two other acting Oscars.

— 1994 —

1994

Italian costume designer **GABRIELLA PESCUCCI** wins the 1994 Best Costume Design Oscar for *The Age of Innocence*. Her two other Oscar nominations are for costume design in *The Adventures of Baron Manchausen* (1990) and *Charlie and the Chocolate Factory* (2006).

A dress (center) by Gabriella Pescucci worn by Winona Ryder in the movie *The Age of Innocence*

1995 Camera operator **BONNIE BLAKE** works on the 1995 Oscar-winning movie *Leaving Las Vegas*. She is hired by Lisa Rinzler (see 2000) after taking the union test to be a camera operator. *True Love*, the first film Blake makes with Rinzler, wins the Grand Jury Prize at the Sundance Film Festival.

> **In this business, your whole ability to make a living is based on the people you meet. You're always building your network from the very, very beginning.**
>
> —BONNIE BLAKE

SHARON CALAHAN joins Pixar in 1994 and serves as the lighting supervisor on the 1995 movie *Toy Story*. As Director of Photography and Lighting Supervisor, she works on movies including *A Bug's Life*, *Toy Story 2* and *Finding Nemo*.

Animator, director, producer, screenwriter and actress **ALISON SNOWDEN** wins the 1995 Best Short Film, Animated Oscar for *Bob's Birthday*. In 1986, she had been nominated in the same category for *Second Class Mail*.

Makeup artist **HALLIE D'AMORE** shares the 1995 Best Makeup Oscar nomination for *Forrest Gump*.

Set decorator **CAROLYN SCOTT** shares the 1995 Best Art Direction, Set Decoration Oscar for *The Madness of King George*.

The Glass Ceiling Commission reports that 95 to 97 percent of the senior management positions in corporate America are held by white men.

Stuntwoman **LaFAYE BAKER** performed stunts for multiple movies in 1995 including *Clueless* and *Se7en*.

Wendy Finerman and Tony Scott on-set of *The Fan*

Costume designer **LIZZY GARDINER** wins the 1995 Best Costume Design Oscar for *The Adventures of Priscilla, Queen of the Desert*.

Producer **WENDY FINERMAN** wins the 1995 Best Picture Oscar for *Forrest Gump*. Also the producer of *The Devil Wears Prada*, she runs her own production company, Wendy Finerman Productions.

Born into an acting dynasty that includes Ethel Barrymore (see 1945), Dolores Costello (see 1926) and Helene Costello (see 1928), actress and producer **DREW BARRYMORE** is a child star in the 1982 movie *E.T. the Extra-Terrestrial*. In 1995, she sets up her own production company, Flower Films, which produces *Charlie's Angels*, *He's Just Not That Into You*, and *Charlie's Angels: Full Throttle*, among other films.

Film editor **SALLY MENKE** is nominated for her first Best Film Editing Oscar in 1995 for *Pulp Fiction*. In 2010, she receives another nomination in the same category for *Inglourious Basterds*. She edited all of Quentin Tarantino's films until her death in 2010.

Director, writer and producer **FREIDA LEE MOCK** wins the Best Documentary, Feature Oscar in 1995 for *Maya Lin: A Strong Clear Vision*. Mock has received four Oscar nominations in the category of Best Documentary, Short Subject in 1983, 1991, 1996 and 2002.

Producer **RUTH KENLEY-LETTS** wins the 1995 Best Short Film, Live Action Oscar for *Franz Kafka: It's a Wonderful Life*.

The June Foray (see 1950) Award is established by the International Animated Film Association. It is given to an individual in recognition of a significant and benevolent or charitable impact on the art and industry of animation. Its recipient, in 1995, is June Foray.

Director and producer **PEGGY RAJSKI** shares the 1995 Best Short Film, Live Action Oscar for *Trevor*.

Singer and songwriter **PATTY SMYTH** shares the 1995 nomination for the Best Music, Original Song Oscar for the song "Look What Love Has Done" from the movie *Junior*.

1995

1996

 Over the course of her almost fifty-year career in the film industry, actress **SUSAN SARANDON** (pictured left with Geena Davis in *Thelma & Louise*) wins one Oscar and is nominated for four others, all in the category of Best Actress in a Leading Role. Her four nominations are for *Atlantic City, USA* (1982), *Thelma & Louise* (1992), *Lorenzo's Oil* (1993) and *The Client* (1995). She wins the Best Actress Oscar in 1996 for *Dead Man Walking*.

A stuntwoman with more than 100 credits and then a stunt coordinator, **LYNN SALVATORI** performs stunts for the 1996 movie *Independence Day*.

Active in the film industry for more than thirty years, stuntwoman **ELIZA COLEMAN** performs stunts in the 1996 movie *Independence Day*.

British makeup artist **LOIS BURWELL** shares the 1996 Best Makeup Oscar for *Braveheart*. In 1999, she shares the Best Makeup Oscar nomination for *Saving Private Ryan*.

Acrobat and stuntwoman **NANCY LEE THURSTON** has more than 100 credits during her long stunting career. In 1996, she performs stunts in *Sgt. Bilko*.

In 1996, sound engineer **ANNA BEHLMER** becomes the first woman to ever receive an Oscar nomination in the Best Sound category. Her ten shared nominations are for *Braveheart* (1996), *Evita* (1997), *L.A. Confidential* (1998), *The Thin Red Line* (1999), *Moulin Rouge!* (2002), *Seabiscuit* (2004), *The Last Samurai* (2004), *War of the Worlds* (2006), *Blood Diamond* (2007), and *Star Trek* (2009). She has more than 150 movie credits.

On the set of *Lemony Snicket's A Series of Unfortunate Events*

Set decorator **CHERYL CARASIK** has shared five nominations for the Best Art Direction Oscar. These are: *A Little Princess* (1996), *The Birdcage* (1997), *Men in Black* (1998), *Lemony Snicket's A Series of Unfortunate Events* (2005), and *Pirates of the Caribbean: Dead Man's Chest* (2007).

JOAN ALLEN receives the first of her three acting Oscar nominations in 1996 for *Nixon* (Supporting Role). Her other Oscar nominations are for *The Crucible* (1997—Supporting Role) and *The Contender* (2001—Leading Role).

Stuntwoman, **JENNIFER LAMB** works in 1996 in both *Independence Day* and *Fargo*.

Director Anna Foerster on the set of *Underworld: Blood Wars*

Cinematographer, visual effects artist, and director **ANNA FOERSTER** serves as the director of photography for the 1996 film *Independence Day*. Her feature film directing debut is the 2016 film *Underworld: Blood Wars*. She is a member of the American Society of Cinematographers.

Studio executive **NIKKI ROCCO** is named president of Distribution for Universal Pictures, a post she will hold for nineteen years. When she retires in 2014, she has been at Universal Pictures for forty-seven years, an amazingly long career in the film industry.

A stuntwoman for about thirty years, **JONI AVERY** performs stunts for the 1997 movie *Titanic*. Later, she is a stunt coordinator. On pay equity, she says, "Typically, men get paid more. I'm like: 'You've got pants and a jacket and pads while she has a miniskirt and high heels. I'm going to pay her more.'"

> "It's a fun job, in that it's never the same."
>
> —JONI AVERY

MIRA SORVINO wins the Best Supporting Actress Oscar in 1996 for *Mighty Aphrodite*.

1996-7

1997 Stuntwoman **SOPHIA CRAWFORD'S** almost thirty years of stunt work includes performing as a stunt double in the 1997 movie *Scream 2*.

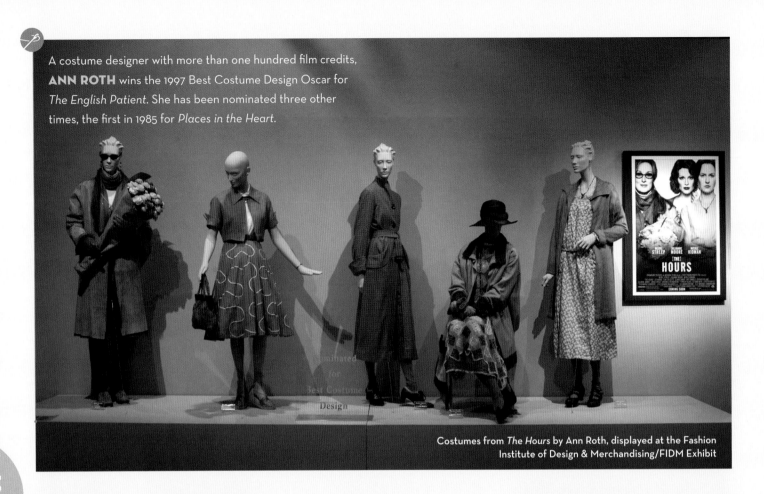

A costume designer with more than one hundred film credits, **ANN ROTH** wins the 1997 Best Costume Design Oscar for *The English Patient*. She has been nominated three other times, the first in 1985 for *Places in the Heart*.

Costumes from *The Hours* by Ann Roth, displayed at the Fashion Institute of Design & Merchandising/FIDM Exhibit

Writer, director and producer **JESSICA YU** wins the Best Documentary, Short Subject Oscar in 1997 for *Breathing Lessons: The Life and Work of Mark O'Brien*.

Actress, writer and director **KASI LEMMONS'S** directorial debut *Eve's Bayou* is released, garnering favorable reviews and awards.

World trampoline champion **LEIGH HENNESSY** has worked as a stunt performer in the film industry for more than twenty years. She serves as the stunt double for Demi Moore in the 1997 movie *G.I. Jane*. She later transitions into stunt coordination and coaching other stunt performers.

In 1997, **FRANCES McDORMAND** wins the Best Actress Oscar for *Fargo*. In 2018, she wins an Oscar in the same category for *Three Billboards Outside Ebbing, Missouri*. She has received three nominations for Best Supporting Actress.

Composer **RACHEL PORTMAN** wins the 1997 Best Music, Original Musical or Comedy Score Oscar in 1997 for the movie *Emma*. She is nominated for two more Oscars in the Best Music, Original Score category in 2000 for *The Cider House Rules* and in 2001 for *Chocolat*.

French actress, artist and dancer **JULIETTE BINOCHE** receives the Best Supporting Actress Oscar in 1997 for her role in *The English Patient*. She is nominated in 2001 for Best Actress for *Chocolat*.

Stuntwoman and coordinator **DORENDA MOORE** performs stunts in the 1997 movie *Alien: Resurrection*. In 2010, she becomes the first woman to win the Outstanding Stunt Coordination Daytime Emmy.

In the business for thirty years, set decorator **STEPHENIE McMILLAN** shares the 1997 Best Art Direction, Set Decoration Oscar for *The English Patient*. She receives four more Oscar nominations in the same category for four Harry Potter movies: *Harry Potter and the Sorcerer's Stone* (2002), *Harry Potter and the Goblet of Fire* (2006), *Harry Potter and the Deathly Hallows: Part 1* (2011), and *Harry Potter and the Deathly Hallows: Part 2* (2012). Said of her: "An eye for even the smallest details—and an understanding of how they swayed the story line—set her body of work apart."

> " I have been so lucky to have had the opportunity to dress these brilliant and huge sets [for the Harry Potter series] with enough time and money to do it properly, so I feel I don't really have any excuse for not getting it right. To have a set that is right for the director and makes the actors feel comfortable, that's really what I strive for. "

—STEPHENIE McMILLAN

Director, writer and editor **PHILIPPA (PIP) KARMEL** is nominated for the Best Film Editing Oscar in 1997 for *Shine*.

1998

British actress **HELENA BONHAM CARTER** has been nominated twice for an Oscar. In 1998, she is nominated for a Best Actress Oscar for *The Wings of the Dove*. The second nomination is for Best Supporting Actress in 2011 for *The King's Speech*. She is a Dame Commander of the Order of the British Empire.

> **"All the ancient, classic fairy tales have always been scary and dark."**
>
> —HELENA BONHAM CARTER

1998

Helen Hunt and Jack Nicholson in *As Good As It Gets*

HELEN HUNT wins a Best Actress Oscar in 1998 for *As Good As It Gets*. Having made movies for more than forty years, Hunt also receives a Best Supporting Actress nomination in 2013 for *The Sessions*.

Cinematographer **NANCY SCHREIBER** shoots *Your Friends & Neighbors* in 1998. The fourth woman to be admitted to the American Society of Cinematographers, she says, "It was very hard for women in those days. The only women shooting were in news and documentaries.

"You have to be thick-skinned, have strength and stamina."

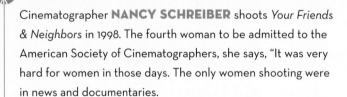

> **"It'll be a tough road. You have to be willing to sacrifice your personal life at the beginning and to take any job to get experience."**
>
> —NANCY SCHREIBER

Lisa Westcott and Julie Dartnell

Movie, television and stage writer and lyricist **LYNN AHRENS** is nominated for two shared Oscars in 1998 for the song "Journey to the Past" from the movie *Anastasia*—for Best Music, Original Song and Best Music, Original Musical or Comedy Score.

A production designer for more than thirty-five years, **JEANNINE CLAUDIA OPPEWALL** has shared four Oscar nominations in Best Art Direction. Her nominations are *L.A. Confidential* (1998), *Pleasantville* (1999), *Seabiscuit* (2004), and *The Good Shepherd* (2007).

Screenwriter **DELIA EPHRON** writes the screenplay for the 1998 movie *You've Got Mail* with her sister Nora Ephron (see 1984). She helps produce the 1993 movie *Sleepless in Seattle*, for which Nora writes the screenplay. Her mother is Phoebe Ephron (see 1964).

British makeup artist **LISA WESTCOTT** shares her first Best Makeup Oscar nomination in 1998 for *Mrs Brown*. She shares another nomination in 1999 in the same category for *Shakespeare in Love* before winning a shared Best Makeup and Hairstyling Oscar in 2013 for *Les Miserables*.

Producer and director **DONNA DEWEY** (pictured) and producer **CAROL PASTERNAK** win the 1998 Best Documentary, Short Subject Oscar for *A Story of Healing*.

Costume designer **DEBORAH LYNN SCOTT** wins the 1998 Best Costume Design Oscar for *Titanic*.

Music composer and orchestrator **DEBORAH LURIE** provides the orchestration for the 1998 movie *The X Files*. She has provided additional music for movies including *Charlotte's Web* and *Dreamgirls*.

Composer **ANNE DUDLEY** wins the 1998 Best Music, Original Music or Comedy Score Oscar for the movie *The Full Monty*. The music she has composed is featured in more than 40 films.

KIM BASINGER wins the Best Supporting Actress Oscar in 1998 for *L.A. Confidential*. Her acting career has now spanned four decades.

Singer ALLISON MOORER shares a nomination for the 1999 Best Music, Original Song Oscar for the song "A Soft Place to Fall" from the movie *The Horse Whisperer*.

Film editor ALISA LEPSELTER begins editing Woody Allen's films, such as *Midnight in Paris* and *Blue Jasmine*.

In 1998, DANIELLE FEINBERG works on *A Bug's Life* doing lighting and visual effects rendering. Later, she is the director of photography and lighting for *Coco* which wins the 2018 Oscar for Best Animated Feature Film.

1999

Nominated for the Best Film Editing Oscar in 1999 for *The Thin Red Line*, LESLIE JONES has edited more than twenty films during her twenty-five year career.

British makeup artist JENNY SHIRCORE wins the Best Makeup Oscar in 1999 for *Elizabeth*. She shares the 2010 nomination for the Best Makeup Oscar for *The Young Victoria*.

Italian SIMONA PAGGI is nominated for the Best Film Editing Oscar for *Life Is Beautiful*. Paggi wins the Donatello in 1991 for her editing of *The Stolen Children*.

1998-9

British actress **JUDI DENCH** wins a Best Supporting Actress Oscar for *Shakespeare in Love* in 1999. She has received multiple Oscar nominations for Best Actress and Best Supporting Actress and has been named a Dame Commander of the Order of the British Empire.

GWYNETH PALTROW wins the Best Actress Oscar in 1999 for *Shakespeare in Love.*

1999

Costume designer **SANDY POWELL** has won three Oscars and has been nominated an additional nine times. Her Best Costume Design Oscar wins are for *Shakespeare in Love* (1999), *The Aviator* (2005) and *The Young Victoria* (2010).

In 1999, the American Film Institute unveils a list of the fifty screen legends (25 women and 25 men) of the first 100 years of the movies. The women listed are, in order:

1. Katharine Hepburn
2. Bette Davis
3. Audrey Hepburn
4. Ingrid Bergman
5. Greta Garbo
6. Marilyn Monroe
7. Elizabeth Taylor
8. Judy Garland
9. Marlene Dietrich
10. Joan Crawford
11. Barbara Stanwyck
12. Claudette Colbert
13. Grace Kelly
14. Ginger Rogers
15. Mae West
16. Vivien Leigh
17. Lillian Gish
18. Shirley Temple
19. Rita Hayworth
20. Lauren Bacall
21. Sophia Loren
22. Jean Harlow
23. Carole Lombard
24. Mary Pickford
25. Ava Gardner

A four-time Oscar-nominated producer **DONNA GIGLIOTTI** wins the 1999 Best Picture Oscar for *Shakespeare in Love*. Her other nominations, all in the same category, are for *The Reader* (2009), *Silver Linings Playbook* (2013) and *Hidden Figures* (2017).

Director, editor and producer **KEIKO IBI** wins the 1999 Oscar for Best Documentary, Short Subject for *The Personals*.

British set decorator **JILL QUERTIER** shares the 1999 Best Art Direction, Set Decoration Oscar for *Shakespeare in Love*. In 2001, she shares an Oscar nomination in the same category for *Quills*.

Producer, writer and director **YVONNE WELBON** is best known for her 1999 documentary *Living with Pride: Ruth C. Ellis @ 100*. She documents the history of African-American female filmmakers in *Sisters in Cinema*.

Judianna Makovsky with the Dumbledore costume she designed for *Harry Potter and the Sorcerer's Stone*

Costume designer **JUDIANNA MAKOVSKY** receives the first of her three Best Costume Design Oscar nominations in 1999 for *Pleasantville*. Active in the business for more than thirty years, her other nominations are for *Harry Potter and the Sorcerer's Stone* (2002) and *Seabiscuit* (2004).

Producer and editor **MARY SWEENEY** is most notably known for *Straight Story* (1999) and *Mulholland Drive* (2001).

Actress **GLORIA FOSTER** appears in films for forty years. She plays the Oracle in 1999 in *The Matrix* and again in 2003 for *The Matrix Reloaded*.

Keanu Reeves and Gloria Foster
in *The Matrix Reloaded*

Director, writer and producer **PATRICIA ROZEMA** directs and writes the 1999 movie *Mansfield Park*. Her 1987 debut film, *I've Heard the Mermaids Singing*, wins multiple awards.

Amy Adams

2000s

BREAKTHROUGHS

A color barrier was finally broken in 2002 when Halle Berry became the first African American to win the Best Actress Oscar for her role in *Monster's Ball*. This decade also saw the first woman nominated for a shared Oscar in the category of Best Animated Feature: Marjane Satrapi for *Persepolis* in 2008.

Woman have been instrumental throughout film history in helping to move forward the technology of the movies and this decade proved no different. Dr. Kristina Johnson worked on technology that helped create RealD 3D imaging, responsible for new and improved 3D movies. It was used for the first time in the movie *Avatar* (2009) and is currently the most widely used technology for watching 3D films in theaters.

Sophia Coppola, daughter of director Francis Ford Coppola, became the third woman to be nominated for the Best Director Oscar in 2004, for *Lost in Translation*. As it was with the previous two nominees for Best Director, she also was nominated for Best Original Screenplay. In that category, Coppola took the Oscar home.

In 2008, Diablo Cody also won an Oscar for Best Original Screenplay, for *Juno*. Women won Oscars in the area of Best Costume Design nine years in a row (from 2000 to 2008) and a woman was nominated in 2009. Thelma Schoonmaker was the only editor to take home the Oscar, with two wins: *The Aviator* in 2005 and *The Departed* in 2007. Women were fabulous in the Best Makeup category with nominations and wins throughout the decade.

Cathy Schulman shared a Best Picture Oscar win for *Crash* in 2006. 2004's *The Lord of the Rings: The Return of the King* brought Fran Walsh two shared Oscar wins. One was for Best Picture and the other was with Philippa Boyens for Best Adapted Screenplay. In that same writing category, Diana Ossana took home the Oscar for *Brokeback Mountain* in 2006.

It was a decade of breakthroughs, in the Oscars and in technology, as women gained ground across the industry.

Named one of the top ten living lyricists by National Public Radio, singer and songwriter **AIMEE MANN** is nominated for the 2000 Best Music, Original Song Oscar for the song "Save Me" from the movie *Magnolia*.

Producer and director **MIMI LEDER** directs the 2000 movie *Pay It Forward*, which stars Helen Hunt (see 1998).

ANGELINA JOLIE wins the Best Supporting Actress Oscar in 2000 for *Girl, Interrupted*. Jolie will later be nominated for the Best Actress Oscar for *Changeling* in 2009, and receives the Jean Hersholt Humanitarian Award (see 1956).

2000

HILARY SWANK wins the first of her two Best Actress Oscars for *Boys Don't Cry*. Her second will come in 2005 for *Million Dollar Baby*.

Stuntwoman **EILEEN WEISINGER** performs stunts in the 2000 movie *Charlie's Angels*.

A television and film actress with almost 100 credits, **LUCY LIU** plays one of the three leading ladies of *Charlie's Angels* in the 2000 movie. She appears in the Kill Bill movies and is a voice actress for the Kung Fu Panda movies.

A stuntwoman who grew up in the circus with an elephant-trainer father, **DARLENE AVA WILLIAMS** stunt doubles for Kate Hudson in the 2000 movie *Almost Famous*. In addition to animal handling and general stunts, she is skilled in aerial acts. Williams has served on the board of the Stuntwoman's Foundation.

Director **BARBARA SCHOCK** and producer **TAMMY TIEHEL STEDMAN** win the 2000 Best Short Film, Live Action Oscar for *My Mother Dreams the Satan Disciples in New York*.

British makeup artist **CHRISTINE BLUNDELL** shares the 2000 Best Makeup Oscar for *Topsy-Turvy*. Blundell has more than 50 movie makeup credits and runs a makeup academy in England.

Producer, writer and director **SUSAN HANNAH HADARY** wins the 2000 Best Documentary, Short Subject Oscar for *King Gimp*.

After shooting her first commercial at age six, **GLORIA O'BRIEN** grows up to be a stuntwoman. A racer, a Scuba diver, a martial artist and a gymnast, O'Brien's many appearances include stunt doubling in *Scream 3* in 2000.

Camera operator **ANNIE McEVEETY** shoots the 2000 movie *The Perfect Storm*.

Film scholar **SHELLEY STAMP** is a leading expert on women and early film culture. Her 2000 book, one of several she has published, is titled *Movie-Struck Girls: Women and Motion Picture Culture after the Nickelodeon*.

A stuntwoman with more than 100 credits, **SHAUNA DUGGINS** stunt doubles for Cameron Diaz in the 2000 movie *Charlie's Angels*.

Over the course of her forty-year stunting career, **LAURI CREACH** has performed in numerous movies including the 2000 movie *Charlie's Angels*.

Lindy Hemming poses in front of her costume designs on display at the DC Comics Exhibition: Dawn Of Super Heroes

Costume designer **LINDY HEMMING** wins the 2000 Best Costume Design Oscar for *Topsy-Turvy*.

British production designer **EVE STEWART** has shared four Oscar nominations for Best Art Direction, Set Decoration or Best Production Design. The nominations are for *Topsy-Turvy* (2000), *The King's Speech* (2011), *Les Miserables* (2013) and *The Danish Girl* (2016).

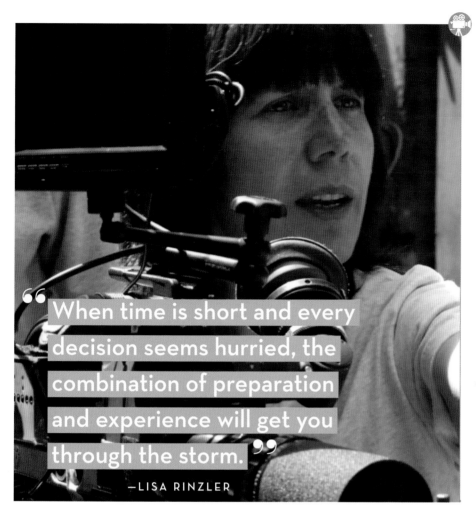

> **When time is short and every decision seems hurried, the combination of preparation and experience will get you through the storm.**
>
> —LISA RINZLER

In 2000, **LISA RINZLER** serves as director of photography for *Pollock*. She says, "A DP's job is to represent, embellish and enhance the director's vision. But you never want to remove yourself, and all your experiences, from the equation. That's why syncing up with the director, finding a chemistry, is critical.... But even if a movie experiences some form of chaos, and that's practically every independent film, you still have a foundation to draw on. You have your creative belief system, coupled with the preparation you and your crew have worked so hard on, and they all come through for you. When time is short and every decision seems hurried, the combination of preparation and experience will get you through the storm. And I'm not talking about just getting the shot. I'm talking about doing beautiful, challenging work that everyone on the film can be proud of."

Canadian animator, director and writer **AMANDA FORBIS** shares two Oscar nominations, both in the category of Best Short Film, Animated. The films are *When the Day Breaks* (2000) and *Wild Life* (2012).

Wendy Tilby (left) and Amanda Forbis (right)

LISA ZENO CHURGIN is nominated for the 2000 Best Film Editing Oscar for *The Cider House Rules*. She has served as president of the Motion Picture Editors Guild and is a member of the American Cinema Editors.

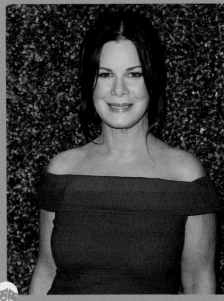

Actress **LAURA LINNEY** has received three acting Oscar nominations—*You Can Count on Me* (2001—Best Actress), *Kinsey* (2005—Best Supporting Actress) and *The Savages* (2008—Best Actress).

MARCIA GAY HARDEN wins a Best Supporting Actress Oscar in 2001 for *Pollock*. She is nominated a second time for that Academy Award in 2004 for *Mystic River*.

Screenwriter, director and producer **SUSANNAH GRANT** is nominated for the 2001 Best Writing, Screenplay Written Directly for the Screen Oscar for *Erin Brockovich*.

2001

JULIA ROBERTS wins the Best Actress Oscar in 2001 for *Erin Brockovich*. She garners three other nominations for Best Actress (*Pretty Woman*, 1991) and Best Supporting Actress (*Steel Magnolias*, 1990 and *August: Osage County*, 2014).

The Curious Case of Benjamin Button

The daughter of a fashion designer, costume designer **JACQUELINE WEST** has been nominated for three Best Costume Design Oscars—*Quills* (2001), *The Curious Case of Benjamin Button* (2009) and *The Revenant* (2016).

Costume designer **JANTY YATES** wins the 2001 Best Costume Design Oscar for *Gladiator*.

Producer and director **TRACY SERETEAN** wins the 2001 Best Documentary, Short Subject Oscar for *Big Mama*.

Producer **DEBORAH OPPENHEIMER** wins the Best Documentary, Feature Oscar for *Into the Arms of Strangers: Stories of the Kindertransport*.

Taiwanese screenwriter **HUI-LING WANG** shares the 2001 Best Writing, Screenplay Based on Material Previously Produced or Published Oscar nomination for *Crouching Tiger, Hidden Dragon*.

A contributing editor for *Elle* magazine, **HOLLY MILLEA** writes extensively about the movie industry. She joins *Elle* in 2001.

Hairdresser **GAIL ROWELL-RYAN** shares the 2001 Best Makeup Oscar for her work on *How the Grinch Stole Christmas*. She has five decades of movie and television hairstyling experience.

2002

French set decorator **MARIE-LAURE VALLA** shares the 2002 Best Art Direction, Set Decoration Oscar with Aline Bonetto for *Amélie*.

Actress and producer **LISA BLOUNT** wins the 2002 Best Short Film, Live Action Oscar for *The Accountant*.

Stuntwoman **SHAWNNA THIBODEAU** doubles for Geena Davis (see 1989) in *Stuart Little 2* in 2002.

Producer **LYNN APPELLE** wins the 2002 Best Documentary, Short Subject for *Thoth*. Later, she produces *Still Alice* for which Julianne Moore (see 2015) wins a Best Actress Oscar.

Considered one of the leading film editors in the world, **JILL BILCOCK** is nominated for the 2002 Best Film Editing Oscar for *Moulin Rouge!* She has been selected for membership in American Cinema Editors.

German-Mexican production designer, set decorator and art director **BRIGITTE BROCH** wins her first Oscar for Best Art Direction, Set Decoration in 2002 (shared with Catherine Martin—see 2002) for *Moulin Rouge!* She was previously nominated in the same category in 1997 for *Romeo + Juliet*, also shared with Catherine Martin.

In 2002, film and sound editor **DODY DORN** is nominated for the Best Film Editing Oscar for *Memento*.

2001-2

♪ In 2002, Irish lyricist **ROMA SHANE RYAN** and Irish songwriter **ENYA** (pictured) are nominated for the Best Music, Original Song Oscar for the song "May It Be" from the movie *The Lord of the Rings: The Fellowship of the Rings*.

2002

Producer, costume designer, set designer and production designer **CATHERINE MARTIN** has won four Oscars and been nominated for two more. She shares two Oscars in 2002 for *Moulin Rouge!*—Best Costume Design and Best Art Direction, Set Decoration (see Brigitte Broch, 2002). In 2014, she wins two Oscars for *The Great Gatsby*—Best Costume Design and Best Production Design (shared with Beverly Dunn, see 2014). Her first Oscar nomination is shared with Brigitte Broch (see 2002) in 1997 for Best Art Direction, Set Decoration for *Romeo + Juliet*.

Producer **LUCY FISHER'S** career includes major executive positions at Sony Studios (vice chairman), Warner Brothers (executive vice president of worldwide production), Zeotrope Studios (head of production), and 20th Century Fox (vice president of production). Films that she has produced, including *The Great Gatsby* and *Memoirs of a Geisha,* have won Academy Awards. In 2002, she produces *Stuart Little 2.* She says that women executives "should foster relationships with women directors. Even though there is no woman at the top at Warner Bros., the presence of three female vice presidents has fostered an atmosphere of acceptance for films made by women."

Lucy Fisher and Jake Gyllenhaal during the filming of *Jarhead*

Actress **AMERICA FERRERA** makes her debut in the 2002 movie *Real Women Have Curves.*

The first African-American woman to win the Academy Award for Best Actress, **HALLE BERRY** receives the honor in 2002 for her role in *Monster's Ball*.

JENNIFER CONNELLY wins the Best Actress Oscar in 2002 for *A Beautiful Mind*. Her film career has extended over thirty years.

2003 **GISELLE CHAMMA** serves as cinematographer for the 2003 movie *Happy Hour*.

A singer, producer and actress, **QUEEN LATIFAH** is nominated for a Best Supporting Actress Oscar in 2003 for *Chicago*.

2003

" I decided early on that I was going to put on my crown and rule my world by acting right and treating myself like a queen. "

—QUEEN LATIFAH

Actress, writer and producer **NIA VARDALOS** is nominated for the 2003 Best Writing, Original Screenplay Oscar for *My Big Fat Greek Wedding*.

Mexican makeup artist **BEATRICE DE ALBA** (pictured left) shares the 2003 Best Makeup Oscar for *Frida* starring Salma Hayek (pictured right).

German director and writer **CAROLINE LINK** wins the 2003 Best Foreign Language Oscar for *Nowhere in Africa*.

Danish producer and writer **MIE ANDREASEN** wins the 2003 Best Short Film, Live Action Oscar for *This Charming Man*.

2003

Actress and director **LISAGAY HAMILTON** directs the 2003 documentary *Beah: A Black Woman Speaks*.

New Zealand-born actress and stuntwoman **ZOE BELL** is a stunt double in both *Kill Bill: Vol. 1* in 2003 and *Kill Bill: Vol. 2* in 2004.

A stuntwoman with more than 100 credits, **STACEY CARINO** performs her first stunts in 2003 for *Bruce Almighty*.

CATHERINE ZETA-JONES wins the Best Supporting Actress award for *Chicago*. Her breakthrough role is in *The Mask of Zorro* in 1998. Zeta-Jones has been named a Dame Commander of the Order of the British Empire.

Director, producer and writer **JULIE TAYMOR,** well-known for her work in the theater, is nominated for the 2003 Best Music, Original Song Oscar for *Frida*, for which she writes the lyrics. The movie, which she also directs, wins the Best Music, Original Score and the Best Makeup Oscars and is also nominated in the Best Art Direction and Best Costume Design categories. In addition, Salma Hayek is nominated in the Best Actress category.

Julie Taymor and Salma Hayek on the set of *Frida*

Costume designer **COLLEEN ATWOOD** has been nominated twelve times for a Best Costume Design Oscar and has won four of those times. Her wins are for *Chicago* (2003), *Memoirs of a Geisha* (2006), *Alice in Wonderland* (2010) and *Fantastic Beasts and Where to Find Them* (2017).

NICOLE KIDMAN wins the Best Actress Oscar in 2003 for *The Hours*. She has three other acting Oscar nominations. Kidman also produces movies.

2004

Actress **KERRY WASHINGTON** receives very positive reviews for her role in the 2004 movie *Ray*.

Actress and composer **ANNETTE O'TOOLE** is nominated for the Best Music, Original Song Oscar in 2004 for "A Kiss at the End of the Rainbow" from the movie *A Mighty Wind*.

Director and producer **MARYANN DELEO** wins the 2004 Best Documentary, Short Subject Oscar for *Chernobyl Heart*.

One of the top stuntwomen in the world, who has doubled for more than 100 actresses, **LISA HOYLE** doubles for Keira Knightley in the 2003 *Pirates of the Caribbean: The Curse of the Black Pearl*. She says, "Stunt people don't have agents so you have to do what we call hustling. The field has gotten more competitive, but there's nothing else I'd rather do. It's the best job in the world."

New Zealand-born screenwriter, producer and lyricist **FRAN WALSH** has been nominated for seven Oscars and won three, most associated with the Lord of the Rings trilogy. In 2004, she wins Best Picture; Best Writing, Adapted Screenplay and Best Music, Original Song Oscars for *The Lord of the Rings: The Return of the King*.

New Zealand-born screenwriter and producer and recipient of the New Zealand Order of Merit, **PHILIPPA BOYENS** wins the Best Writing, Adapted Screenplay Oscar for *The Lord of the Rings: Return of the King*. Boyens receives a 2002 Oscar nomination for Best Writing, Screenplay Based on Materials Previously Produced or Published for *The Lord of the Rings: The Fellowship of the Ring*.

New Zealand costume designer **NGILA DICKSON** wins the 2004 Best Costume Design Oscar for *Lord of the Rings: The Return of the King*. She is also nominated for the same award in that year for *The Last Samurai*. In 2002, she is nominated in the same category for *Lord of the Rings: The Fellowship of the Ring*.

2004

Scottish singer and songwriter and Dame Officer of the Order of the British Empire, **ANNIE LENNOX** shares the 2004 Best Music, Original Song Oscar for the song "Into the West" from the movie *The Lord of the Rings: The Return of the King*.

Nominated for three Oscars, **RENÉE ZELLWEGER** wins the Best Supporting Actress Oscar in 2004 for *Cold Mountain*. In 2007, she is one of Hollywood's highest paid actresses.

South African-born **CHARLIZE THERON** wins the Best Actress Oscar in 2004 for *Monster*. A second nomination in 2006 for *North Country* follows. She founds and owns a production company.

Sofia Coppola (center)
on the set of *Marie Antionette*

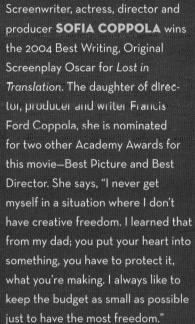

Screenwriter, actress, director and producer **SOFIA COPPOLA** wins the 2004 Best Writing, Original Screenplay Oscar for *Lost in Translation*. The daughter of director, producer and writer Francis Ford Coppola, she is nominated for two other Academy Awards for this movie—Best Picture and Best Director. She says, "I never get myself in a situation where I don't have creative freedom. I learned that from my dad; you put your heart into something, you have to protect it, what you're making. I always like to keep the budget as small as possible just to have the most freedom."

Nominated twice for the Best Actress Oscar, British actress and producer **NAOMI WATTS** receives her first nomination in 2004 for *21 Grams*. Her second nomination is for *Lo imposible* in 2013.

Naomi Watts and Jack Black in *King Kong*

2004

On the set of
The Phantom of the Opera

2005

British set decorator and art director **CELIA BOBAK** shares two Oscar nominations. The first, in 2005, is for Best Art Direction for *The Phantom of the Opera*. The second, in 2016, is for Best Production Design for *The Martian*.

Stuntwoman **JENNIFER CAPUTO** stunt doubles for Rosario Dawson (see 2006) in the 2005 movie *Rent*.

British director, writer and cinematographer **ZANA BRISKI** shares the 2005 Best Documentary, Feature Oscar for *Born Into Brothels: Calcutta's Red Light Kids*.

Makeup artist **VALLI O'REILLY** shares the 2005 Best Makeup Oscar for *Lemony Snicket's A Series of Unfortunate Events*.

Australian actress **CATE BLANCHETT** wins her first Oscar for Best Supporting Actress for *The Aviator*. Her first Oscar nomination was for Best Actress in 1999 for *Elizabeth*. She wins the 2014 Best Actress Oscar for *Blue Jasmine*.

Over her thirty-five year career, Italian set decorator **FRANCESCA LO SCHIAVO** has won three shared Oscars and been nominated an additional five times, each with her husband Dante Ferretti. The three Oscar wins are all in the category of Best Art Direction and are for the movies *The Aviator* (2005), *Sweeney Todd: The Demon Barber of Fleet Street* (2008) and *Hugo* (2012).

Actress, director, producer, screen-writer and songwriter **JULIE DELPY** shares nominations for two Best Writing, Adapted Screenplay Oscars. The Oscar nominations are for *Before Sunset* (2005) and *Before Midnight* (2014). She also stars in Angieszka Holland's (see 1992) Oscar-nominated *Europa Europa*.

2005

Actress and producer **ANDREA ARNOLD** wins an Oscar in 2005 for Best Short Film, Live Action for *Wasp*. She then turns her focus to feature-length films.

66 Dramatically, I like darkness, I like conflict— but I don't see the world as defined by them. 99

—ANDREA ARNOLD

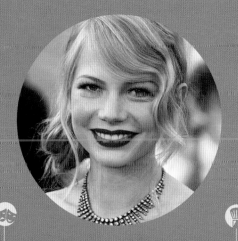

MICHELLE WILLIAMS receives the first of her four Oscar nominations in 2006 for Best Supporting Actress for her role in *Brokeback Mountain*. Her subsequent nominations are for Best Actress in 2011 for *Blue Valentine*, for Best Actress in 2012 for *My Week with Marilyn*, and for Best Supporting Actress in 2017 for *Manchester by the Sea*.

Prosthetic makeup artist **TAMI LANE** shares the 2006 Best Makeup Oscar for *The Chronicles of Narnia: The Lion, the Witch and the Wardrobe*. She is the lead prosthetic artist for the movie, directing a team of 42 people. In 2013 she shares the Oscar nomination for Best Makeup and Hairstyling for *The Hobbit: An Unexpected Journey*.

Actress **AMY ADAMS** receives her first of four Oscar nominations for Best Supporting Actress in 2006 for *Junebug*. The others are for *Doubt* (2009), *The Fighter* (2011) and *The Master* (2013). Her 2014 Oscar nomination is for Best Actress for her role in the movie *American Hustle*. Her film debut is in 1999 with *Drop Dead Gorgeous* and her breakout role comes in the 2007 movie *Enchanted*.

2006

2006

Actress **ROSARIO DAWSON,** who debuts in the 1995 movie *Kids*, receives critical acclaim for her work in 2006 for *Rent*.

Producer **CATHY SCHULMAN** wins the 2006 Best Picture Oscar for *Crash*. She is also known for *The Illusionist* and *The Foreigner*.

Producer and business executive **AMY PASCAL** serves as the chairperson of the Motion Pictures Group of Sony Pictures and co-chair of Sony Pictures from 2006 to 2015. The films she develops while at Sony include *Spider-Man, The Da Vinci Code* and *Zero Dark Thirty*.

Actress and producer **REESE WITHERSPOON** wins the Best Actress Oscar in 2006 for *Walk the Line*. She will be nominated in the same category for *Wild* in 2015. She owns a production company and is an advocate for women and children.

2006

Stuntwoman and actress **NATASCHA HOPKINS** performs stunts for the 2006 movie *Dreamgirls*.

Memoirs of a Geisha

Prosthetic makeup (also called special effects makeup or SFX) involves molding, sculpting and casting techniques to create cosmetic effects. This type of makeup was revolutionized for the movies *Planet of the Apes* and *Little Big Man*.

Set decorator **GRETCHEN RAU** shares the 2006 Best Art Direction Oscar for *Memoirs of a Geisha*. She shares a 2004 nomination in the Best Art Direction, Set Decoration category for *The Last Samurai* and shares another nomination for Best Art Direction in 2007 for *The Good Shepherd*.

A former Ultimate Pro Wrestler, stuntwoman **CARYN MOWER** has over 100 stunt credits and performs stunts for the 2006 movie *Poseidon*.

Producer and director **PEGGY STERN** wins the 2006 Best Short Film, Animated Oscar for *The Moon and the Son: An Imagined Conversation.*

Screenwriter Alejandro Amenábar and Rachel Weisz on the set of *Agora*

Production designer **SARAH GREENWOOD** and set decorator **KATIE SPENCER** have shared six Oscar nominations. The first in 2006 is for Best Art Direction for *Pride & Prejudice.* The other two in that same Oscar category are *Atonement* (2008) and *Sherlock Holmes* (2010). Their three shared Oscar nominations in the category of Best Production Design are *Anna Karenina* (2013), *Beauty and the Beast* (2018) and *Darkest Hour* (2018).

British actress **RACHEL WEISZ,** who made her Hollywood debut in 1996 in *Chain Reaction* wins the Best Supporting Actress Oscar in 2006 for *The Constant Gardener.*

Sarah Greenwood (left) and Katie Spencer (right)

Screenwriter and producer **DIANA OSSANA** shares the 2006 Best Writing, Adapted Screenplay Oscar for *Brokeback Mountain.* She is also nominated for Best Picture for the same movie.

Diana Ossana and co-writer Larry McMurty

2006

Character actress, lyricist and composer **KATHLEEN YORK** shares the 2006 Best Original Song Oscar nomination for the song "In the Deep" from the movie *Crash*.

Producer **CORINNE MARRINAN** shares the 2006 Best Documentary, Short Subject Oscar for *A Note of Triumph: The Golden Age of Norman Corwin*.

2007 Spanish makeup artist **MONTSE RIBE** shares the 2007 Best Makeup Oscar for *Pan's Labyrinth*.

Irish costume designer **CONSOLATA BOYLE** is nominated for the first of three Best Costume Design Oscars in 2007 for *The Queen*.

In 2007, singer and songwriter **SIEDAH GARRETT** shares her first Best Original Song Oscar nomination for the song "Love You I Do" from *Dreamgirls*. Her second shared nomination comes in 2012 for the song "Real in Rio" from the movie *Rio*. She writes the lyrics for both songs.

Writer **IRIS YAMASHITA** shares the 2007 Best Writing, Original Screenplay Oscar nomination for *Letters from Iwo Jima*.

Cinematographer **POLLY MORGAN** is the assistant camera for the 2007 movie *Hairspray*. She is named as one of *Variety*'s Ten Cinematographers to Watch (2016).

Singer and songwriter **MELISSA ETHERIDGE** wins the Best Music Written for Motion Pictures, Original Song Oscar for the song "I Need to Wake Up" from the movie *An Inconvenient Truth*.

Composer **ANNE PREVEN** is nominated for the 2007 Best Music Written for Motion Pictures, Original Song Oscar for the song "Listen" in *Dreamgirls*.

2007

Spanish Set decorator **PILAR REVUELTA** shares the 2007 Best Art Direction Oscar for *Pan's Labyrinth*.

Pilar Revuelta and co-winner Eugenio Caballero

British actress **HELEN MIRREN** wins the Best Actress Oscar in 2007 for *The Queen*. She receives three other nominations in the categories of Best Actress or Best Supporting Actress—*The Madness of King George* (1995), *Gosford Park* (2002) and *The Last Station* (2010) over a fifty-year career and is named a Dame Commander of the Order of the British Empire.

Singer and actress **JENNIFER HUDSON** wins the Best Supporting Actress Oscar for *Dreamgirls* in 2007.

Film editor **DANA GLAUBERMAN** edits *Juno* in 2007 and *Up in the Air* in 2009.

Originally from Hong Kong, editor, director and producer **RUBY YANG** wins the 2007 Best Documentary, Short Subject Oscar for *The Blood of Yingzhou District*. She is nominated again in 2011 in the same Oscar category for *The Warriors of Qiugang*. A member of the Directors Guild of America, she heads the Hong Kong Documentary Initiative at the University of Hong Kong.

Writer, director and producer **FRANCES-ANNE SOLOMON,** in addition to her film projects, is the founder and CEO of CaribbeanTales. This group of companies produces film festivals, provides marketing training for producers and provides sales and marketing for Caribbean-themed films. In 2007, she directs *A Winter Tale*.

Norwegian-born Canadian animator **TORILL KOVE** wins the 2007 Best Short Film, Animated Oscar for *The Danish Poet*. She receives additional nominations in the same category for *My Grandmother Ironed the King's Shirts* (2000) and *Me and My Moulton* (2015).

2008
A stunt performer for more than fifteen years, **KIMBERLY SHANNON MURPHY** is a member of the team that receives the 2008 Screen Actors Guild Award for Outstanding Performance by a Stunt Ensemble in a Motion Picture for *I Am Legend*.

TILDA SWINTON wins the Best Supporting Actress Oscar in 2008 for *Michael Clayton*.

2007-8

Producer and director **EVA ORNER** wins the 2008 Best Documentary, Feature Oscar for *Taxi to the Dark Side*.

Writer, director and producer **GINA PRINCE-BLYTHEWOOD** directs the 2008 film *The Secret Life of Bees*.

In 2008, **MARION COTILLARD** becomes the first French actress to win a Best Actress Oscar for a French-speaking role, for her performance in *La Vie en Rose*.

Screenwriter **DIABLO CODY** wins the 2008 Best Writing, Original Screenplay Oscar for *Juno*.

In 2008, actress, director and writer **DARNELL MARTIN** writes and directs *Cadillac Records*. With this movie, she becomes the first African-American woman to direct a feature film produced by a major Hollywood Studio.

Cinematographer and director **REED MORANO** is the Director of Photography for the 2008 film *Frozen River* which is nominated for two Academy Awards. At age 36, she is the youngest member of the American Society of Cinematographers when she is invited to join in 2013.

The documentary *Pray the Devil Back to Hell*, produced by **ABIGAIL DISNEY,** is released in 2008. The great-niece of Walt Disney, she is passionate about advocating for women and advancing their interests.

British costume designer **ALEXANDRA BYRNE** wins the 2008 Best Costume Design Oscar for *Elizabeth: The Golden Age*. Her previous Oscar nominations in the same category include *Hamlet* (1997), *Elizabeth* (1999) and *Finding Neverland* (2005).

2008

Makeup artist **JAN ARCHIBALD** shares the 2008 Best Makeup Oscar for *La Vie en Rose*.

Producer **VANESSA ROTH** shares the 2008 Best Documentary, Short Subject Oscar for *Freeheld* with Cynthia Wade (see 2008).

An Iranian-born film director who lives in France, **MARJANE SATRAPI** becomes the first woman nominated for Best Animated Feature Film when she shares a nomination for *Persepolis*.

Director, producer and cinematographer **CYNTHIA WADE** shares the 2008 Best Documentary, Short Subject Oscar for *Freeheld*. She is nominated again in 2013 in the same category for *Mondays at Racine*. Wade co-produces the 2015 feature film *Freeheld*, starring Julianne Moore (see 2015), with Vanessa Roth (see 2008). The film is distributed by Lionsgate and is based on Wade's Oscar-winning documentary.

Director, writer and editor **KELLY REICHARDT** is known for *Wendy and Lucy*, an award-winning movie starring Michelle Williams (see 2006), for which she writes the screenplay, directs and edits.

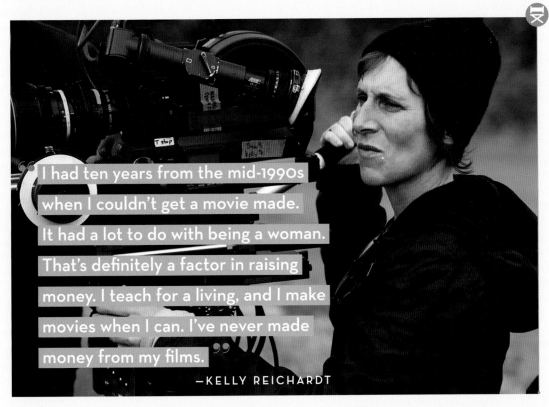

I had ten years from the mid-1990s when I couldn't get a movie made. It had a lot to do with being a woman. That's definitely a factor in raising money. I teach for a living, and I make movies when I can. I've never made money from my films.

—KELLY REICHARDT

Director, producer, writer and production designer **CATHERINE HARDWICKE** directs the 2008 movie *Twilight*, an international commercial success. The 2003 movie *Thirteen*, which she wrote and directed, resulted in a Best Supporting Actress Oscar nomination for Holly Hunter (see 1994).

Kristen Stewart, Catherine Hardwicke and Robert Pattinson in a promotional photograph for *Twilight*

Irish actress **SAOIRSE RONAN** receives the first of her three Oscar nominations in 2008. The first, for Best Supporting Actress, is for *Atonement*. Her subsequent nominations are both in the category of Best Actress, for *Brooklyn* (2016) and *Lady Bird* (2018).

British director and writer **SUZIE TEMPLETON** shares the 2008 Best Short Film, Animated Oscar for *Peter & The Wolf.*

A sound editor with more than 90 credits, **KAREN BAKER LANDERS** shares two Best Sound Editing Oscars. Her Oscar wins are in 2008 for *The Bourne Ultimatum* and in 2013 for *Skyfall.*

Athlete and stuntwoman **LUCI ROMBERG** has earned her nickname, "Steel." She has performed stunts in many movies including, in 2008, *Indiana Jones and the Kingdom of the Crystal Skull.*

2009 **TARAJI P. HENSON** is nominated in 2009 for the Best Supporting Actress Oscar for her role in the 2009 movie *The Curious Case of Benjamin Button.* She has acted in movies for twenty years.

Markéta Irglová and Glen Hansard

Czech composer **MARKÉTA IRGLOVÁ** shares the 2008 Best Original Song Oscar for the song "Falling Slowly," from the movie *Once,* with Glen Hansard.

KRISTINA JOHNSON'S work on polarization-control technology, which is integrated into RealD 3D imaging, is used for the first time in the movie *Avatar.* Dr. Johnson is inducted into the National Inventors Hall of Fame for her contribution in 2015.

Cinematographer **ELLEN KURAS** is nominated for the Best Documentary, Feature Oscar in 2009 for *The Betrayal—Nerakhoon* which she co-writes, co-directs, co-produces and shoots. A member of the American Society of Cinematographers, Kuras has won multiple awards at the Sundance Film Festival.

British rapper and songwriter **MAYA ARULPRAGASAM**, known by her stage name M.I.A., shares the 2009 Best Original Song Oscar nomination for the song "O Saya" from *Slumdog Millionaire*.

A stuntwoman with more than 100 credits, **ANGELA MERYL** doubles for Beyoncé in the 2009 movie *Obsessed*.

PAULA DUPRÉ PESMEN produces *The Cove*, which wins the 2009 Best Documentary, Feature Oscar. She is the associate producer for *Mrs. Doubtfire* and the first three Harry Potter movies.

Producer and director **MEGAN MYLAN** wins the 2009 Best Documentary, Short Subject Oscar for *Smile Pinki*.

British actress **KATE WINSLET** has been nominated a total of seven times for either the Best Actress or Best Supporting Actress Oscar. She wins the Best Actress Oscar in 2009 for *The Reader*. She has been awarded Dame Commander of the Order of the British Empire.

2009

PENELOPE CRUZ receives the Best Supporting Actress Oscar in 2009 for her role in *Vicky Cristina Barcelona*.

Ava DuVernay

2010s

AND STILL WOMEN RISE

S tarting the decade with a bang, Kathryn Bigelow became the fourth woman nominated and the first woman to win the Best Director Oscar for *The Hurt Locker* in 2010. That night she also took home a shared Oscar for Best Picture for the same film. Greta Gerwig became the fifth woman nominated for the Best Director Oscar in 2018 for *Lady Bird*. Like three of the four preceding female nominees, she, too, was nominated for Best Original Screenplay for her film.

2018 brought Rachel Morrison the first nomination for a woman in the Best Cinematography category, for *Mudbound*. This decade also landed Lora Hirschberg the first Oscar win for a woman in the category of Best Sound Mixing, for *Inception* in 2011.

The second shared Oscar win, and the third nomination for a woman in the category of Best Visual Effects, went to Sara Bennett for *Ex Machina* in 2016. Women began to pick up speed in the Best Animated Feature category, with three shared wins: Brenda Chapman for *Brave* (2013), Jennifer Lee for *Frozen* (2014) and Darla K. Anderson for Coco (2018).

Women in the Best Costume Design category showed no signs of slowing down with seven Oscar wins. Women celebrated six Oscar wins in Best Art Direction, which was renamed Best Production Design in 2012. In both of these categories, women received nominations every year.

Women dominated in the Best Makeup and Hairstyling category with nominations and wins. They also demonstrated staying power in the Best Documentary Feature and Documentary Short Subject categories. Patty Jenkins directed a *Wonder Woman* (2017) blockbuster, which became the highest-grossing superhero origin film in history.

These victories were the culmination of years of hard work by women in the industry, but the 2010s may come to be defined by the social change it led toward the decade's end. The Time's Up movement was founded in January 2018 to address inequity in opportunities, benefits and pay in the entertainment industry. Systemic harassment that had previously gone unacknowledged, and had been tolerated for too long, came to the public's attention and began to be addressed as well.

For more than a hundred years, women have enhanced the movie industry with their incredible accomplishments. They are to be celebrated for their achievements. Hope abounds that they will be able to fulfill their dreams and thrive in the decades to come.

SANDRA BULLOCK receives the Academy Award for Best Actress for her role in *The Blind Side*. She receives another nomination for Best Actress in 2014 for *Gravity*.

A sound editor with more than 100 movie credits, **GWENDOLYN YATES WHITTLE** shares two Oscar nominations for Best Sound Editing for *Avatar* (2010) and *Tron* (2011).

Mo'NIQUE wins a Best Supporting Actress Oscar for *Precious*.

2010

In 2010, **ANNA KENDRICK** is nominated for a Best Supporting Actress Oscar for *Up in the Air*. She appears in each of the Pitch Perfect movies and in The Twilight Saga.

A makeup artist for more than thirty years, **MINDY HALL** shares the 2010 Best Makeup Oscar for *Star Trek*. She oversees a team of more than forty makeup artists and leads the redesign of the Romulan race portrayed in the movie.

Producer **ELINOR BURKETT** shares the 2010 Best Documentary, Short Subject Oscar for *Music by Prudence*.

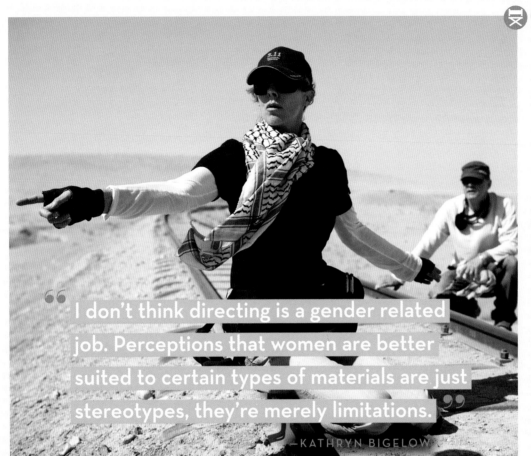

> I don't think directing is a gender related job. Perceptions that women are better suited to certain types of materials are just stereotypes, they're merely limitations.
> —KATHRYN BIGELOW

In 2010, director, writer and producer **KATHRYN BIGELOW** becomes the first woman in the history of the Oscars to win Best Director for *The Hurt Locker*. She also wins the Best Picture Oscar in 2010 for the same movie. Bigelow is nominated for the 2013 Best Picture Oscar for *Zero Dark Thirty* which she directs and produces. She says, "If there's specific resistance to women making movies, I just choose to ignore that as an obstacle for two reasons: I can't change my gender and I refuse to stop making movies."

2011 **MARTHA LAUZEN** is the Executive Director of the Center for the Study of Women in Television and Film and a professor at San Diego State University. She serves on the Advisory Board for the Center for the Study of Women in Television and Film and is interviewed for the 2011 documentary *Miss Representation*.

CIRA FELINA BOLLA serves as cinematographer for *Life of Lemon* in 2011.

German cinematographer **UTA BRIESEWITZ** (pictured right) shoots *Arthur* in 2011.

Award-winning cinematographer **AMY VINCENT** serves as the director of photography for the 2011 movie *Footloose*. She receives the 2005 Sundance Film Festival Cinematography award.

Songwriter **HILLARY LINDSEY** shares the 2011 Best Music, Original Song Oscar nomination for the song "Coming Home" from *Country Strong*.

British singer and songwriter **DIDO** shares the 2011 Best Music, Original Song nomination for the song "If I Rise" from *127 Hours*, for which she writes the lyrics.

Producer and writer **ANNE ROSELLINI** shares nominations for two 2011 Oscars for *Winter's Bone*—Best Picture and Best Writing, Adapted Screenplay.

MELISSA LEO wins the Best Supporting Actress Oscar in 2011 for *The Fighter*. An actress with more than 100 credits, she was nominated in 2009 for the Best Actress Oscar for *Frozen River*.

2011

Stuntwoman **CHRISSY WEATHERSBY BALL** is a member of the team that wins the 2011 Screen Actors Guild Award for Outstanding Performance by a Stunt Ensemble in a Motion Picture for *Inception*.

Selected as a member of the American Cinema Editors, **PAMELA MARTIN** is nominated in 2011 for the Best Film Editing Oscar for *The Fighter*. Previously, she had edited the 2006 movie *Little Miss Sunshine*.

Director, producer and writer **LYNNE RAMSAY** does all three for the 2011 movie *We Need to Talk About Kevin*.

Producer **AUDREY MARIE MARRS** wins the 2011 Best Documentary, Feature Oscar for *Inside Job*. Her previous nomination in the same category is in 2008 for *No End in Sight*.

Writer and director **DEE REES** is known for her 2011 film *Pariah*. In 2018, she is nominated for the Best Adapted Screenplay Oscar for *Mudbound*. This is the movie that earns Rachel Morrison (see 2018) a nomination for the Best Achievement in Cinematography Oscar, the first woman to be nominated in that category in the history of the Oscars.

Producer **DARLA ANDERSON** shares the 2018 Best Animated Feature Film Oscar for Coco. Formerly a film producer at Pixar, she is nominated in 2011 for Best Picture for *Toy Story 3*. She is active in the Producers Guild of America, having sat on their national board of directors.

Director, writer, and cinematographer **DEBRA GRANIK** shares a nomination for the 2011 Best Adapted Screenplay Oscar for *Winter's Bone*. This is the movie for which actress Jennifer Lawrence (see 2013) receives her first Academy Award nomination for Best Actress.

A set decorator for more than thirty years, **KAREN O'HARA** shares the 2011 Best Art Direction Oscar for *Alice in Wonderland*. She shared a previous nomination for the 1987 Best Art Direction, Set Decoration Oscar for *The Color of Money*.

Producer and director **KAREN GOODMAN** wins the 2011 Best Documentary, Short Subject Oscar for *Strangers No More*. She has three previous Oscar nominations over her illustrious career, all in the same category: *The Children's Storefront* (1989), *Chimps: So Like Us* (1991) and *Rehearsing a Dream* (2007). She and her husband Kirk Simon have their own production company, Simon & Goodman Picture Company.

NATALIE PORTMAN wins the 2011 Best Actress Oscar for her role in *Black Swan*. She is nominated twice more—once for Best Actress (*Jackie*, 2017) and once for Best Supporting Actress (*Closer*, 2005).

A sound engineer who has worked on more than 100 films, **LORA HIRSCHBERG** shares the 2011 Best Sound Mixing Oscar for *Inception*. She is the first woman to win an Oscar in this category. In 2009, she shares an Oscar nomination in the same category for *The Dark Knight*.

2012

Pakistani director and producer **SHARMEEN OBAID-CHINOY** shares two Best Documentary, Short Subject Oscars: in 2012 for *Saving Face* and in 2016 for *A Girl in the River: The Price of Forgiveness*. Obaid-Chinoy has been honored with the second highest civilian honor given by the country of Pakistan and has been named by *Time* Magazine as one of the 100 most influential people in the world.

2012

OCTAVIA SPENCER wins the Best Supporting Actress Oscar in 2012 for *The Help*. She is nominated again in 2017 for *Hidden Figures*, making her the first African-American actress to be nominated for an Academy Award after already winning one. In 2018, she is nominated for the same Oscar category for *The Shape of Water*.

Sound engineer **DEB ADAIR** shares a nomination for the 2012 Best Sound Mixing Oscar for the movie *Moneyball*.

Irish-born producer **OORLAGH MARIE GEORGE** shares the 2013 Best Short Film, Live Action Oscar for *The Shore*.

JESSICA CHASTAIN receives her first Oscar nomination in 2012 for Best Supporting Actress in *The Help*. Her second nomination is for Best Actress in 2013 for *Zero Dark Thirty*.

Kristen Wiig (left) and Annie Mumolo

Actress, writer and producer **ANNIE MUMOLO** and actress, writer and producer **KRISTEN WIIG** share the 2012 Best Writing, Original Screenplay Oscar nomination for *Bridesmaids*.

French editor **ANNE-SOPHIE BION** is nominated for the 2012 Best Film Editing Oscar for *The Artist*, which wins the Best Picture Oscar.

Director and animator **JENNIFER YUH NELSON** becomes the first woman to solely direct an animated film with the very financially successful *Kung Fu Panda 2*. She is nominated for the Best Animated Feature Film Oscar for it in 2012. Subsequently, she directs *Kung Fu Panda 3* in 2016.

Producer **MEGAN ELLISON** founds Annapurna Pictures in 2011. Since that time, she has been nominated for four shared Oscars for Best Picture: *Zero Dark Thirty* (2013), *Her* (2104), *American Hustle* (2014), and *Phantom Thread* (2018).

JENNIFER LAWRENCE wins the Best Actress Oscar in 2013 for *Silver Linings Playbook*. She has garnered three additional Oscar nominations for *Winter's Bone* (2011), *American Hustle* (2014) and *Joy* (2016).

Director of Photography **CHRISTINA VOROS** shoots the 2013 movie *As I Lay Dying*.

2013

Producer, director and writer **ANDREA NIX FINE** wins the 2013 Best Documentary, Short Subject Oscar for *Inocente*. She received a nomination for Best Documentary, Feature Oscar in 2008 for *War Dance*.

Artist and animator **LORELAY BOVE** shares a nomination for the Annie Award (see 1972) for *Wreck-It Ralph*. She has worked at Pixar Animation Studios and Walt Disney Animation Studios.

Writer and animator **BRENDA CHAPMAN** shares the 2013 Best Animated Feature Oscar for *Brave*. She is the first woman to win an Oscar in this category.

Songwriter and singer **ADELE** shares the 2013 Best Music, Original Song Oscar for "Skyfall" from the movie of the same title.

British writer, director and actress **AMMA ASANTE** (pictured center) directs the 2013 movie *Belle*. She has been awarded the Most Excellent Order of the British Empire.

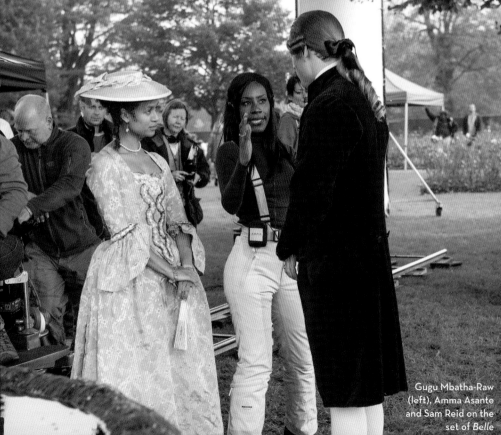

Gugu Mbatha-Raw (left), Amma Asante and Sam Reid on the set of *Belle*

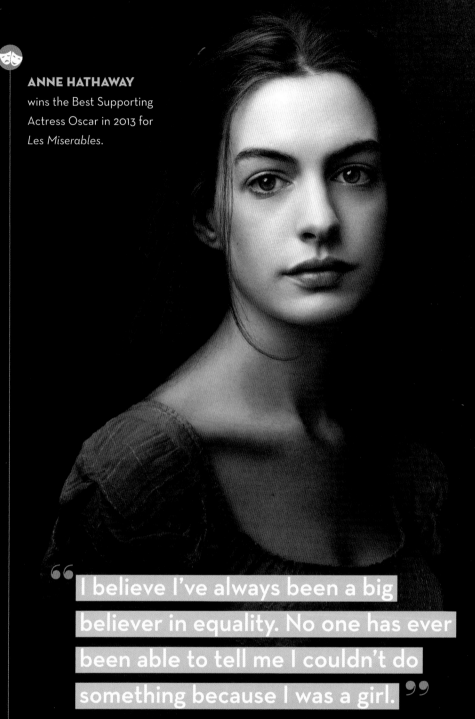

British makeup artist **JULIE DARTNELL**, who has worked in films for forty years, shares the 2013 Best Makeup and Hairstyling Oscar for *Les Miserables*.

ANNE HATHAWAY wins the Best Supporting Actress Oscar in 2013 for *Les Miserables*.

Costume designer **JACQUELINE DURRAN** wins the 2013 Best Costume Design Oscar for *Anna Karenina*. She has received five other nominations in the same category: *Pride & Prejudice* (2006), *Atonement* (2008), *Mr. Turner* (2015), *Darkest Hour* (2018) and *Beauty and the Beast* (2018).

2013

> " I believe I've always been a big believer in equality. No one has ever been able to tell me I couldn't do something because I was a girl. "
>
> —ANNE HATHAWAY

Keira Knightley and Jacqueline Durran with costume from *Anna Karenina*

A Professor of Film at Columbia University's School of the Arts, **JANE GAINES** receives a Scholarly Award in 2013 from the Academy of Motion Picture Arts and Sciences to support her book *Pink-Slipped: What Happened to Women in the Silent Film Industries?* (2018) and her work on the Women Film Pioneers Project digital archive at Columbia University. In 2018 she wins the Society for Cinema and Media Studies Distinguished Career Award.

2014 **LUPITA NYONG'O** wins the Best Supporting Actress Oscar in 2014 for *12 Years a Slave*.

Award-winning cinematographer **NATASHA BRAIER** is the director of photography for the 2014 movie *The Rover*.

Art director and set decorator **BEVERLY DUNN** shares the 2014 Best Production Design Oscar for *The Great Gatsby*.

Stuntwoman **NICOLE CALLENDER** performs stunts in the 2014 movie *Birdman or (The Unexpected Virtue of Innocence)*.

Animator **LISA KEENE** shares a 2014 Annie Award (see 1972) for production design for the movie *Frozen*.

DEDE GARDNER is the first female producer to win two Best Picture Oscars. Nominated five times, her two wins are in 2014 for *12 Years a Slave* and in 2017 for *Moonlight*. Her other nominations are in 2012 for *The Tree of Life*, 2015 for *Selma* and 2016 for *The Big Short*. Gardner is the president of the production company Plan B Entertainment.

Dorothy McKim (left) and Lauren MacMullan

2014

Director and animator **LAUREN MacMULLAN** shares a Best Short Film, Animated Oscar nomination in 2014 for the film *Get a Horse!* with producer **DOROTHY McKIM**.

Songwriter **KRISTEN ANDERSON-LOPEZ** shares the 2014 Best Music, Original Song Oscar with her husband, Robert Lopez, for the song "Let it Go" from the movie *Frozen*. They win an Oscar in the same category in 2018 for the song "Remember Me" from the movie Coco.

British actress **SALLY HAWKINS** is nominated for the 2014 Best Supporting Actress Oscar for *Blue Jasmine*. In 2018, she is nominated for the Best Actress Oscar for *The Shape of Water*.

Writer and director **JENNIFER LEE** wins the Best Animated Feature Film Oscar in 2014 for *Frozen*. She is also the first female director whose feature film earns more than $1 billion in gross box office revenue.

Producer **CAITRIN ROGERS** wins the 2014 Best Documentary, Feature Oscar for *Twenty Feet from Stardom*.

Korean-American **KAREN O**, shares the 2014 Best Music, Original Song Oscar nomination for "The Moon Song" from *Her*, for which she writes the music and lyrics.

Named president of Sony Animation in 2015, film producer **KRISTINE BELSON** formerly worked for Dreamworks Animation. She shares a 2014 Best Animated Feature Film Oscar nomination for *The Croods*.

Hairstylist **ADRUITHA LEE** and makeup artist **ROBIN MATHEWS** share the 2014 Best Makeup and Hairstyling Oscar for *Dallas Buyers Club*.

Adruitha Lee (left) and Robin Mathews

Writer and producer **AMANDA SILVER**, in collaboration with her husband Rick Jaffa, revives the Planet of the Apes franchise. In addition, in 2015, they write the screenplay for *Jurassic World*.

Singer and songwriter **DANIELLE BRISEBOIS** shares the 2015 Best Music, Original Song Oscar nomination for the song "Lost Stars" from *Begin Again*.

Producer and editor **SANDRA ADAIR** is nominated in 2015 for the Best Film Editing Oscar for *Boyhood*.

2015

Makeup, hair and prosthetics artist **FRANCES HANNON** shares the 2015 Best Makeup and Hairstyling Oscar for *The Grand Budapest Hotel*.

After thirty years in the industry, **BECKY SULLIVAN** becomes a sound editor. With her shared 2015 nomination in the Best Sound Editing category for *Unbroken*, she becomes the fifth woman nominated for an Oscar in this category.

Producer and visual effects artist **KRISTINA REED** wins the 2015 Best Short Film, Animated Oscar for *Feast*.

An actress who makes her film debut in 1987, **PATRICIA ARQUETTE** wins the Best Supporting Actress Oscar in 2015 for the film *Boyhood*.

Dana Perry (left) and Ellen Goosenberg Kent

In 2015, **BONNIE ARNOLD** is named co-president of feature animation for Dreamworks Animation. Her film producing career begins in 1984 with *The Slugger's Wife*. She has worked at Columbia, Disney and Pixar. In 2015, she shares the Best Animated Feature Film Oscar nomination for *How to Train Your Dragon*.

French editor and director **MATHILDE BONNEFOY** shares the 2015 Best Documentary, Feature Oscar for *Citizenfour* with Laura Poitras (see 2015).

Producer and director **ELLEN GOOSENBERG KENT** and producer and director **DANA PERRY** win the 2015 Best Documentary, Short Subject for *Crisis Hotline: Veterans Press 1*.

MacArthur Fellow, producer, cinematographer and director **LAURA POITRAS** shares the 2015 Best Documentary, Feature Oscar for *Citizenfour*, with Mathilde Bonnefoy (see 2015). She received a nomination for the 2007 Oscar in the same category for *My Country, My Country*.

JULIANNE MOORE receives four Oscar nominations before winning the Best Actress Oscar in 2015 for *Still Alice*. Her other nominations are for *Boogie Nights* (1998), *The End of the Affair* (2000), *The Hours* (2003), and *Far from Heaven* (2003).

Set decorator **ANNA PINNOCK** shares the 2015 Best Production Design Oscar for *The Grand Budapest Hotel*. She is also nominated that year for a shared Oscar in the same category for *Into the Woods*. She has four other shared Oscar nominations: *Gosford Park* (2002), *The Golden Compass* (2008), *Life of Pi* (2003) and *Fantastic Beasts and Where to Find Them* (2017).

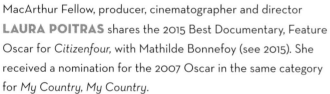

2016 Swedish actress **ALICIA VIKANDER** receives the Best Supporting Actress Oscar in 2016 for *The Danish Girl*.

Nicole Rocklin (left) and
Blye Pagon Faust

Producers **BLYE PAGON FAUST** and **NICOLE ROCKLIN** win the 2016 Best Picture Oscar for *Spotlight*. Both former practicing attorneys, they form the production firm Rocklin/Faust in 2009. *Spotlight* is Faust's first film and was seven years in the making. Up for six Academy Awards, it also wins the Best Writing, Original Screenplay Oscar.

The documentary *Cameraperson* is released in 2016 by cinematographer and producer **KIRSTEN JOHNSON**. She serves as cinematographer for *Citizenfour*, which wins an Oscar for Best Documentary, Feature in 2015 (see Laura Poitras—2015 and Mathilde Bonnefoy—2015).

Elka Wardega (left) and
Lesley Vanderwalt

New Zealand hairstylist and makeup artist **LESLEY VANDERWALT** and Australian prosthetic makeup artist **ELKA WARDEGA** share the 2016 Best Makeup and Hairstyling Oscar for *Mad Max: Fury Road*.

Producer and visual effects artist **NICOLE PARADIS GRINDLE** is nominated for the 2016 Best Short Film, Animated Oscar for *Sanjay's Super Team*. Grindle produces *The Incredibles*, *Monsters, Inc.*, and *Toy Story 3*, among others.

The first African-American female editor to be elected a member of the American Cinema Editors (an honorary editing society), **LILLIAN BENSON** edits the American Masters documentary *Maya Angelou: And Still I Rise* which is shown at the Sundance Film Festival in 2016.

Mary Jo Markey (left) and Maryann Brandon

In 2016, editors **MARYANN BRANDON** and **MARY JO MARKEY** are nominated for the Best Film Editing Oscar for *Star Wars: Episode VII—The Force Awakens*.

2016

Stop-motion animator and producer **ROSA TRAN** is nominated for the 2016 Best Animated Feature Film of the Year for *Anomalisa*.

Editor **MARGARET SIXEL** wins the 2016 Best Film Editing Oscar for *Mad Max: Fury Road*.

British singer and composer **ANOHNI** shares the 2016 Best Music, Original Song Oscar nomination for the song "Manta Ray," from *Racing Extinction*, for which she wrote the lyrics.

A set decorator for twenty-five years, **LISA THOMPSON** shares the 2016 Best Production Design Oscar for *Mad Max: Fury Road*.

In 2016, **BRIE LARSON** wins the Best Actress Oscar for *Room*.

Brie Larson and Jacob Tremblay

Writer **MEG LeFAUVE** shares the 2016 Best Writing, Original Screenplay Oscar nomination for *Inside Out*. She previously ran Jodie Foster's (see 1989) Egg Productions Company.

" What I feel I can do personally to help with diversity is to mentor those younger female writers and writers of color who are coming up so we can hear their voices, because when you can hear them, they can get made into these films, which is incredibly exciting. "

—MEG LeFAUVE

Singer, songwriter and composer **LADY GAGA** shares the 2016 Best Music, Original Song Oscar nomination for the song "Til It Happens to You" from *The Hunting Ground*.

RACHEL McADAMS wins the Best Supporting Actress Oscar in 2016 for *Spotlight*.

Director and producer **SERENA ARMITAGE** wins the 2016 Best Short Film, Live Action Oscar for *Stutterer*.

Visual effects artist **SARA BENNETT** shares the 2016 Best Visual Effects Oscar for *Ex Machina*.

2017 **VIOLA DAVIS** wins the 2017 Best Actress Oscar for her performance in *Fences*. She has two previous nominations, one for Best Actress (*The Help*, 2012) and one for Best Supporting Actress (*Doubt*, 2009).

> "The only thing that separates women of color from anyone else is opportunity.

—VIOLA DAVIS

Director **PATTY JENKINS** brings *Wonder Woman* to the screen in 2017. It becomes the top-grossing superhero origin movie of all time. On taking on a $149 million budget, she says, "People always want to know what it's like to take on such a huge budget. I still have 20 percent too little money and 20 percent too little time to do what I'm trying to do."

On women directors and money, "Women's movies have been more financially sound and bigger moneymakers across the board. That's the conundrum in this business—are you guys about money, or are you not?"

Gal Gadot (left) and Patty Jenkins while filming *Wonder Woman*

Set decorator **SANDY REYNOLDS-WASCO** shares the 2017 Best Production Design Oscar for the movie *La La Land* with her husband and collaborator David Wasco.

EMMA STONE wins the Best Actress Oscar in 2017 for *La La Land*. In 2015, she is nominated for the Best Supporting Actress Oscar for *Birdman or (The Unexpected Virtue of Innocence)*.

British composer **MICA LEVI** (also known as Micachu) is nominated for the 2017 Best Music, Score Oscar for *Jackie*. The fifth woman nominated in the category, she had begun composing for films in 2014.

British producer, director and writer **JOANNA NATASEGARA** wins the 2017 Oscar for Best Documentary, Short Subject for *The White Helmets*. She was nominated in 2015 for Best Documentary, Feature Oscar for *Virunga*.

2017

Producer **CAROLINE WATERLOW** wins the Academy Award for Best Documentary, Feature in 2017 for *O.J.: Made in America*.

Animator and producer **ARIANNE SUTNER** is nominated for the 2017 Best Animated Feature Film for *Kubo and the Two Strings*.

Producer **ADELE ROMANSKI** wins the 2017 Best Picture Oscar for *Moonlight*.

Hungarian producer **ANNA UDVARDY** wins the 2017 Best Live Action, Short Film Oscar for *Mindenki*.

Ava DuVernay with Storm Reid during filming of *A Wrinkle in Time*.

The first African-American woman to be nominated for a Best Director, Motion Picture Golden Globe, writer, director and producer **AVA DuVERNAY** is nominated for a Best Documentary Feature Oscar in 2017 for *13th*. DuVernay directs the movie *Selma* which is nominated for the 2015 Best Picture Oscar. In 2018, when *A Wrinkle in Time* is released, she becomes the first African-American woman to direct a movie with a $100 million budget. She says, "Ignore the glass ceiling and do your work. If you're focusing on the glass ceiling, focusing on what you don't have, focusing on the limitations, then you will be limited. My way was to work, make my short ... make my documentary ... make my small films ... use my own money ... raise money myself ... and stay shooting and focused on each project."

She also says: "As an artist, I am grateful that I live at a time when access to cameras and distribution platforms and ways to reach audiences outside of the normal Hollywood infrastructure are more possible for me, a black person, a woman, than ever before. My voice as a storyteller and vision as a filmmaker can be amplified without the permission of the privileged few who have held marginalized creators at arm's distance for decades."

> "Ignore the glass ceiling and do your work. If you're focusing on the glass ceiling, focusing on what you don't have, focusing on the limitations, then you will be limited."
>
> —AVA DuVERNAY

In 2017, editor **JOI McMILLON** becomes the first African-American woman nominated for the Best Film Editing Oscar with her shared nomination for *Moonlight*.

Mildred Iatrou Morgan (left) and Ai-Ling Lee

The first all-female team ever nominated for the Best Sound Editing Oscar consists of **MILDRED IATROU MORGAN** and **AI-LING LEE**. The nomination is for *La La Land* in 2017. Lee also shares a 2017 nomination in the category of Best Sound Mixing for the same movie.

Joaquin Phoenix and Carla Hacken at the premiere of *Walk The Line*

Producer **CARLA HACKEN** shares the nomination for the 2017 Best Picture Oscar for *Hell or High Water*. She works at Fox 2000 for fifteen years, first as senior vice president of production and later as executive vice president of production. In 2014, she becomes president of production for Sidney Kimmel Entertainment.

Stuntwoman Deven MacNair files a complaint with the Equal Employment Opportunity Commission claiming sex discrimination against stuntwomen over "wigging," a technique in which men perform stunts for women actors wearing wigs and dresses. At the time the complaint is filed, none of the four main stuntmen's associations allows women as members.

British makeup artist **LUCY SIBBICK** shares the 2018 Best Makeup and Hairstyling Oscar for her work on *Darkest Hour*.

Sound designer **MARY H. ELLIS,** who has been in the business for thirty years, shares the 2018 Best Sound Mixing Oscar nomination for *Baby Driver*. Ellis is one of the very few women who has been nominated in the sound mixing category.

Writer **VANESSA TAYLOR** shares the 2018 Oscar nomination for Best Original Screenplay for *The Shape of Water*.

2018

In her directorial debut, actress, writer and director **GRETA GERWIG** receives two 2018 Oscar nominations for *Lady Bird*: Best Directing and Best Original Screenplay. Gerwig is the fifth woman in the history of the Oscars to be nominated for the Best Directing Oscar.

ALLISON JANNEY wins the Best Supporting Actress Oscar for *I, Tonya*.

British actress and writer **RACHEL SHENTON** shares the 2018 Best Live Action Short Film Oscar for *The Silent Child*, which she writes and stars in. After having experienced her father's loss of hearing when she was in her teens, Shenton becomes an advocate for deaf causes.

In 2018, the first woman to be nominated for an Oscar in the category of Best Cinematography, **RACHEL MORRISON** receives that recognition for *Mudbound*.

Actress, singer and songwriter **MARY J. BLIGE** is nominated for two Oscars in 2018. She shares the nomination for Best Music, Original Song for "Mighty River" from the movie *Mudbound* with songwriter **TAURA STINSON.** Her second nomination is for Supporting Actress for the same movie. She is the first woman to receive an acting and music Oscar nomination in the same year. Her acting nomination makes Dee Rees (see 2011) the first African-American woman to direct a movie for which an actor or actress is nominated for an Academy Award.

> " You can't get around pain and opposition, but you can try to be joyful in the trial, and thank yourself for the trial and thank God for the strength to get through it. "
>
> —MARY J. BLIGE

2018

Mary J. Blige

Taura Stinson

Agnes Varda and JR filming *Faces Places*

Legendary French film director, editor, writer and producer **AGNES VARDA** receives an Honorary Academy Award in 2018. She is the first female director to be so honored. She says, "You ask me 'Is it difficult to be a woman director?' I'd say it is difficult to be a director period! It is difficult to be free; it is difficult not to be drowned in the system. We have a lot of women in the film industry—It is in terms of consciousness that we have not got it right.

"There's a difference between Hollywood films and mine. Hollywood is doing them because they will make money. Mine will make money too, but that is not my motivation. My pleasure is to show women in their totality—their joys, problems, potentials. And above all, the unique rhythms by which they live their lives.

"I am a feminist, I am a filmmaker, I am a woman. That doesn't make me a feminist-woman-filmmaker. Filmmaking is specific work. I do it. I try to do it well. But it includes the fact that my opinions as a woman, as a feminist, sometimes show up, sometimes are explicit, sometimes are implicit . . . But filmmaking is filmmaking. Do you ask a man who doesn't have hair if he considers himself a bald filmmaker? He's a man with no hair, and he's a filmmaker.

"Do you know any intelligent woman? Intelligent women exist, don't they? Why aren't they ever in films? There are always stories about virile male friendships, Brando and Nicholson, Newman and Redford, and so on, but not about friendship between women. The women are always motherly or tarty."

> " I am a feminist, I am a filmmaker, I am a woman. That doesn't make me a feminist-woman-filmmaker. "
>
> —AGNES VARDA

Actress Piper Laurie standing on soundstage.

INDEX

†Bickel, Moidele (1937-2016)
†Bickford, Laura (?-)
†Bier, Susanne (1960-)
*Bigelow, Kathryn, 2010 (1951-)
†Bilcock, Jill, 2002 (1948-)
Billington, Francelia, 1912 (1895-1934)
†Binda, Beverly (?-)
Binney, Constance, 1920 (1896-1989)
Binney, Faire, 1919 (1900-1957)
*Binoche, Juliette, 1997 (1964-)
†Bion, Anne-Sophie, 2012 (?-)
Birdwell, Mabel "Mimi" Condon, 1916 (1887-1965)
†Bjork (1965-)
†Black, Karen, 1971 (1939-2013)
†Blackie-Goodine, Janice (?-)
Blackton, Marian Constance, 1924 (1901-1993)
Blackton, Paula, 1919 (1881-1930)
†Blair, Betsy (1923-2009)
†Blair, Linda (1959-)
Blair, Mary, 1946 (1911-1978)
Blake, Bonnie, 1995 (?-)
*Blake, Yvonne, 1972 (1940-2018)
†Blakley, Ronee (1945-)
*Blanchett, Cate, 2005 (1969-)
†Blaugrund, Andrea (?-)
Bleecker, Katherine, 1915 (1893-1996)
†Blethyn, Brenda (1946-)
†Blige, Mary J., 2018 (1971-)
Bliss, Lucille, 1950 (1916-2012)
Blodgett, Katharine, 1939 (1898-1979)
†Blondell, Joan, 1930 (1906-1979)
*Blount, Lisa, 2002 (1957-2010)
*Blundell, Christine, 2000 (1961-)
†Blyth, Ann (1928-)
Blythe, Betty, 1921 (1893-1972)
Boardman, Eleanor, 1928 (1898-1991)
†Bobak, Celia, 2005 (?-)
†Bochner, Sally (?-)
†Bode (Tyson), Susan (1952?-)
†Bohlen, Anne (?-)
Boisseree, Simone, 1985 (1947-)
†Boisson, Noelle (1944-)
†Boland, Bridget (1913-1988)
Boland, Mary, 1939 (1882-1965)
Bolla, Cira Felina, 2011 (1973?-2014)
†Bondi, Beulah (1889-1981)
†Bonetto, Aline (?-)
†Bonham Carter, Helena, 1998 (1966-)
*Bonnefoy, Mathilde, 2015 (1972-)
*Bonnot, Françoise, 1970 (1939-2018)
*Booth, Margaret, 1936 (1898-2002)
*Booth, Shirley, 1953 (1898-1992)
Borden, Olive, 1922 (1906-1947)
*Borders, Gloria, 1992 (?-)
†Bortnik, Aida, 1986 (1938-2013)
Boss, May, 1952 (1924-2015)
†Boswell, Merideth (?-)
Bove, Lorelay, 2013 (1985?-)
Bow, Clara, 1927 (1905-1965)
Bowser, Pearl, 1994 (1931-)
†Box, Betty (?-)
*Box, Muriel, 1947 (1905-1991)\
*Boyens, Philippa, 2004 (?-)
†Boyle, Consolata, 2007 (?-)
†Bracco, Lorraine (1954-)
Brackett, Leigh, 1946 (1915-1978)
Braier, Natasha, 2014 (1974-)
*Brady, Alice, 1938 (1892-1939)

Brady, Janet, 1980 (?-)
Brandeis, Madeline, 1918 (1897-1937)
†Brandon, Maryann, 2016 (?-)
*Braun, Ewa, 1994 (1944-)
†Brebner, Veronica (?-)
†Breier, Betsy Broyles (?-)
†Brennan, Eileen (1932-2013)
†Brenner, Robbie (?-)
Brent, Evelyn, 1928 (1895-1975)
†Breslin, Abigail (1996-)
†Brezis, Mihal (1977-)
Brian, Mary, 1924 (1906-2002)
*Bridge, Joan, 1967 (1912-2009)
Briesewitz, Uta, 2011 (1967-)
*Brisebois, Danielle, 2015 (1969-)
*Briski, Zana, 2005 (1966-)
*Broch, Brigitte, 2002 (1943-)
Brockwell, Gladys, 1922 (1894-1929)
†Brodksy, Irene Taylor (?-)
†Brokman, Dea (?-)
Bromberg, Betzy, 1991 (?-)
Bronson, Betty, 1924 (1906-1971)
Brooks, Louise, 1929 (1906-1985)
†Brown, Kerrie (?-)
Brown, Winna "Winnie", 1913 (?-)
†Browne, Leslie (1957-)
Bruce, Kate, 1910 (1860-1946)
†Bruce, Lisa (?-)
†Buchanan, Ann (?-)
Buffington, Adele, 1919 (1900-1973)
†Bujold, Genevieve (1942-)
*Bullock, Sandra, 2010 (1964-)
Burbridge, Elizabeth (Betty), 1917 (1895-1987)
†Burke, Billie, 1939 (1884-1970)
†Burke, Marcella (?-)
*Burke, Michèle, 1983 (1959-)
*Burkett, Elinor, 2010 (1946-)
†Burns, Catherine (1945-)
Burson, Polly, 1947 (1919-2006)
†Burstein, Nanette (1970-)
*Burstyn, Ellen, 1975 (1932-)
*Burwell, Lois, 1996 (1960-)
Bush, Anita, 1921 (1883-1974)
†Bush, Nan (?-)
Bute, Mary Ellen, 1940 (1906-1983)
†Byington, Spring (1886-1971)
*Byrne, Alexandra, 2008 (1962-)

Calahan, Sharon, 1995 (?-)
†Callaghan, Colleen (?-)
Callender, Nicole, 2014 (?-)
†Cammisa, Rebecca (1966-)
*Campion, Jane, 1994 (1954-)
†Cannarozzi, Antonella (?-)
†Cannon, Dyan, 1970 (1937-)
*Canonero, Milena, 1976 (1946-)
Caputo, Jennifer, 2005 (1971-)
*Cara, Irene, 1984 (1959-)
†Carasik, Cheryl, 1996 (1952-)
†Carey, Altina (1907-1999)
†Carey, Vivien (?-)
Carino, Stacey, 2003 (?-)
Carley, Gladys, 1943 (?-)
†Carlin, Lynn (1938-)
Carol, Sue, 1927 (1906-1982)
†Caron, Leslie (1931-)
†Carr, Cindy, 1992 (?-)
Carr, Mary, 1920 (1874-1973)

†Carranza, Bernadette (?-)
†Carroll, Diahann, 1975 (1935-)
†Carroll, Nancy (1903-1965)
Carson, Jo, 1986 (?-)
†Carstensen, Kira (?-)
†Carter, Ruth E., 1993 (1960-)
Caspary, Vera, 1949 (1899-1987)
†Cass, Peggy (1924-1999)
Cassinelli, Dolores, 1919 (1888-1984)
Castle, Irene, 1917 (1893-1969)
†Castle-Hughes, Keisha (1990-)
†Causey, Gigi (?-)
†Chaffin, Cean (1957-)
Chamma, Giselle, 2003 (?-)
†Channing, Carol, 1968 (1921-)
†Channing, Stockard (1944-)
*Chapman, Brenda, 2013 (1962-)
†Chapman, Jan (1950-)
†Chapman, Linda (?-)
*Chasnoff, Debra, 1992 (1957-2017)
†Chastain, Jessica, 2012 (1977-)
†Chatterton, Ruth (1892-1961)
†Checkoway, Laura (?-)
Chenzira, Ayoka, 1982 (1953-)
*Cher, 1988 (1946-)
Chester, Lillian, 1920 (1887-1961)
†Cholodenko, Lisa (1964-)
Chopra, Joyce, 1986 (1936-)
†Choy, Christine, 1989 (1952-)
*Christie, Julie, 1966 (1940-)
†Christl, Lisy (1964-)
†Churgin, Lisa Zeno, 2000 (1955-)
†Cilento, Diane (1933-2011)
†Clark, Candy (1947-)
†Clark, Chris (1946-)
Clark, Marguerite, 1914 (1883-1940)
†Clarke, Shirley, 1960 (1919-1997)
†Clarkson, Patricia (1959-)
†Clayburgh, Jill, 1979 (1944-2010)
Clayton, Ethel, 1909 (1882-1966)
†Clemente, Pia (?-)
Clifford, Kathleen, 1919 (1887-1962)
Clifford, Ruth, 1917 (1900-1998)
†Close, Glenn, 1983 (1947-)
*Coates, Anne V., 1963 (1925-2018)
*Cody, Diablo, 2008 (1978-)
†Coffee, Lenore, 1939 (1896-1984)
*Colbert, Claudette, 1935 (1903-1996)
†Cole, Janet (?-)
Coleman, Eliza, 1996 (1956?-)
†Collette, Toni (1972-)
Collier, Constance, 1928 (1878-1955)
†Collinge, Patricia (1892-1974)
†Collingwood, Monica, 1948 (1908-1989)
†Collins, Judy, 1975 (1939-)
Collins, Kathleen, 1980 (1942-1988)
†Collins, Pauline (1940-)
†Colman, Sharon (1978-)
†Comandini, Adele, 1937 (1898-1987)
†Comden, Betty, 1954 (1917-2006)
†Comencini, Cristina (1956-)
Compson, Betty, 1919 (1897-1974)
Compton, Joyce, 1937 (1907-1997)
*Conn, Pamela, 1988 (?-)
*Connelly, Jennifer, 2002 (1970-)
Connors, Carol, 1977 (1940-)
Coolidge, Martha, 1991 (1946-)
†Cooper, Dorree (1953-)

†Cooper, Gladys, 1943 (1888–1971)
Cooper, Miriam, 1915 (1891–1976)
Cooper, Olive, 1938 (1892–1987)
†Cooperman, Kahane (1965–)
*Coppola, Sofia, 2004 (1971–)
Corbin, Virginia Lee, 1926 (1910–1942)
†Corby, Ellen (1911–1999)
†Cornell, Pamela (?–)
†Cortese, Valentina (1923–)
†Cory, Judith A., 1994 (?–)
†Costello, Dianna (?–)
Costello, Dolores, 1926 (1903–1979)
Costello, Helene, 1928 (1906–1957)
*Cotillard, Marion, 2008 (1975–)
Coulter, Jean, 1977 (?–)
Courtot, Marguerite, 1922 (1897–1986)
Cowan, Sada, 1920 (1882–1943)
Craig, Phyllis, 1953 (1929–1997)
†Crain, Jeanne (1925–2003)
†Cram, Mildred, 1940 (1889–1985)
*Crawford, Joan, 1946 (1905–1977)
Crawford, Sophia, 1997 (1966–)
Creach, Lauri, 2000 (?–)
Crenshaw, Michelle, 1990 (?–)
*Cristiani, Gabriella, 1988 (1949–)
†Crossley, Callie (1951–)
†Crouse, Lindsay (1948–)
Crowell, Josephine, 1915 (1859–1932)
*Cruz, Penélope, 2009 (1974–)
Cuffee, Evelyne, 1978 (1933–)
†Cummings, Quinn (1967–)
Cunard, Grace, 1917 (1893–1967)
†Cunningham, Carolynne (?–)
Curley, Pauline, 1918 (1903–2000)
†Curtin, Valerie (1945–)
†Cusack, Joan (1962–)
†Cusack, Pud (?–)

†Daelemans, Anja (1967–)
Dalton, Dorothy, 1915 (1893–1972)
*Dalton, Phyllis, 1966 (1925–)
†d'Amico, Suso Cecchi (1914–2010)
†D'Amore, Hallie, 1995 (1942–2006)
Dana, Viola, 1917 (1897–1987)
†Dandridge, Dorothy, 1955 (1922–1965)
†Danevic, Nena, 1985 (?–)
Daniels, Bebe, 1910 (1901–1971)
Danko, Betty, 1939 (1903–1979)
†Danon, Ambra (?–)
Darmond, Grace, 1917 (1893–1963)
*Dartnell, Julie, 2013 (1963–)
*Darwell, Jane, 1941 (1879–1967)
Dash, Julie, 1991 (1952–)
Dashnaw, Tracy Keehn, 1988 (?–)
†Davaa, Byambasuren (1971–)
David, Jadie, 1979 (1951?–)
Davies, Marion, 1917 (1897–1961)
†Davies, Suzie (?–)
†Davies, Tessa, 1984 (1940–1988)
Davis, Alice, 1960 (1929–)
*Davis, Bette, 1936 (1908–1989)
*Davis, Geena, 1989 (1956–)
†Davis, Judy (1955–)
†Davis, Kate (1960–)
†Davis, Sharen (1957–)
Davis, Sonja, 1993 (1962–1994)
*Davis, Viola, 2017 (1965–)
Daw, Marjorie, 1917 (1902–1979)

†Dawson, Beatrice (1908–1976)
Dawson, Rosario, 2006 (1979–)
†Day, Doris, 1960 (1922 –)
Day, Marceline, 1928 (1908–2000)
Dayton, Helena Smith, 1917 (1879–1960)
*De Alba, Beatrice, 2003 (?–)
†Dean, Lisa (?–)
Dean, Priscilla, 1917 (1896–1987)
†DeAngelo, Rena (?–)
†Dee, Ruby, 1950 (1922–2014)
Dee, Sandra, 1957 (1942–2005)
De Fina, Barbara, 1986 (1949–)
DeFreest, Babe, 1937 (1907–1986)
*de Havilland, Olivia, 1947 (1916–)
†Delamare, Rosine (1911–2013)
*DeLeo, Maryann, 2004 (?–)
Dell, Paula, 1963 (1926–2017)
†Delmar, Vina (1903–1990)
†Delpy, Julie, 2005 (1969–)
Del Rio, Dolores, 1925 (1904–1983)
†De Matteis, Maria (1898–1988)
Dempster, Carol, 1920 (1901–1991)
†Denaver, Deborah LaMia (?–)
*Dench, Judi, 1999 (1934–)
†Deneuve, Catherine (1943–)
*Dennis, Sandy, 1967 (1937–1992)
†De Passe, Suzanne, 1973 (1946–)
Deren, Maya, 1947 (1917–1961)
†Dern, Laura, 1992 (1967–)
†DeScenna, Linda, 1980 (1949–)
†Deutsch, Helen, 1954 (1906–1992)
Devereaux, Minnie, 1914 (1891–1984)
Devore, Dorothy, 1918 (1899–1976)
†De Waele, Ellen (1973–)
*Dewey, Donna, 1998 (1947?–)
De Wolf, Karen, 1934 (1909–1989)
†Dickson, Deborah, 1988 (?–)
*Dickson, Ngila, 2004 (1958–)
Didion, Joan, 1976 (1934–)
†Dido, 2011 (1971–)
†Dietrich, Marlene, 1931 (1901–1992)
†di Florio, Paola (?–)
*Dillon, Carmen, 1949 (1908–2000)
†Dillon, Melinda, 1978 (1939–)
†Dine, Nancy (?–)
Di Novi, Denise, 1990 (1956–)
Disney, Abigail, 2008 (1960–)
Dix, Beulah Marie, 1917 (1876–1970)
Dixon, Leslie, 1987 (?–)
†Djordjadze, Nana (1948–)
†Djurkovic, Maria (?–)
Doherty, Ethel, 1925 (1889–1974)
†Dolgin, Gail (1945–2010)
†Donoghue, Emma (1969–)
Donoghue, Mary Agnes, 1988 (1943–)
†Donovan, Arlene (?–)
†Doran, Lindsay (1948–)
†Dorn, Dody, 2002 (1955–)
Dougherty, Kathryn, 1932 (?–)
†Douglas, Clare (1944–2017)
Dove, Billie, 1927 (1903–1997)
*Dowd, Nancy, 1979 (1945–)
†Dreiband-Burman, Bari, 1989 (?–)
†Dresser, Louise (1878–1965)
*Dressler, Marie, 1931 (1868–1934)
†Driver, Minnie (1970–)
†Dryfoos, Susan W. (1946–)
†Dubreuil, Helene (?–)

Du Brey, Claire, 1917 (1892–1993)
Ducey, Lillian, 1923 (1878–1952)
*Dudley, Anne, 1998 (1956–)
Duggins, Shauna, 2000 (?–)
*Dukakis, Olympia, 1988 (1931–)
*Duke, Patty, 1963 (1946–2016)
*Dunaway, Faye, 1977 (1941–)
†Dundas, Sally (?–)
Dunham, Katherine, 1948 (1909–2006)
*Dunn, Beverly, 2014 (?–)
Dunn, Dorothy, 1917 (?–)
Dunn, Winifred, 1926 (1898–1977)
†Dunne, Irene, 1932 (1898–1990)
†Dunnock, Mildred (1901–1991)
†Duras, Marguerite (1914–1996)
*Durbin, Deanna, 1939 (1921–2013)
Durfee, Minta, 1914 (1889–1975)
*Durran, Jacqueline, 2013 (?–)
†Durrin, Ginny (?–)
†DuVernay, Ava, 2017 (1972–)
Dwan, Dorothy, 1925 (1906–1981)
†Dwyer, Finola (?–)

†Eagels, Jeanne (1890–1929)
†Easley, Pamela, 1994 (?–)
†Earnshaw, Tina (?–)
Eastman, Carole, 1971 (1934–2004)
Eddy, Helen Jerome, 1919 (1897–1990)
†Edwards, Trisha (?–)
†Edzard, Christine (1945–)
†Eggar, Samantha (1939–)
Egleston, Rita, 1982 (?–)
†Ehrlich, Judith (?–)
†Elliott, Alice (1950–)
Ellis, Annie, 1987 (1956–)
†Ellis, Mary H., 2018 (?–)
†Ellison, Megan, 2013 (1986–)
†Emerson, Hope (1897–1960)
†Enya, 2002 (1961–)
†Enyedi, Ildiko (1955–)
Ephron, Delia, 1998 (1944–)
†Ephron, Nora, 1984 (1941–2012)
†Ephron, Phoebe, 1964 (1914–1971)
Epper, Eurlyne, 1983 (1960–)
Epper, Jeannie, 1969 (1941–)
Epper, Stephanie, 1970 (1943–)
†Ergüven, Deniz Gamze (1978–)
†Erskine, Karin (1945–)
†Esson, Katja (1966–)
†Estabrook, Helen (?–)
*Etheridge, Melissa, 2007 (1961–)
Evans, Debbie, 1991 (1958–)
Evans, Delight, 1917 (1902–1985?)
Evans, Donna, 1987 (?–)
†Evans, Edith, 1964 (1888–1976)
†Ewing, Heidi (?–)
Eyton, Bessie, 1914 (1890–1965)

†Fadiman, Dorothy (?–)
Fairfax, Marion, 1922 (1875–1970)
†Farmiga, Vera (1973–)
Farnum, Dorothy, 1926 (1900–1970)
†Farr, Judy (?–)
Farrar, Geraldine, 1915 (1882–1967)
*Faust, Blye Pagon, 2016 (?–)
Faye, Alice, 1938 (1915–1998)
Faye, Julia, 1926 (1892–1966)
*Fazan, Adrienne, 1959 (1906–1986)

Fazenda, Louise, 1917 (1895–1962)

†Fehr, Kaja (1950–)

Feinberg, Danielle, 1998 (1974?–)

Ferguson, Helen, 1933 (1901–1977)

Ferrera, America, 2002 (1984–)

†Ferri, Elda (?–)

†Ferry, April (1932–)

†Fialon, Estelle (1969–)

†Field, Connie (?–)

†Field, Fern (1934–)

†Field, Patricia (1941–)

*Field, Sally, 1980 (1946–)

†Fielder, Angie (?–)

*Fields, Dorothy, 1937 (1904–1974)

*Fields, Verna, 1976 (1918–1982)

Finch, Flora, 1908 (1867–1940)

*Fine, Andrea Nix, 2013 (?–)

†Fine, Sylvia, 1954 (1913–1991)

*Finerman, Wendy, 1995 (1960–)

Finley, Evelyn, 1941 (1916–1989)

Finn, Lila, 1939 (1909–1996)

Finochio, Stephanie, 1987 (1971–)

Fioramonti, Glory, 1976 (?–)

Fischer, Margarita, 1913 (1886–1975)

Fisher, Carrie, 1977 (1956–2016)

Fisher, Lucy, 2002 (1949–)

†Fitzgerald, Geraldine (1913–2005)

†Flagg, Fannie, 1992 (1944–)

†Flaherty, Frances (1883–1972)

*Fletcher, Louise, 1976 (1934–)

*Florio, Maria, 1986 (?–)

Flugrath, Edna, 1916 (1893–1966)

†Foch, Nina (1924–2008)

Foerster, Anna, 1996 (?–)

Folkerson, Cindy, 1982 (?–)

*Fonda, Jane, 1972 (1937–)

†Foner, Naomi (1946–)

*Fontaine, Joan, 1942 (1917–2013)

†Fontaine, Lynn (1887–1983)

†Fontaine, Madeline (?–)

Foray, June, 1950 (1917–2017)

†Forbis, Amanda, 2000 (1963–)

Forsyte, Joey, 1993 (?–)

†Forte, Lori (?–)

Foster, Gloria, 1999 (1933–2001)

*Foster, Jodie, 1989 (1962–)

†Foster, Lesley (?–)

†Foster, Lilibet (?–)

†Fowler, Marjorie (1920–2003)

†Fox, Jennifer (?–)

†Frank Jr., Harriet, 1964 (1917–)

†Frederick, Ericka (?–)

Frederick, Pauline, 1915 (1883–1938)

*Fricker, Brenda, 1990 (1945–)

Friedman (Astor), Lillian, 1934 (1912–1989)

†Friedman, Sonya (1932–)

†Froemke, Susan (?–)

*Fruchtman, Lisa, 1984 (1948–)

†Fryday, Robin (?–)

Fuller, Mary, 1914 (1888–1973)

Fulton, Maude, 1931 (1881–1950)

*Furse, Margaret, 1970 (1911–1974)

†Gaga, Lady, 2016 (1986–)

Gaines, Jane, 2013 (?–)

*Garbo, Greta, 1931 (1905–1990)

†Garbus, Liz (?–)

†Gardiner, Ainsley (?–)

*Gardiner, Lizzy, 1995 (1966–)

†Gardner, Ava, 1946 (1922–1990)

*Gardner, Dede, 2014 (1967–)

Gardner, Helen, 1912 (1884–1968)

†Garey, Diane (?–)

*Garland, Judy, 1940 (1922–1969)

*Garner, Peggy Ann, 1946 (1932–1984)

†Garr, Teri (1944–)

†Garrett, Siedah, 2007 (1960–)

*Garson, Greer, 1943 (1904–1996)

Gauntier, Gene, 1907 (1885–1966)

*Gaynor, Janet, 1929 (1906–1984)

†George, Gladys (1904–1954)

George, Hazel, 1957 (1904–1996)

George, Maude, 1915 (1888–1963)

*George, Oorlagh Marie, 2012 (1980–)

†Georges, Emilie (?–)

Geraghty, Carmelita, 1925 (1901–1966)

Gerber, Neva, 1917 (1894–1974)

†Gerwig, Greta, 2018 (1983–)

Gibson, Helen, 1915 (1892–1977)

*Gigliotti, Donna, 1999 (1955–)

†Gilliatt, Penelope (1932–1993)

†Gilman, Sari (1969–)

Gimpel, Sandra Lee, 1980 (1939–)

Gish, Dorothy, 1918 (1898–1968)

*Gish, Lillian, 1912 (1893–1993)

Gist, Eloyce King Patrick, 1933 (1892–1974)

†Glatter, Lesli Linka (1953–)

†Glatzer, Jocelyn (?–)

Glauberman, Dana, 2007 (1968–)

Glaum, Louise, 1920 (1888–1970)

Glover, Kristin, 1993 (?–)

Glyn, Elinor, 1921 (1864–1943)

†Goddard, Paulette, 1936 (1910–1990)

Godino, Grace, 1974 (1915–2011)

†Godmilow, Jill, 1975 (1943–)

†Goffe, Sue (1964–)

†Goffette, Vivian (?–)

†Goldberg, Tikki (?–)

*Goldberg, Whoopi, 1991 (1955–)

†Golden, Kit (?–)

†Goldfarb, Lyn (?–)

†Goldstein, Abbee (?–)

Gonzalez, Myrtle, 1916 (1891–1918)

†Goodman, Julie (?–)

*Goodman, Karen, 2011 (?–)

†Goodrich, Frances, 1935 (1890–1984)

Goodwin, Aline, 1933 (1887–1980)

†Goodwin, Rosie (?–)

†Gooley, Nikki (?–)

†Gordon, Emily V. (1979–)

*Gordon, Ruth, 1969 (1896–1985)

†Gore, Lesley, 1981 (1946–2015)

*Gorris, Marleen (1948–)

Goudal, Jetta, 1925 (1891–1985)

Grable, Betty, 1940 (1916–1973)

†Grady, Rachel (?–)

*Grahame, Gloria, 1953 (1923–1981)

†Granik, Debra, 2011 (1963–)

*Grant, Lee, 1976 (1925–)

Grant, Nellie, 1916 (?–)

†Grant, Susannah, 2001 (1963–)

†Granville, Bonita (1923–1988)

*Gratz, Joan, 1993 (1941–)

†Gray, Lorraine (?–)

†Gray, Maggie (?–)

Green, Marian, 1984 (1959–)

†Green, Sarah (?–)

†Green, Steph (1979–)

Greenberger, Lillian, 1919 (?–)

†Greenwood, Sarah, 2006 (?–)

Greenwood, Winifred, 1910 (1885–1961)

†Gregory, Grace (1901–1985)

†Gresham, Gloria (?–)

Grier, Pam, 1974 (1949–)

*Griffin, Eleanore, 1939 (1904–1995)

†Griffith, Corinne, 1930 (1894–1979)

†Griffith, Melanie (1957–)

†Griffiths, Mildred, 1946 (1894–1949)

†Griffiths, Rachel (1968–)

†Grigg, Sian (?–)

†Grindle, Nicole Paradis, 2016 (?–)

†Grossman, Nora (1983–)

†Grote, Ulrike (1963–)

Guenther, Ann, 1973 (1937–2017)

Guihan, Frances, 1920 (1890–1951)

Gulliver, Dorothy, 1932 (1908–1997)

Guy-Blaché, Alice, 1896 (1873–1968)

†Gyllenhaal, Maggie (1977–)

†Hacken, Carla, 2017 (1961–)

†Hackett, Joan (1934–1983)

*Hadary, Susan Hannah, 2000 (?–)

Haellmigk, Anette, 1990 (?–)

*Haffenden, Elizabeth, 1960 (1906–1976)

†Hagen, Jean (1923–1977)

*Haigh, Nancy, 1992 (1948?–)

Haines, Randa, 1986 (1945–)

†Hale, Nancy (?–)

†Halfon, Lianne (1953–)

*Hall, Cecelia, 1991 (?–)

Hall, Donna, 1953 (1928–2002)

Hall, Ella, 1913 (1897–1981)

†Hall, Grayson (1922–1985)

*Hall, Mindy, 2010 (?–)

†Hallinan, Eda Godel (1943?–)

Hamilton, LisaGay, 2003 (1964–)

*Hamilton, Nancy, 1956 (1908–1985)

Hammer, Barbara, 1992 (1939–)

Hammerstein, Elaine, 1924 (1897–1948)

†Hamzavi, Talkhon (1979–)

*Hannon, Frances, 2015 (?–)

Hansberry, Lorraine, 1961 (1930–1965)

Hansen, Juanita, 1915 (1895–1961)

Happy, Bonnie, 1985 (1954–)

Happy (Connelly), Edith, 1951 (1925–1999)

Happy, Marguerite, 1991 (?–)

*Harden, Marcia Gay, 2001 (1959–)

†Harding, Ann (1902–1981)

Harding, LaVerne, 1934 (1905–1984)

Hardwicke, Catherine, 2008 (1955–)

Harlow, Jean, 1930 (1911–1937)

Harper, Patricia, 1938 (?–)

†Harper, Tess (1950–)

Harris, Barbara, 1972 (1935–2018)

*Harris, Julie, 1966 (1921–2015)

†Harris, Julie (1925–2013)

Harris, Leslie, 1992 (1959–)

Harris, Mildred, 1914 (1901–1944)

†Harris, Naomie (1976–)

†Harris, Rosemary (1927–)

†Harrison, Joan, 1941 (1907–1994)

†Hartman, Elizabeth (1943–1987)

†Harwood, Shuna (1940–)

Haskell, Molly, 1974 (1939–)

*Hathaway, Anne, 2013 (1982–)
†Hawkins, Sally, 2014 (1976–)
*Hawn, Goldie, 1970 (1945–)
†Hayek, Selma (1966–)
*Hayes, Helen, 1933 (1900–1993)
†Hayward, Debra (?–)
Hayward, Lillie, 1943 (1891–1977)
*Hayward, Susan, 1959 (1917–1975)
Hayworth, Rita, 1946 (1918–1987)
*Head, Edith, 1950 (1897–1981)
*Heckart, Eileen, 1973 (1919–2001)
†Heckel, Sally (?–)
Heckerling, Amy, 1982 (1954–)
†Hegedus, Chris (1952–)
†Heideman, Cecile (?–)
Heims, Jo, 1971 (1930–1978)
†Heller, Caryl (?–)
Heller, Rosilyn, 1973 (1937–)
*Hellman, Lillian, 1942 (1905–1984)
†Hemingway, Mariel (1961–)
†Hemming, Carol (?–)
*Hemming, Lindy, 2000 (1948–)
Henie, Sonja, 1939 (1912–1969)
†Henkin, Hilary (1952–)
†Henley, Beth (1952–)
Hennessy, Leigh, 1997 (?–)
Henry, Gale, 1918 (1893–1972)
Henson, Lisa, 1993 (1960–)
†Henson, Taraji P., 2009 (1970–)
*Hepburn, Audrey, 1954 (1929–1993)
*Hepburn, Katharine, 1934 (1907–2003)
*Herbert, Jocelyn, 1964 (1917–2003)
†Herbich, Barbara (1954–2009)
*Heron, Julia, 1942 (1897–1977)
Herrick, Margaret (Gledhill), 1936 (1902–1976)
†Hershey, Barbara (1948–)
†Heyman, Norma (1940–)
†Hibbert-Jones, Dee (?–)
†Hill, Elizabeth, 1939 (1901–1978)
Hill, Ethel, 1939 (1898–1954)
†Hill, Gladys, 1976 (1916–1981)
*Hiller, Wendy, 1959 (1912–2003)
Hilliker, Katherine, 1925 (1885–1965)
*Hirschberg, Lora, 2011 (1963–)
†Hobby, Amy (?–)
Hoffman, Leslie, 1976 (1955–)
†Hoffmann, Deborah (?–)
†Høgh, Dorte (1968–)
†Holland, Angieszka, 1992 (1948–)
†Holleran, Leslie (?–)
*Holliday, Judy, 1951 (1921–1965)
†Holliman, Elaine (?–)
*Holm, Celeste, 1948 (1917–2012)
Holmes, Helen, 1914 (1891 or 1892–1950)
†Honan, Robin (?–)
†Hopkins, Miriam (1902–1972)
Hopkins, Natascha, 2006 (?–)
Hopper, Hedda, 1938 (1885–1966)
†Horovitz, Rachael (1961–)
†Horvath, Joan (?–)
House, Lucille, 1950 (1910–2008)
†Houston, Dianne (1954–)
Howard, Linda Fetters, 1989 (?–)
Howell, Alice, 1917 (1886–1961)
Howell, Dorothy, 1931 (1899–1971)
Hoyle, Lisa, 2003 (1971–)
†Hoyt, Judie C. (?–)
*Hubley, Faith, 1963 (1924–2001)

*Hudson, Jennifer, 2007 (1981–)
†Hudson, Kate (1979–)
†Huffman, Felicity (1962–)
*Huguenot van der Linden, Martina, 1973 (?–1988)
*Hull, Josephine, 1951 (1877–1957)
†Humes, Immy (?–)
†Hunt, Courtney (1964–)
*Hunt, Helen, 1998 (1963–)
*Hunt, Linda, 1984 (1945–)
*Hunt, Marjorie, 1985 (1954–)
*Hunter, Holly, 1994 (1958–)
*Hunter, Kim, 1952 (1922–2002)
†Huppert, Isabelle (1953–)
Hurd, Gale Anne, 1984 (1955–)
†Hussey, Ruth (1911–2005)
*Huston, Anjelica, 1986 (1951–)
Hutton, Betty, 1944 (1921–2007)
Hyams, Nessa, 1971 (1941–)
†Hyde, Margaret (?–)
†Hyer, Martha (1924–2014)
Hyland, Frances, 1926 (1904–?)
Hyson, Roberta, 1929 (1905–1989)

*Ibi, Keiko, 1999 (1967–)
*Innis, Chris (?–)
†Irene, 1949, (1901–1962)
*Irglová, Markéta, 2008 (1988–)
†Irving, Amy (1953–)
†Ishaq, Sara (1984–)
*Ishioka, Eiko, 1993 (1938–2012)
Ivers, Julia Crawford, 1916 (1867–1930)
†Iwerks, Leslie (1970–)
Izzolena, Sonia (Sonia Jo McDancer), 1991 (?–)

†Jackson, Gemma (1951–)
*Jackson, Glenda, 1971 (1936–)
*Jackson, Janet, 1994 (1966–)
Jacobs, Daisy, 2015 (1988–)
*Janney, Allison, 2018 (1959–)
†Jaoui, Agnes (1964–)
†Jayashri, Bombay (?–)
*Jeakins, Dorothy, 1949 (1914–1995)
†Jean-Baptiste, Marianne (1967–)
†Jenet, Veronika, 1994 (?–)
Jenkins, Patty, 2017 (1971–)
†Jenkins, Tamara (1962–)
*Jenssen, Elois, 1951 (1922–2004)
Jessye, Eva, 1929 (1895–1992)
*Jhabvala, Ruth Prawer, 1987 (1927–2013)
†Joffe, Carol, 1987 (?–)
†Johns, Glynis (1923–)
†Johnson, Bridget (?–)
†Johnson, Celia (1908–1982)
Johnson, Diane, 1980 (1934–)
Johnson, Edith, 1916 (1894–1969)
Johnson, Julie Ann, 1967 (1939–)
Johnson, Kirsten, 2016 (1965–)
Johnson, Kristina, 2009 (1957–)
†Johnson, Lynn (?–)
Johnson, Osa, 1921 (1894–1953)
Johnston, Agnes Christine, 1927 (1896–1978)
†Johnston, Becky (?–)
†Johnston, Joanna (?–)
†Johnstone, Anna Hill (1913–1992)
*Jolie, Angelina, 2000 (1975–)
Jones, Amy Holden, 1988 (1955–)
†Jones, Carolyn (1930–1983)
†Jones, Felicity (1983–)

*Jones, Jennifer, 1944 (1919–2009)
†Jones, Leslie, 1999 (?–)
†Jones, Natalie R. (?–)
*Jones, Shirley, 1961 (1934–)
†Jordan, Jeanne (?–)
Jordan (Mason), Jewell, 1937 (1917–2009)
†Jorry, Corinne (?–)
Joy, Leatrice, 1917 (1893–1985)
†Joyce, Adrien, see Carole Eastman
Joyce, Alice, 1910 (1890–1955)
†Jurado, Katy (1924–2002)

Kael, Pauline, 1965 (1919–2001)
†Kahn, Madeline, 1974 (1942–1999)
†Kalinina, Irina (?–)
Kalmus, Natalie, 1939 (1882–1965)
†Kaminska, Ida (1899–1980)
†Kane, Carol (1952–)
†Kanin, Fay, 1959 (1917–2013)
*Karinska, Barbara, 1949 (1886–1983)
†Karlin, Meg (also Marsha Karlin) (?–)
†Karmel, Philippa (Pip), 1997 (1963–)
†Karrell, Matia (?–)
†Kasdan, Meg (?–)
†Katz, Gloria, 1974 (1942–)
Kaus, Gina, 1953 (1893–1985)
Kavanaugh, Frances, 1945 (1915–2009)
†Kavanaugh, Lisa Dean, 1991 (?–)
*Keaton, Diane, 1978 (1946–)
*Kedrova, Lila, 1965 (1909–2000)
Keegan, Donna, 1984 (1959–)
Keeler, Ruby, 1933 (1910–1993)
Keene, Lisa, 2014 (?–)
†Keener, Catherine (1959–)
Keller, Helen, 1918 (1880–1968)
Kellerman, Annette, 1916 (1887–1975)
†Kellerman, Sally (1937–)
†Kellogg, Virginia, 1950 (1907–1981)
*Kelly, Grace, 1955 (1929–1982)
†Kelly, Nancy (1921–1995)
†Kendrick, Anna, 2010 (1985–)
*Kenley-Letts, Ruth, 1995 (?–)
†Kennedy, Kathleen, 1983 (1953–)
Kennedy, Madge, 1917 (1891–1987)
†Kennedy, Rory (1968–)
*Kent, Ellen Goosenberg, 2015 (?–)
Kenyon, Doris, 1924 (1897–1979)
*Kernochan, Sarah, 1973 (1947–)
*Kerr, Deborah, 1950 (1921–2007)
*Khouri, Callie, 1992 (1957–)
*Kidman, Nicole, 2003 (1967–)
†Kikuchi, Rinko (1981–)
†Kilvert, Lilly (1950–)
Kingsley, Dorothy, 1955 (1909–1997)
Kingsley, Grace, 1914 (1873–1962)
Kingston, Natalie, 1926 (1905–1991)
†Kirkland, Sally (1941–)
Kissane, Ruth, 1978 (1929–1990)
†Klapper-McNally, Lianne (?–)
Klick, Laurel, 1984 (?–)
†Klingman, Lynzee, 1976 (1943–)
†Klotz, Florence (1920–2006)
†Knight, Amanda (?–)
†Knight, Shirley (1936–)
†Knightley, Keira (1985–)
†Kobiela, Dorota (1978–)
*Koch, Norma, 1963 (1898–1979)
†Kohner, Susan (1936–)

†Kopacz, Aneta (1975-)
*Kopple, Barbara, 1977 (1946-)
†Korjus, Miliza (c.1905–1980)
†Koskoff, Emma Tillinger (1972-)
*Kove, Torill, 2007 (1958-)
†Kowarsky, Philippa (?-)
†Krieger, Kristie Macosko (1970-)
†Krizan, Kim (1961-)
Kroyer, Sue, 1992 (?-)
†Kuljian, Anne, 1990 (1949-)
†Kuras, Ellen, 2009 (1959-)
†Kuwahata, Ru (?-)
†Kymry, Tylwyth (see Meg Karlin)

La Badie, Florence, 1909 (1888–1917)
†Ladd, Diane, 1975 (1935-)
†LaGarde, Jocelyne (1924–1979)
*Lahti, Christine, 1985 (1950-)
La Marr, Barbara, 1921 (1896–1926)
Lamarr, Hedy, 1938 (1914–2000)
Lamb, Jennifer, 1996 (?-)
Lamour, Dorothy, 1940 (1914–1996)
†Lanchester, Elsa (1902–1986)
*Landers, Karen Baker, 2008 (?-)
†Landis, Deborah Nadoolman (1952-)
†Landis, Ilene (?-)
†Lane, Diane (1965-)
*Lane, Tami, 2006 (1974-)
†Langan, Christine (1965-)
†Langdon, Dory (see Dory Previn)
†Lange, Hope (1933–2003)
*Lange, Jessica, 1983 (1949-)
*Lansbury, Angela, 1945 (1925-)
†Lansing, Sherry, 1980 (1944-)
La Plante, Laura, 1926 (1904–1996)
*Larson, Brie, 2016 (1989-)
†Latifah, Queen, 2003 (1970-)
†Laurie, Piper, 1962 (1932-)
Lauzen, Martha, 2011 (?-)
La Verne, Lucille, 1937 (1872–1945)
Lawrence, Florence, 1907 (1886–1938)
*Lawrence, Jennifer, 2013 (1990-)
†Lawrence, Viola, 1958 (1894–1973)
†Lazaridi, Christina (1970-)
*Lazarus, Margaret, 1994 (1949-)
†Lazin, Lauren (1960-)
*Leachman, Cloris, 1972 (1926-)
†Leaf, Caroline, 1977 (1946-)
Leahy, Agnes Brand, 1925 (1893–1934)
Learn, Bessie, 1914 (1888–1987)
†LeBlanc, Pam (?-)
Le Blond, Mrs. Aubrey, 1898 (1860–1934)
Leder, Mimi, 2000 (1952-)
*Lee, Adruitha, 2014 (?-)
†Lee, Ai-Ling, 2017 (?-)
*Lee, Jennifer, 2014 (1971-)
Lee, Lila, 1918 (1905–1973)
†Lee, Peggy (1920–2002)
†Leeds, Andrea (1914–1984)
†LeFauve, Meg, 2016 (?-)
†Le Gallienne, Eva (1899–1991)
†Lehman, Gladys, 1945 (1892–1993)
†Leigh, Janet, 1961 (1927–2004)
†Leigh, Jennifer Jason (1962-)
*Leigh, Vivien, 1940 (1913–1967)
†Leighton, Margaret (1922–1976)
Lemmons, Kasi, 1997 (1961-)
†Lennart, Isobel, 1956 (1915–1971)

*Lennox, Annie, 2004 (1954-)
†Lense-Møller, Lise (1957-)
†Lentz, Irene (see Irene)
†Lenya, Lotte (1898–1981)
*Leo, Melissa, 2011 (1960-)
†Leonard, Judith (?-)
Lepselter, Alisa, 1999 (1963-)
†Lerner, Gail (?-)
†Lessin, Tia (?-)
†Leterrier, Catherine (1942-)
*Levien, Sonya, 1956 (1888–1960)
*Levinson, Shelley, 1982 (1943-)
†Levitt, Helen, 1950 (1913–2009)
†Levitt, Ruby, 1960 (1907–1992)
†Lewis, Juliette (1973-)
†Lewis, Mildred (?-)
*Light, Allie, 1992 (?-)
†Lindsey, Hillary, 2011 (?-)
*Lingheim, Susanne, 1984 (1954-)
*Link, Caroline, 2003 (1964-)
†Linney, Laura, 2001 (1964-)
†Lins, Gabriele (?-)
Little, Ann, 1911 (1891–1984)
†Littleton, Carol, 1983 (1948-)
*Littman, Lynne, 1977 (1941-)
Liu, Lucy, 2000 (1968-)
†Llosa, Claudia (1976-)
Loden, Barbara, 1970 (1932–1980)
†Loeb, Janice, 1949 (1902–1996)
†Loeffler, Heather (?-)
*Lombard, Carole, 1937 (1908–1942)
Loos, Anita, 1912 (1889–1981)
Loos, Mary, 1955 (1910–2004)
*Loren, Sophia, 1962 (1934-)
†Lorenz, Barbara (?-)
Loring, Jane, 1928 (1890–1983)
Lorraine, Louise, 1921 (1904–1981)
†Lorring, Joan (1926–2014)
*Lo Schiavo, Francesca, 2005 (1948-)
Louise, Ruth Harriet, 1925 (1903–1940)
†Love, Bessie, 1930 (1898–1986)
†Lovett, Josephine, 1928 (1877–1958)
†Lowell, Carol (?-)
Lowell, Louise, 1920 (?-)
*Loy, Myrna, 1934 (1905–1993)
*Lucas, Marcia, 1978 (1945-)
Lucas, Sharon, 1948 (1928–2006)
†Luce, Clare Boothe, 1950 (1903–1987)
Lupino, Ida, 1941 (1918–1995)
Lurie, Deborah, 1998 (1974-)
†Lynch-Robinson, Anna (?-)

Maas, Frederica Sagor, 1925 (1900–2012)
*Macaulay, Eunice, 1979 (1923–2013)
*MacAvin, Josie, 1986 (1919–2005)
MacDonald, Jeanette, 1929 (1903–1965)
†Macdonald, Tatiana (?-)
†MacGraw, Ali, 1971 (1939-)
MacKaill, Dorothy, 1924 (1903–1990)
*MacLaine, Shirley, 1984 (1934-)
MacLaren, Mary, 1916 (1896–1985)
†MacMahon, Aline (1899–1991)
†MacMullan, Lauren, 2014 (1964-)
MacPherson, Jeanie, 1913 (1886–1946)
†Macrorie, Alma, 1956 (1904–1970)
†Madigan, Amy (1950-)

†Madigan-Yorkin, Alix (?-)
Madison, Cleo, 1914 (1883–1964)
†Madsen, Virginia (1961-)
*Magnani, Anna, 1956 (1908–1973)
*Main, Marjorie (1890–1975)
Majolie, Bianca, 1940 (1900–1997)
*Makovsky, Judianna, 1999 (1955 or 1967-)
*Malone, Dorothy, 1957 (1924–2018)
†Mann, Aimee, 2000 (1960-)
Mansfield, Martha, 1920 (1899–1923)
†Manville, Lesley (1956-)
Maple, Jessie, 1981 (1947-)
†Mara, Rooney (1985-)
†Marchand, Anne-Marie (1927–2005)
†Marchand, Colette (1925–2015)
*Marion, Frances, 1931 (1888–1973)
†Markey, Mary Jo, 2016 (?-)
†Marks, Gertrude Ross (1916–1994)
†Marre, Elizabeth (?-)
*Marrinan, Corinne, 2006 (1974-)
*Marrs, Audrey Marie, 2011 (1970-)
†Marsh, Courtney (1986-)
Marsh, Mae, 1912 (1894–1968)
Marshall, Penny, 1988 (1943-)
*Martin, Catherine, 2002 (1965-)
Martin, Darnell, 2008 (1964-)
†Martin, Pamela, 2011 (?-)
Martin, Vivian, 1919 (1893–1987)
†Marvin, Niki (1951-)
*Marx, Sue, 1988 (?-)
†Masaro, Anastasia (1974-)
†Mason, Marsha, 1974 (1942-)
*Mason, Sarah Y., 1934 (1896–1980)
Mason, Shirley, 1917 (1900–1979)
†Mastrantonio, Mary Elizabeth (1958-)
*Mathews, Robin, 2014 (?-)
Mathis, June, 1918 (1887–1927)
†Mathison, Melissa, 1983 (1950–2015)
*Matlin, Marlee, 1987 (1965-)
†Matziaraki, Daphne (?-)
†May, Elaine, 1978 (1932-)
*McAdams, Rachel, 2016 (1978-)
McAvoy, May, 1925 (1899–1984)
†McBride, Elizabeth (1955–1997)
McCall, Cheryl (1950–2005)
McCall Jr., Mary C., 1935 (1904–1986)
*McCambridge, Mercedes, 1950 (1916–2004)
†McCarthy, Melissa (1970-)
McCartney, Linda, 1974 (1941–1998)
†McCormack, Patty (1945-)
*McDaniel, Hattie, 1940 (1895–1952)
†McDonnell, Mary (1952-)
*McDormand, Frances, 1997 (1957-)
McEveety, Annie, 2000 (?-)
†McGovern, Elizabeth (1961-)
†McGuire, Dorothy (1916–2001)
McGuire, Kathryn, 1924 (1903–1978)
†McGuire, Michele (?-)
†McKim, Dorothy, 2014 (1961-)
McKinney, Nina Mae, 1929 (1912–1967)
*McLean, Barbara, 1945 (1903–1996)
†McLeod, Sandy (?-)
*McMillan, Stephenie, 1997 (1942–2013)
†McMillon, Joi, 2017 (?-)
†McNamara, Maggie (1929–1978)
†McTeer, Janet (1961-)
McVey, Lucille, 1915 (1890–1925)
McWade, Margaret, 1921 (1871–1956)

†Medford, Kay (1919–1980)

†Mehta, Deepa (1950–)

*Memel, Jana Sue, 1988 (?–)

†Menegoz, Margaret (1941–)

†Menke, Sally, 1995 (1953–2010)

Menken, Marie, 1957 (1909–1970)

Mercer, Beryl, 1930 (1882–1939)

†Merchant, Vivien (1929–1982)

†Mercouri, Melina (1920–1994)

†Meredyth, Bess, 1930 (1890–1969)

†Merkel, Una, 1962 (1903–1986)

Merman, Ethel, 1936 (1908–1984)

Mersereau, Violet, 1909 (1892–1975)

Meryl, Angela, 2009 (?–)

†Metcalf, Laurie (1955–)

†Meyers, Nancy, 1983 (1949–)

†M.I.A. (see Maya Arulpragasam)

†Micheli, Amanda (?–)

†Midler, Bette, 1980 (1945–)

Miles, Frances, 1932 (1907–2004)

†Miles, Sarah (1941–)

†Miles, Sylvia (1924–)

†Milford, Penelope (1948–)

Millea, Holly, 2001 (1961–)

Miller, Patsy Ruth, 1923 (1904–1995)

*Mills, Hayley, 1961 (1946–)

*Minnelli, Liza, 1973 (1946–)

Minter, Mary Miles, 1919 (1902–1984)

*Mirren, Helen, 2007 (1945–)

Mitchell, Dora, 1921 (1891–1970)

†Mnouchkine, Ariane (1939–)

Moberly-Holland, Sylvia, 1940 (1900–1974)

*Mock, Freida Lee, 1995 (?–)

†Mollo, Anne (1933–)

*Mo'Nique, 2010 (1967–)

Monroe, Marilyn, 1959 (1926–1962)

†Montell, Judith (?–)

†Montenegro, Fernanda (1929–)

Montgomery, "Baby Peggy," 1923 (1918–)

†Monzani, Sarah, 1983 (1949–)

Moody, Paula, 1982 (1951–2007)

Moore, Colleen, 1923 (1899–1988)

Moore, Dorenda, 1997 (?–)

†Moore, Grace (1898–1947)

†Moore, Juanita, 1960 (1914–2014)

*Moore, Julianne, 2015 (1960–)

†Moore, Mary Tyler, 1981 (1936–2017)

†Moore, Terry (1929–)

†Moorcroft, Judy (1933–1991)

†Moorehead, Agnes, 1943 (1900–1974)

†Moorer, Allison, 1999 (1972–)

Moran, Polly, 1930 (1883–1952)

Morano, Reed, 2008 (1977–)

†Moreno, Catalina Sandino (1981–)

*Moreno, Rita, 1962 (1931–)

Morgan, Marion, 1935 (1881–1971)

†Morgan, Mildred Iatrou, 2017 (?–)

Morgan, Polly, 2007 (?–)

†Moriarty, Cathy (1960–)

†Morley, Angela, 1975 (1924–2009)

†Morley, Ruth (1925–1991)

Morra, Irene, 1942 (1893–1978)

†Morrison, Rachel, 2018 (1978–)

†Morse, Susan E., 1987 (1952–)

†Morton, Samantha (1977–)

†Mosbacher, Dee (1949–)

Most, Madelyn, 1980 (?–)

Mower, Caryn, 2006 (1965–)

*Mudd, Victoria, 1986 (1946–)

†Mueller, Lynn (?–)

Muir, Florabel , 1935 (1889–1970)

†Mulford, Marilyn (?–)

†Mulligan, Carey (1985–)

†Mumolo, Annie, 2012 (1973–)

†Munoz, Susana (1954?–)

†Muraki, Shinobu, 1986 (1923–1997)

†Murfin, Jane, 1933 (1884–1955)

Murillo, Mary, 1914 (1888–1944)

Murphy, Brianne, 1982 (1933–2003)

Murphy, Edna, 1925 (1899–1974)

Murphy, Kimberly Shannon, 2008 (1974–)

†Murray, Dana (?–)

Murray, Mae, 1925 (1889–1965)

Myerhoff, Barbara, 1977 (1935–1985)

Myers, Carmel, 1925 (1899–1980)

†Myers, Ruth (1940–)

Myers, Stevie, 1969 (1929–1991)

*Mylan, Megan, 2009 (1969–)

†Nagy, Phyllis (1962–)

†Nair, Mira (1957–)

†Naito, Ramey Ann (?–)

Naldi, Nita, 1922 (1894–1961)

†Napier, Sheena (?–)

Nasatir, Marcia, 1974 (1926–)

*Nash, Terre, 1983 (1949–)

*Natasegara, Joanna, 2017 (?–)

†Natwick, Mildred (1905–1994)

Nazimova, Alla, 1916 (1879–1945)

*Neal, Patricia, 1964 (1926–2010)

†Negga, Ruth (1982–)

Negri, Pola, 1924 (1897–1987)

†Neihausen, Raphaela (1976–)

*Neill, Ve, 1989 (1951–)

†Nelligan, Kate (1950–)

†Nelson, Kay (1909–2003)

†Nesson, Sara (?–)

Nevins, Sheila, 1979 (1939–)

†Newman, Eve, 1969 (1915–2003)

†Nigh-Strelich, Alison (?–)

Nilsson, Anna, 1911 (1888–1974)

†Nini, Diane (1951?–)

Nixon, Marian, 1932 (1904–1983)

Nixon, Marni, 1956 (1930–2016)

†Noremark, Henny (1942–)

Normand, Mabel, 1914 (1892–1930)

†Norris, Patricia, 1979 (1931–2015)

†Norton, Rosanna (?–)

†Noujaim, Jehane (1974–)

Novak, Jane, 1913 (1896–1990)

Novak, Kim, 1955 (1933–)

†Nyberg, Mary Ann (1923–1979)

†Nye, Nancy (?–)

*Nyong'o, Lupita, 2014 (1983–)

†O, Karen, 2014 (1978–)

*Obaid-Chinoy, Sharmeen, 2012 (1978–)

†Oberon, Merle (1911–1979)

O'Brien, Gloria, 2000 (?–)

*O'Brien, Margaret, 1945 (1937–)

†O'Brien, Sheila (1902–1983)

Obst, Lynda, 1992 (1950–)

†Ochipinti, Julie (?–)

†O'Connor, Bridget (1961–2010)

O'Connor, Mary H., 1921 (1872–1959)

O'Day, Molly, 1927 (1911–1998)

*Oestreicher, Christine, 1983 (1940–)

*O'Hara, Karen, 2011 (?–)

*O'Hara, Maureen, 1939 (1920–2015)

†O'Hara, Meghan (?–)

†Ohayon, Michèle (1960–)

†O'Kane, Eimear (?–)

†Okonedo, Sophie (1968–)

†Olin, Lena (1955–)

†Oliver, Edna May (1883–1942)

†Oliver, Nancy (1955–)

†Olson, Nancy (1928–)

*O'Neal, Tatum, 1974 (1963–)

†O'Neil, Barbara (1910–1980)

O'Neil, Kitty, 1975 (1946–)

*O'Neill, Evelyn (?–)

*Oppenheimer, Deborah, 2001 (?–)

†Oppewall, Jeannine Claudia, 1998 (1946–)

Ordway, Margery, 1916 (?–?)

†Oreck, Sharon (1955–)

†O'Reilly, Fodhla Cronin (1986–)

*O'Reilly, Valli, 2005 (?–)

†Orkin, Ruth, 1954 (1921–1985)

Ormonde, Czenzi, 1951 (1906–2004)

*Orner, Eva, 2008 (1969–)

†Orzolek, Karen (see Karen O)

Osborne, Florence M., 1925 (?–)

*Ossana, Diana, 2006 (1949–)

Ostriche, Muriel, 1913 (1896–1989)

†O'Toole, Annette, 2004 (1952–)

†Ouspenskaya, Maria (1876–1949)

†Owen, Alison (1961–)

Owen, Seena, 1915 (1894–1966)

†Page, Ellen (1987–)

*Page, Geraldine, 1986 (1924–1987)

†Paggi, Simona, 1999 (1962–)

Palcy, Euzhan, 1989 (1958–)

†Palermo, Donatella (?–)

†Palmer, Adele (1915–2008)

*Paltrow, Gwyneth, 1999, (1972–)

*Paquin, Anna, 1994 (1982–)

†Parent, Mary (1968–)

Park, Ida May, 1917 (1879–1954)

Parker, Claire, 1935 (1906–1981)

†Parker, Dorothy, 1938 (1893–1967)

†Parker, Eleanor, 1951 (1922–2013)

*Parsons, Estelle, 1968 (1927–)

Parsons, Harriet, 1948 (1906–1983)

Parsons, Louella, 1914 (1881–1972)

†Parton, Dolly, 1981 (1946–)

Parton, Regina, 1971 (1945–)

†Partridge, Meg (?–)

Pascal, Amy, 2006 (1958–)

†Pascale, Jan (?–)

†Pasqua-Casny, Gloria (?–)

*Pasternak, Carol, 1998 (?–)

†Patterson, Janet, 1994 (1956–2016)

†Pavan, Marisa (1932–)

†Pavignano, Anna (1955–)

†Pavlatova, Michaela, 1993 (1961–)

*Paxinou, Katina, 1944 (1900–1973)

†Pearlstein, Elise (?–)

Pearson, Virginia, 1919 (1886–1958)

†Perez, Rosie, 1994 (1964–)

†Perlman, Janet (1954–)

†Peroni, Geraldine (1953–2004)

†Perrine, Valerie (1943–)

*Perry, Dana, 2015 (?–)

†Perry, Eleanor (1914–1981)
*Pescucci, Gabriella, 1994 (1943–)
*Pesmen, Paula DuPré, 2009 (1962–)
Peters (Scannell), Mary, 1976 (1949–)
†Peters, Susan (1921–1952)
Petrova, Olga, 1914 (1884–1977)
†Pfeiffer, Michelle, 1989 (1958–)
†Phelan, Anna Hamilton, 1989 (?–)
Philbin, Mary, 1925 (1903–1993)
†Phillips, Arianne (1963–)
Phillips, Dorothy, 1911 (1889–1980)
*Phillips, Julia, 1974 (1944–2002)
Pickett Chevalier, Elizabeth, 1925 (1896–1984)
Pickford, Lottie, 1915 (1895–1936)
*Pickford, Mary, 1909 (1892–1979)
†Pike, Rosamund (1979–)
†Pilcher, Lydia Dean (?–)
*Pillsbury, Sarah, 1980 (1951–)
*Pinnock, Anna, 2015 (?–)
Pitts, ZaSu, 1919 (1894–1963)
*Platt, Janice, 1984 (?–)
†Platt, Polly, 1984 (1939–2011)
†Plowright, Joan (1929–)
*Poitras, Laura, 2015 (1964–)
†Polak, Hanna (1967–)
†Polley, Sarah (1979–)
†Pope, Leslie (?–)
†Portillo, Lourdes (1944–)
*Portman, Natalie, 2011 (1981–)
*Portman, Rachel, 1997 (1960–)
†Posey, Amanda (?–)
*Powell, Sandy, 1999 (1960–)
Preer, Evelyn, 1920 (1896–1932)
Pretty, Arline, 1913 (1885–1978)
†Preven, Anne, 2007 (?–)
†Previn, Dory, 1961 (1925–2012)
Prevost, Marie, 1919 (1898–1937)
Price, Gertrude, 1912 (?–)
Prince-Blythewood, Gina, 2008 (1969–)
Pringle, Aileen, 1924 (1895–1989)
Printzlau, Olga, 1920 (1891–1962)
†Prudhomme, Monique (?–)
Purcell, Gertrude, 1937 (1895–1963)
Purviance, Edna, 1915 (1895–1958)

*Quertier, Jill, 1999 (1936–)
†Querzola, Alessandra (?–)
Questel, Mae, 1931 (1908–1998)
†Quinlan, Kathleen (1954–)
†Quinn, Joanna (1962–)

†Radin, Helen Kristt (?–)
*Rainer, Luise, 1937 (1910–2014)
*Rajski, Peggy, 1995 (?–)
Ralston, Esther, 1924 (1902–1994)
†Rambeau, Marjorie, 1941 (1889–1970)
Rambova, Natacha, 1922 (1897–1966)
†Rampling, Charlotte (1946–)
Ramsay, Lynne, 2011 (1969–)
†Ramsey, Anne (1929–1988)
Rand, Ayn, 1949 (1905–1982)
†Randall, Terri (?–)
†Random, Ida (1945–)
Rasch, Albertina, 1934 (1891–1967)
†Rattray, Celine (1975–)
*Rau, Gretchen, 2006 (1939–2006)
Ray, Allene, 1924 (1901–1979)
Raye, Martha, 1969 (1916–1994)

*Raymond, Susan, 1994 (?–)
†Redfearn, Jennifer (1975–)
*Redgrave, Lynn, 1967 (1943–2010)
†Redgrave, Vanessa, 1978 (1937–)
†Redman, Joyce (1915–2012)
Red Wing, Princess, 1914 (1884–1974)
*Reed, Donna, 1954 (1921–1986)
*Reed, Kristina, 2015 (?–)
†Rees, Dee, 2011 (1977–)
Reichardt, Kelly, 2008 (1964–)
†Reichert, Julia, 1978 (1946?–)
Reid, Alison, 1987 (?–)
Reid, Dorothy Davenport, 1923 (1895–1977)
†Reid, Frances (?–)
†Reinhardt, Elizabeth, 1945 (1909–1954)
Reiniger, Lotte, 1926 (1899–1981)
Remick, Lee (1935–1991)
*Renié, 1964 (1901–1992)
Resnick, Patricia, 1980 (1953–)
†Reticker, Gini (?–)
Revere, Anne, 1946 (1903–1990)
Reville, Alma, 1941 (1899–1982)
*Revuelta, Pilar, 2007 (?–)
Reynolds, Debbie, 1965 (1932–2016)
Reynolds, Vera, 1927 (1899–1962)
*Reynolds-Wasco, Sandy, 2017 (?–)
Rhodes, Billie, 1913 (1894–1988)
*Rhodes, Leah, 1950 (1902–1986)
*Ribe, Montse, 2007 (1972–)
Rich, Irene, 1925 (1891–1988)
†Richards, Beah, 1968 (1920–2000)
Richardson, Miranda (1958–)
†Rickards, Jocelyn (1924–2005)
Ricksen, Lucille, 1923 (1910–1925)
†Riegel, Tatiana S. (?–)
Rinehart, Mary Roberts, 1914 (1876–1958)
Rinzler, Lisa, 2000 (1955–)
†Ripps, Hillary (1944?–)
†Ritter, Thelma, 1951 (1902–1969)
†Riva, Emmanuelle (1927–2017)
†Roach, Janet, 1986 (?–)
†Robbie, Margot (1990–)
†Robbins, Ayn, 1977 (?–)
*Roberts, Julia, 2001 (1967–)
Roberts, Marguerite, 1933 (1905–1989)
†Roberts, Rachel (1927–1980)
†Robinson, Jane (?–)
†Robinson, Susan (1942–2007)
†Robledo, Hania (?–)
†Robson, Flora (1902–1984)
†Robson, May (1858–1942)
Rocco, Nikki, 1996 (1950?–)
*Rocklin, Nicole, 2016 (1979–)
†Rodgers, Aggie Guerard (1943–)
*Rogers, Caitrin, 2014 (?–)
*Rogers, Ginger, 1941 (1911–1995)
Roland, Ruth, 1909 (1892–1937)
*Romanski, Adele, 2017 (1983?–)
Romberg, Luci, 2008 (1981–)
†Ronan, Saoirse, 2008 (1994–)
†Ronell, Ann, 1946 (1905–1993)
†Root, Joan (1936–2006)
†Rose, Alexandra (1946–)
*Rose, Helen, 1953 (1904–1985)
*Rose, Kay, 1985 (1922–2002)
Rose, Ruth, 1933 (1896–1978)
†Rosellini, Anne, 2011 (?–)
Rosenberg, Jeanne, 1979 (1950–)

†Rosenblum, Nina (?–)
†Ross, Diana, 1973 (1944–)
†Ross, Katharine, 1968 (1940–)
*Roth, Ann, 1997 (1931–)
*Roth, Vanessa, 2008 (?–)
Rothman, Stephanie, 1965 (1936–)
Rowell, Kathleen, 1984 (?–)
*Rowell-Ryan, Gail, 2001 (1939–)
*Rowlands, Gena, 1975 (1930–)
Royer, Fanchon, 1928 (1902–1986)
Rozema, Patricia, 1999 (1958–)
Rubens, Alma, 1916 (1897–1931)
Rubin, Glynn, 1980 (?–)
†Rubino, Beth (?–)
*Ruehl, Mercedes, 1992 (1948–)
Russel, Tanya Sandoval, 1980 (1956–)
†Russell, Erica (1951–)
Russell, Jane, 1943 (1921–2011)
†Russell, Rosalind, 1943 (1907–1976)
†Russell, Shirley (1935–2002)
*Rutherford, Margaret, 1964 (1892–1972)
†Ryack, Rita (?–)
†Ryan, Amy (1969–)
†Ryan, Joy (?–)
Ryan, Meg, 1990 (1961–)
†Ryan, Roma Shane, 2002 (?–)
†Ryder, Winona (1971–)
Ryerson, Florence, 1939 (1892–1965)

†Saari, Kirsikka (1973–)
*Sager, Carole Bayer, 1982 (1947–)
*Saint, Eva Marie, 1955 (1924–)
*Sainte-Marie, Buffy, 1983 (1941–)
Sais, Marin, 1910 (1890–1971)
Salvatori, Lynn, 1996 (1954–)
†Samuelson, Kristine (?–)
†Sanders, Jessica (?–)
*Sarandon, Susan, 1996 (1946–)
*Satrapi, Marjane, 2008 (1969–)
†Savone, Pilar (1971–)
†Sawyer, Joan (?–)
Scarwid, Diana (1955–)
†Schachter, Julia (?–)
Schaffer, Sharon, 1980 (1958–)
†Schaffler, Annette (1967–)
†Schiffman, Suzanne, 1974 (1929–2001)
*Schock, Barbara, 2000 (?–)
*Schoonmaker, Thelma, 1981 (1940–)
Schreiber, Nancy, 1998 (1949–)
†Schroeder, Allison (?–)
Schroeder, Doris, 1935 (1893–1981)
*Schulman, Cathy, 2006 (1965–)
†Schutt, Debra (?–)
†Schwartz, Vanessa (?–)
Scola, Kathryn, 1938 (1891–1982)
*Scott, Carolyn, 1995 (?–)
*Scott, Cynthia, 1984 (1939–)
*Scott, Deborah Lynn, 1998 (1954–)
†Scott, Jane (?–)
†Scott, Martha (1912–2003)
Scott, Retta, 1942 (1916–1990)
†Seaward, Tracey (1965–)
Sedgwick, Eileen, 1918 (1898–1991)
Sehring, Alicia Craft, 1987 (?–)
†Seibel, Anne (?–)
†Seidelman, Susan, 1994 (1952–)
†Sellar, JoAnne (1963–)
†Senior, Anna (1941–)

*Seretean, Tracy, 2001 (?–)
†Serreau, Coline (1947–)
†Sevigny, Chloë (1974–)
Sewell, Blanche, 1939 (1898–1949)
*Shaffer, Beverly, 1978 (1945–)
*Shapiro, Justine (?–)
*Sharaff, Irene, 1952 (1910–1993)
*Shearer, Norma, 1931 (1902–1983)
*Shedd, Jacqueline Phillips, 1979 (?–)
†Sheldon, Elaine McMillion (?–)
*Shenton, Rachel, 2018 (1987–)
†Sheppard, Anna B., 1994 (1946–)
†Sheppard, Loulia (Lou Sheppard) (?–)
†Sher, Stacey (1962–)
†Sheridan, Kirsten (1976–)
†Sheridan, Naomi (?–)
†Sherman, Stacy (?–)
Shipman, Nell, 1914 (1892–1970)
*Shircore, Jenny, 1999 (?–)
†Shire, Talia, 1975 (1946–)
†Shirley, Anne (1918–1993)
†Short, Marjorie Anne (Marjie) (?–)
†Shue, Elizabeth (1963–)
Shuler Donner, Lauren, 1985 (1949–)
†Shurer, Osnat (1970?–)
*Sibbick, Lucy, 2018 (?–)
†Sibley, Amber (?–)
†Sidibe, Gabourey (1983–)
†Sidney, Sylvia (1910–1999)
†Siegel-Magness, Sarah (?–)
Sigall, Martha, 1936 (1917–2014)
*Signoret, Simone, 1960 (1921–1985)
Silver, Amanda, 2015 (?–)
Silver, Joan Micklin, 1975 (1935–)
†Simmons, Jean, 1949 (1929–2010)
Simmons, Sabrina, 1992 (?–)
*Simon, Carly, 1989 (1945–)
*Simpson, Claire, 1987 (?–)
†Simpson, Susanne (?–)
*Sixel, Margaret, 2016 (?–)
†Skala, Lilia (1896–1994)
*Slesin, Aviva, 1988 (?–)
†Slesinger, Tess, 1946 (1905–1945)
†Sloss, Nancy (?–)
†Smilow, Margaret (?–)
†Smith, Caroline (?–)
†Smith, Christina, 1992 (1945–)
*Smith, Maggie, 1970 (1934–)
Smith, Rose, 1915 (1897–1962)
†Smith, Yvonne (?–)
†Smyth, Patty, 1995 (1957–)
†Snodgrass, Carrie (1945–2004)
Snow, Marguerite, 1911 (1889–1958)
*Snowden, Alison, 1995 (1958–)
†Sobieski, Carol, 1992 (1939–1990)
*Söderlund, Ulla-Britt, 1976 (1943–1985)
Solomon, Frances-Anne, 2007 (1966–)
*Sondergaard, Gale, 1937 (1899–1985)
†Sonneborn, Barbara (1944–)
†Sopher, Sharon I. (?–)
†Sørensen, Signe Byrge, (1970–)
*Sorvino, Mira, 1996 (1967–)
†Sothern, Ann (1909–2001)
Souders, Tressie, 1922 (1897–1995)
†Spacek, Sissy, 1981 (1949–)
†Speller, Cara (?–)
†Spencer, Dorothy, 1940 (1909–2002)
Spencer, Jeanne, 1928 (1897–1986)

†Spencer, Katie, 2006 (?–)
*Spencer, Octavia, 2012 (1972–)
†Spewack, Bella, 1941 (1899–1990)
Spielberg, Anne, 1989 (1949–)
Spheeris, Penelope, 1992 (1945–)
*Squarciapino, Franca, 1991 (1940–)
†Squibb, June (1929–)
Stamp, Shelley, 2000 (1963–)
*Stanley, Kim (1925–2001)
*Stanwyck, Barbara, 1938 (1907–1990)
*Stapleton, Maureen, 1959 (1925–2006)
Starke, Pauline, 1919 (1901–1977)
†Staunton, Imelda (1956–)
Stedman, Myrtle, 1915 (1883–1938)
*Stedman, Tammy Tiehel, 2000 (1964–)
Steel, Dawn, 1987 (1946–1997)
*Steenburgen, Mary, 1981 (1953–)
*Stein, Joan (?–)
†Steinfeld, Hailee (1996–)
†Sterling, Jan (1921–2004)
†Stern, Cori Shepherd (1968–)
*Stern, Joan Keller, 1970 (?–)
†Stern, Peggy, 2006 (?–)
†Stevens, Freddi (?–)
†Steward, Kimberly (1981–)
Stewart, Anita, 1918 (1895–1961)
†Stewart, Eve, 2000 (1961–)
†Stinson, Taura, 2018 (?–)
†Stites, Wendy (1949–)
†St. Johns, Adela Rogers, 1933 (1894–1988)
*Stone, Emma, 2017 (1988–)
†Stone, Sharon (1958–)
Stonehouse, Ruth, 1907 (1892–1941)
Storey, Edith, 1909 (1892–1967)
*Straight, Beatrice, 1977 (1914–2001)
*Streep, Meryl, 1980 (1949–)
*Streisand, Barbra, 1969 (1942–)
†Stuart, Gloria (1910–2010)
Stubbs, Melissa, 1990 (1970–)
Suesse, Dana, 1931 (1909–1987)
†Sullavan, Margaret (1909–1960)
†Sullivan, Becky, 2015 (?–)
Sul-Te-Wan, Madame, 1943 (1873–1959)
†Sutherland, Cathleen (?–)
†Sutner, Arianne, 2017 (?–)
†Sutton, Imogen (?–)
†Suzman, Janet (1939–)
*Swank, Hilary, 2000 (1974–)
†Swanson, Gloria, 1929 (1899–1983)
Sweeney, Mary, 1999 (1953–)
Sweet, Blanche, 1914 (1896–1986)
†Sweete, Barbara Willis (?–)
†Swicord, Robin (1952–)
*Swinton, Tilda, 2008 (1960–)
†Switzgable, Meg (?–)
†Sylbert, Anthea (1939–)

†Tajima, Renee (?–)
Takagi, Tokuko Nagai, 1911 (1891–1919)
Taliaferro, Mabel, 1912 (1887–1979)
†Talisman, Nomi (1966–)
Talmadge, Constance, 1916 (1898–1973)
Talmadge, Natalie, 1920 (1896–1969)
Talmadge, Norma, 1911 (1894–1957)
†Tana, Gabrielle (?–)
*Tandy, Jessica, 1990 (1909–1994)
Tashman, Lilyan, 1922 (1896–1934)
†Tatchell, Terri (1978–)

*Taylor, Elizabeth, 1961 (1932–2011)
†Taylor, Renee (1933–)
†Taylor, Vanessa, 2018 (1970–)
†Taymor, Julie, 2003 (1952–)
†Tegnell, Ann (?–)
*Temple Black, Shirley, 1935 (1928–2014)
*Templeton, Suzie, 2008 (1967–)
Terry, Alice, 1921 (1900–1987)
Tewkesbury, Joan, 1975 (1936–)
Theby, Rosemary, 1918 (1892–1973)
*Theron, Charlize, 2004 (1975–)
Thibodeau, Shawnna, 2002 (?–)
†Thomas, Anna (1948–)
†Thomas, Emma (1968–)
†Thomas, Kristin Scott (1960–)
Thomas, Olive, 1917 (1894–1920)
Thomas Quee, Betty, 1985 (?–)
†Thompson, Betsy (?–)
Thompson, Caroline, 1990 (1956–)
†Thompson, Danièle, 1977 (1942–)
*Thompson, Emma, 1993 (1959–)
†Thompson, Linda, 1993 (1950–)
*Thompson, Lisa, 2016 (?–)
Thurman, Mary, 1921 (1895–1925)
Thurman (Brackenbury), Sammy, 1980 (1933–)
†Thurman, Uma (1970–)
Thurston, Helen, 1938 (1909–1979)
Thurston, Nancy Lee, 1996 (?–)
*Tiehel, Tammy see Tammy Tiehel Stedman
Tierney, Gene (1920–1991)
Tilby, Wendy, 1992 (1960–)
†Tilly, Jennifer (1958–)
†Tilly, Meg (1960–)
Tincher, Fay, 1914 (1884–1983)
†Title, Stacy (1970–)
†Todd, Susan (?–)
Todd, Thelma, 1931 (1906–1935)
*Tomei, Marisa, 1993 (1964–)
†Tomblin, Lisa (?–)
†Tomlin, Lily, 1976 (1939–)
†Tondelli, Renée (?–)
†Topping, Jenno (?–)
*Toussieng, Yolanda, 1994 (1949–)
†Tran, Rosa, 2016 (?–)
*Trent, Barbara, 1993 (?–)
*Trevor, Claire, 1939 (1910–2000)
Trunnelle, Mabel, 1911 (1879–1981)
Tuchock, Wanda, 1934 (1898–1985)
Tully, May, 1921 (1884–1924)
Turner, Florence, 1907 (1885–1946)
†Turner, Kathleen, 1987 (1954–)
†Turner, Lana, 1958 (1921–1995)
Turney, Catherine, 1947 (1906–1998)
†Twomey, Nora (1971–)
†Tyrrell, Susan (1945–2012)
†Tyson, Cicely, 1973 (1924–)

*Udvardy, Anna, 2017 (?–)
†Ullman, Liv, 1973 (1938–)
*Umeki, Miyoshi, 1958 (1929–2007)
Unger, Gladys, 1935 (1885–1940)
Unsell, Eve, 1914 (1887–1937)
†Ure, Mary (1933–1975)

†Vaccaro, Brenda (1939–)
Vale, Vola, 1917 (1897–1970)
Valkyrien, Valda, 1916 (1895–1956)
†Valla, Marie-Laure, 2002 (?–)

Valli, Virginia, 1925 (1895–1968)
Van, Beatrice, 1930 (1890–1983)
†Vance-Straker, Marilyn (?–)
Vanderkloot, Victoria, 1983 (?–)
†van der Oest, Paula (1965–)
*Vanderwalt, Lesley, 2016 (?–)
†Van Dijk, Cilia (1941–)
*Van Fleet, Jo, 1956 (1915–1996)
Van Riper, Kay, 1939 (1907–1948)
†Van Runkle, Theadora, 1968 (1928–2011)
*Van Tulden, Linda, 1987 (1952–)
Van Upp, Virginia, 1934 (1902–1970)
*Varda, Agnes, 2018 (1928–)
†Varda, Rosalie (1958–)
†Vardalos, Nia, 2003 (1962–)
†Varsi, Diane (1938–1992)
†Vega, Isabel (?–)
Velez, Lupe, 1933 (1908–1944)
*Verdon-Roe, Vivienne, 1987 (?–)
†Vesth, Louise (1973–)
Vidor, Florence, 1917 (1895–1977)
Viertel, Salka, 1935 (1889–1978)
*Vikander, Alicia, 2016 (1988–)
†Vilhunen, Selma (1976–)
†Viljoen, Tina (?–)
Vincent, Amy, 2011 (1959–)
†Von Bahr, Eva (1968–)
von Beltz, Heidi, 1981 (1955–2015)
*von Brandenstein, Patrizia, 1985 (1943–)
†von Cube, Irma, 1949 (1899–1977)
Voros, Christina, 2013 (?–)

*Wada, Emi, 1986 (1937–)
*Wade, Cynthia, 2008 (?–)
Wagner, Jane, 1981 (1935–)
†Waite, Samantha (?–)
*Wakeling, Gwen, 1951 (1901–1982)
Walcamp, Marie, 1913 (1894–1936)
†Walker, Lucy (1970–)
Walker, Nellie, 1933 (1902–1980)
*Wallace, Pamela, 1986 (1949–)
†Wallack, Melisa (1968–)
†Wallis, Quvenzhané (2003–)
*Walsh, Fran, 2004 (1959–)
Walsh, Susan, 1985 (?–)
†Walters, Julie (1950–)
†Wang, Hui-Ling, 2001 (?–)
Ward, Fannie, 1915 (1872–1952)
Ward, Luci, 1942 (1907–1969)
*Wardega, Elka, 2016 (?–)
Warp, Hazel Hash, 1939 (1914–2008)
†Warren, Diane, 1988 (1956–)
†Warren, Lesley Ann (1946–)
Warrenton, Lule, 1917 (1862–1932)
Washington, Kerry, 2004 (1977–)
Washington Longino, Kym, 1985 (1957–)

Waterbury, Ruth, 1961 (1896–1982)
*Waterlow, Caroline, 2017 (?–)
†Waters, Ethel, 1950 (1896–1977)
†Watson, Emily (1967–)
†Watson, Lucile (1879–1962)
†Watts, Charlotte (?–)
†Watts, Naomi, 2004 (1968–)
†Wayne, June (1918–2011)
†Weaver, Jacki (1947–)
†Weaver, Sigourney, 1987 (1949–)
Weber, Lois, 1916 (1879–1939)
†Weil, Cynthia, 1987 (1940–)
Weill, Claudia, 1979 (1947–)
†Weinberg, Wendy (?–)
†Weinstein, Lisa (?–)
Weinstein, Paula, 1981 (1945–)
Weisinger, Eileen, 2000 (?–)
†Weiss, Fredda (1941–)
†Weiss, Julie (?–)
*Weisz, Rachel, 2006 (1970–)
Welbon, Yvonne, 1999 (?–)
Welcome, Madame E. Toussaint, 1916 (1885–1956)
†Weld, Tuesday (1943–)
†Welfling, Juliette (1956–)
†Wertmuller, Lina, 1977 (1928–)
West, Clare, 1920 (1889–1980)
*West, Claudine, 1943 (1890–1943)
†West, Jacqueline, 2001 (?–)
West, Mae, 1932 (1893–1980)
West, Vera, 1934 (1900–1947)
†Westcott, Lisa, 1998 (?–)
†Weston, Maggie (?–)
*White, Onna, 1969 (1922–2005)
White, Pearl, 1914 (1889–1938)
†Whitney, Helen (1943?–)
†Whittle, Gwendolyn Yates, 2010 (1961–)
†Whitty, May (1865–1948)
*Wiest, Dianne, 1987 (1948–)
Wiggins, Mary, 1934 (1909–1945)
†Wiig, Kristen, 2012 (1973–)
*Wilbur, Claire, 1976 (1933–2004)
Wilde, Hagar, 1938 (1905–1971)
†Williams, Cara (1925–)
Williams, Darlene Ava, 2000 (?–)
Williams, Esther, 1949 (1921–2013)
Williams, Frances E., 1979 (1905–1995)
†Williams, JoBeth (1948–)
Williams, Kathlyn, 1913 (1879–1960)
†Williams, Megan (?–)
†Williams, Michelle, 2006 (1980–)
*Wills, Mary, 1963 (1914–1997)
Wilson, Elsie Jane, 1917 (1885–1965)
†Wilson, Juanita (?–)
Wilson, Lois, 1926 (1894–1988)
Wilson, Margery, 1916 (1896–1986)
Windsor, Claire, 1921 (1892–1972)

†Winfrey, Oprah, 1986 (1954–)
†Wingate, Ann (?–)
†Winger, Debra, 1983 (1955–)
Winkler, Margaret, 1924 (1895–1990)
†Winningham, Mare (1959–)
*Winslet, Kate, 2009 (1975–)
†Winter, Rachel (?–)
*Winters, Shelley, 1960 (1920–2006)
Withers, Jane, 1934 (1926–)
*Witherspoon, Reese, 2006 (1976–)
†Wittlinger, Heidi (1978–)
Wong, Anna May, 1922 (1905–1961)
Wong, Marion, 1916 (1895–1969)
†Wood, Natalie, 1956 (1938–1981)
†Wood, Peggy (1892–1978)
†Woodard, Alfre, 1984 (1952–)
Woodruff, Eleanor, 1913 (1891–1980)
*Woodward, Joanne, 1958 (1930–)
*Woollard, Joanne, 1988 (?– 2015)
Woolverton, Linda, 1991 (1952–)
Wray, Fay, 1933 (1907–2004)
*Wright, Teresa, 1943 (1918–2005)
*Wurzburg, Gerardine, 1993 (?–)
†Wycherly, Margaret (1881–1956)
†Wydra, Anna (1979–)
*Wyman, Jane, 1949 (1917–2007)
Wynyard, Diana (1906–1964)

†Yamashita, Iris, 2007 (1965–)
*Yang, Ruby, 2007 (?–)
†Yasui, Lise (?–)
*Yates, Janty, 2001 (1950–)
Yeats, Marie Osborne, 1916 (1911–2010)
†Yianni-Georgiou, Elizabeth (?–)
†York, Kathleen, 2006 (?–)
†York, Susannah (1939–2011)
†Yorn, Julie (1967–)
*Yoshida, Yuki, 1978 (?–)
Yost, Dorothy, 1920 (1899–1967)
Young, Clara Kimball, 1914 (1890–1960)
†Young, Erin Faith (?–)
*Young, Loretta, 1948 (1913–2000)
*Yu, Jessica, 1997 (1966–)
†Yuh Nelson, Jennifer, 2012 (1972–)

†Zamparelli, Elsa (1944–)
*Zanuck, Lili Fini, 1990 (1954–)
†Zea, Kristi (1948–)
*Zellweger, Renee, 2004 (1969–)
*Zeta-Jones, Catherine, 2003 (1969–)
Zetterling, Mai, 1944 (1925–1994)
Ziegler, Liz (Elizabeth), 1990 (?–)
†Ziering, Amy (1962–)
Ziskin, Laura, 1990 (1950–2011)
†Zophres, Mary (1964–)

BIBLIOGRAPHY

Acker, Ally, *Reel Women: Pioneers of the Cinema, The First Hundred Years (Volume 1: 1890's – 1950's; Volume II: 1960's – 2010*. Reel Women Media Publishing: Roslyn Heights, New York, 2012.

Bobo, Jacqueline, Editor. *Black Women Film & Video Artists*. Routledge: New York, New York, 1998.

Bridges, Melody and Cheryl Robson, Silent Women: Pioneers of Cinema. Supernova Books: Twickenham, United Kingdom, 2016.

Francke, Lizzie, *script girls: Women Screenwriters in Hollywood*, British Film Institute: London, United Kingdom, 1994.

Gregory, Mollie, *Stuntwomen: The Untold Hollywood Story*. University Press of Kentucky: Lexington, Kentucky, 2015.

Kelly, Gabrielle and Cheryl Robson, Editors. Celluloid Ceiling: *Women Film Directors Breaking Through*. Supernova Books: Twickenham, United Kingdom, 2014.

Krasilovsky, Alexis, *Women Behind the Camera: Conversations with Camerawomen*. Praeger Publishers: Westport, Connecticut, 1997.

Lowe, Denise, *An Encyclopedic Dictionary of Women in Early American Films: 1895-1930*. The Haworth Press: Binghamton, New York, 2005.

Margolis, Harriet, Alexis Krasilovsky and Julia Stein, *Shooting Women: Behind the Camera, Around the World*. Intellect and The University of Chicago Press: Bristol, United Kingdom and Chicago, Illinois, 2015.

Meuel, David, *Women Film Editors: Unseen Artists of American Camera*, McFarland & Company, Inc. Publishers: Jefferson, North Carolina: , 2016.

Slide, Anthony, *The Silent Feminists: America's First Women Directors*. The Scarecrow Press, Inc.: Lanham, Maryland, 1996.

Sova, Dawn B., *Women in Hollywood: From Vamp to Studio Head*, Fromm International: New York, 1998.

Stamp, Shelley, *Movie-Struck Girls: Women and Motion Picture Culture After the Nickelodeon*, Princeton University Press: Princeton, New Jersey, 2000.

Academy of Motion Picture Arts and Sciences: www.oscars.org

IMDB: www.imdb.com

Wikipedia: en.Wikipedia.org

Women Film Pioneers Project, https://wfpp.cdrs.columbia.edu/

IMAGE CREDITS

Page 1
Mary Pickford: Courtesy of the Library of Congress

Page 2
Dorothy Dandridge: see 1955
Anna May Wong: see page 72
Elizabeth Taylor: Silver Screen Collection/Getty Images
Florence Vidor: see 1917
America Ferrera: see 2002
Hattie Mc Daniel: Everett Collection
Marilyn Monroe: see 1959
Edith Head: see 1950
Julia Roberts: see 2001
Greta Garbo: PictureLux/The Hollywood Archive/Alamy Stock Photo
Sharmeen Obaid-Chinoy: see 2012
Louise Brooks: Courtesy of the Library of Congress

Page 4-5
Everett Collection

Page 12
Julia Roberts: Francois Durand/Getty Images

Page 14
Alice Guy-Blaché: Wikipedia

1893
Edison's Vitascope: Courtesy of the Library of Congress
Kinetoscope, by Thomas Edison: INTERFOTO/Alamy Stock Photo

1896
Alice Guy-Blaché: PD-US
Pathe: Album/Alamy Stock Photo

1898
Aubrey Le Blond: PD-US

Page 20
Mary Pickford: Courtesy of the Library of Congress

1907
Ruth Stonehouse: Everett Collection
Florence Lawrence: Courtesy of The New York Public Library
Florence Turner: Everett Collection
Gene Gauntier: Chronicle/Alamy Stock Photo

1908
Linda Arvidson: Everett Collection
Flora Finch: Courtesy of The New York Public Library

1909
Mary Pickford: Courtesy of the Library of Congress
Stella Adams: Wikipedia
Ethel Clayton: Courtesy of the Library of Congress
Ruth Roland: Courtesy of the Library of Congress

Florence LaBadie: Courtesy of The New York Public Library
Violet Mersereau: © 20th Century Fox Film Corp. All rights reserved/Courtesy of The Everett Collection
Edith Storey: PD-US

Page 30
Lillian Gish: Courtesy of the Library of Congress

1910
Eugenie Besserer: PD-US
Kate Bruce: Courtesy of the Library of Congress
Bebe Daniels: Courtesy of the Library of Congress
Marin Sais: Wikipedia
Winifred Greenwood: Wikipedia
Alice Joyce: Courtesy of the Library of Congress

1911
Leah Baird: Courtesy of the Library of Congress
Norma Talmadge: Courtesy of the Library of Congress
Anna Nilsson: Courtesy of the Library of Congress
Dorothy Phillips: PD-US
Ann Little: Wikipedia
Marguerite Snow: Wikipedia
Tokuko Nagai Takagi: Wikipedia
Mabel Trunnelle: Wikipedia

1912
Mae Marsh: Wikipedia
Francelia Billington: Glasshouse Images/Alamy Stock Photo
Lillian Gish: Courtesy of the Library of Congress
Beverly Bayne: Wikipedia
Anita Loos: Wikipedia
Mabel Taliaferro: Courtesy of the Library of Congress
Helen Gardner: Courtesy of the Library of Congress

1913
Jeanie MacPherson: Everett Collection
Margarita Fischer: Photo 12/Alamy Stock Photo
Ella Hall: Wikipedia
Jane Novak: Wikipedia
Billie Rhodes: Wikipedia
Marie Walcamp: Popperfoto/Getty Images
Eleanor Woodruff: Courtesy of the Library of Congress
Kathlyn Williams: Wikipedia
Muriel Ostriche: History and Art Collection/Alamy Stock Photo
Arline Pretty: Hulton Archive/Getty Images

1914
Fay Tincher: Wikipedia
Minta Durfee: Wikipedia
Clara Kimball Young: Wikipedia
Phyllis Allen: Everett Collection
Tsuru Aoki: Vintage Images/Alamy Stock Photo

Marguerite Clark: Courtesy of the Library of Congress
Mary Murillo: Courtesy of The New York Public Library
Olga Petrova: Courtesy of the Library of Congress
Minnie Devereaux: Everett Collection
Eve Unsell: Historic Collection/Alamy Stock Photo
Nell Shipman: RGR Collection/Alamy Stock Photo
Bessie Eyton: Everett Collection
Cleo Madison: RGR Collection/Alamy Stock Photo
Louella Parsons: Archive PL/Alamy Stock Photo
Mabel Normand: Courtesy of the Library of Congress
Helen Holmes: Courtesy of the Library of Congress
Blanche Sweet: Courtesy of the Library of Congress
Mildred Harris: Courtesy of the Library of Congress
Pearl White: Courtesy of the Library of Congress
Princess Red Wing: Wikipedia
Mary Roberts Rinehart: Wikipedia

1915
Ouida Bergere: Everett Collection
Geraldine Farrar: Courtesy of the Library of Congress
Mary Alden: Wikipedia
Miriam Cooper: © 20th Century Fox Film Corp. All rights reserved/Courtesy of The Everett Collection
Josephine Crowell: Everett Collection
Pauline Frederick: Courtesy of the Library of Congress
Maude George: John Springer Collection/Getty Images
Juanita Hansen: Wikipedia
Dorothy Dalton: Wikipedia
Fannie Ward: Everett Collection
Seena Owen: Everett Collection
Gertrude Astor: Courtesy of the Library of Congress
Helen Gibson: Wikipedia
Lucille McVey: Wikipedia
Rose Smith: Everett Collection
Myrtle Stedman: Courtesy of the Library of Congress
Edna Purviance: Wikipedia

1916
Alma Rubens: Glasshouse Images/Alamy Stock Photo
Mary MacLaren: Archive PL/Alamy Stock Photo
Edith Johnson: Everett Collection
Edna Flugrath: Bettmann/Getty Images
Lois Weber: Courtesy of the Library of Congress
Baby Marie Osborne Yeats: Hulton Archive/Getty Images
Alla Nazimova: Courtesy of the Library of Congress
Marion Wong: Everett Collection
Hettie Grey Baker: Wikipedia
Valda Valkyrien: Courtesy of The New York Public Library
Constance Talmadge: Courtesy of the Library of Congress
Myrtle Gonzalez: Glasshouse Images/Alamy Stock Photo

Margery Wilson: Everett Collection
Margery Ordway: Courtesy of the Library of Congress
Annette Kellerman: Courtesy of the Library of Congress

1917
Marion Davies: Courtesy of the Library of Congress
Viola Dana: Courtesy of the Library of Congress
Marjorie Daw: John Springer Collection/Getty Images
Neva Gerber: Wikipedia
Delight Evans: Wikipedia
Olive Thomas: Wikipedia
Alice Howell: American Stock Archive/Getty Images
Grace Darmond: Ronald Grant Archive/Alamy Stock Photo
Grace Cunard: John Springer Collection/CORBIS/Corbis via Getty Images
Vola Vale: Wikipedia
Theda Bara: Everett Collection
Louise Fazenda: AF archive/Alamy Stock Photo
Leatrice Joy: Courtesy of the Library of Congress
Shirley Mason: Courtesy of The New York Public Library
Madge Kennedy: Courtesy of the Library of Congress
Priscilla Dean: Courtesy of the Library of Congress
Claire Du Brey: Hulton Archive/Getty Images
Dorothy Dunn: Wikipedia
Ruth Clifford: Everett Collection
Irene Castle: Courtesy of the Library of Congress
Florence Vidor: Everett Collection
Beulah Marie Dix: Courtesy of The New York Public Library
Mabel Ballin: Archive PL/Alamy Stock Photo

1918
Helen Keller: Courtesy of the Library of Congress
Bessie Barriscale: Bettmann/Getty Images
Eileen Sedgwick: Archive PL/Alamy Stock Photo
Anita Stewart: Courtesy of the Library of Congress
Dorothy Devore: Albert Witzel/Everett Collection
Rosemary Theby: Popperfoto/Getty Images
Dorothy Gish: Adolph de Meyer/Condé Nast/Getty Images
Lila Lee: Oscar White/Corbis/VCG/Getty Images
Gale Henry: American Stock/Getty Images
June Mathis: Ronald Grant Archive/Alamy Stock Photo

1919
Faire Binney: Everett Collection
Kathleen Clifford (left): Wikipedia
Kathleen Clifford (right): Historic Images/Alamy Stock Photo
Vivian Martin: Courtesy of the Library of Congress
Virginia Pearson: Courtesy of the Library of Congress
Marie Prevost: Courtesy of the Library of Congress
Pauline Starke: Courtesy of the Library of Congress
Betty Compson: Courtesy of the Library of Congress
Dolores Cassinelli: Courtesy of the Library of Congress
Mary Miles Minter: Courtesy of the Library of Congress
ZaSu Pitts: Wikipedia
Helen Jerome Eddy: Everett Collection
Paula Blackton: Courtesy of the Library of Congress

Anna May Wong: Edward Steichen/Condé Nast via Getty Images

1920
Mary Carr: Sueddeutsche Zeitung Photo/Alamy Stock Photo
Louise Glaum: Courtesy of the Library of Congress
Evelyn Preer: Courtesy of The New York Public Library
Natalie Talmadge: Courtesy of the Library of Congress
Constance Binney: Courtesy of the Library of Congress
Carol Dempster: Chronicle/Alamy Stock Photo
Martha Mansfield: Courtesy of the Library of Congress
Lillian Chester: Everett Collection
Frances Guihan: Wikipedia
Clara Beranger: Archive PL/Alamy Stock Photo
Clare West: Glasshouse Images/Alamy Stock Photo

1921
Barbara La Marr: ullstein bild Dtl./Getty Images
Agnes Ayres: Courtesy of the Library of Congress
Betty Blythe: Courtesy of the Library of Congress
Alice Terry: Courtesy of the Library of Congress
Mary Thurman: Courtesy of the Library of Congress
Claire Windsor: Courtesy of the Library of Congress
Louise Lorraine: Everett Collection
Anita Bush: Courtesy of the Library of Congress
Margaret McWade: Everett Collection
Elinor Glyn: Courtesy of the Library of Congress
Osa Johnson: George Eastman House/Getty Images

1922
Marguerite Courtot: Everett Collection
Gladys Brockwell: Everett Collection
Nita Naldi: Courtesy of the Library of Congress
Lilyan Tashman: Courtesy of the Library of Congress
Anna May Wong: Courtesy of the Library of Congress
Madge Bellamy: Courtesy of the Library of Congress
Marion Fairfax: Everett Collection
Olive Borden: John Springer Collection/CORBIS/Getty Images
Enid Bennett: United Artists/Getty Images
Natacha Rambova: Keystone-France/Gamma-Keystone via Getty Images

1923
Dorothy Davenport Reid: Everett Collection
Patsy Ruth Miller: Courtesy of the Library of Congress
Baby Peggy Montgomery: Courtesy of the Library of Congress
Lucille Ricksen: Hulton Archive/Getty Images
Colleen Moore: Wikipedia

1924
Margaret Winkler: Wikipedia
Pola Negri: Courtesy of the Library of Congress
Aileen Pringle: Courtesy of the Library of Congress
Esther Ralston: Wikipedia
Betty Bronson: Courtesy of the Library of Congress
Elaine Hammerstein: Wikipedia
Doris Kenyon: Courtesy of the Library of Congress
Allene Ray: United Archives GmbH/Alamy Stock Photo
Dorothy Mackaill: AF archive/Alamy Stock Photo

Marian Constance Blackton: Courtesy of the Library of Congress
Mary Brian: Courtesy of the Library of Congress
Kathryn McGuire: Courtesy of the Library of Congress

1925
Katherine Hilliker: Wikipedia
Frederica Sagor Maas: Wikipedia
Edna Murphy: Everett Collection
Mary Philbin: Courtesy of the Library of Congress
Belle Bennett: John Springer Collection/CORBIS/Getty Images
Dorothy Dwan: John Springer Collection/CORBIS/Getty Images
Renee Adoree: Courtesy of the Library of Congress
Vilma Banky: Courtesy of the Library of Congress
Dolores Del Rio: Wikipedia
Jetta Goudal: Pictorial Press Ltd/Alamy Stock Photo
Mae Murray: Courtesy of the Library of Congress
Carmel Myers: Courtesy of the Library of Congress
Irene Rich: Courtesy of the Library of Congress
Virginia Valli: Courtesy of the Library of Congress
Ethel Doherty: Academy of Motion Picture Arts and Sciences
May McAvoy: Wikipedia
Carmelita Geraghty: Everett Collection
Ruth Harriet Louise: Wikipedia

1926
Lotte Reiniger: ZUMA Press, Inc./Alamy Stock Photo
Lois Wilson: Courtesy of the Library of Congress
Dorothy Farnum: Bettmann/Getty Images
Dolores Costello: Courtesy of the Library of Congress
Winifred Dunn: Wikipedia
Frances Hyland: Mary Evans/Ronald Grant/Everett Collection
Natalie Kingston: Wikipedia
Julia Faye: Glasshouse Images/Alamy Stock Photo
Laura La Plante: Hulton Archive/Getty Images
Virginia Lee Corbin: Film Favorites/Getty Images

1927
Billie Dove: Everett Collection, Inc./Alamy Stock Photo
Molly O'Day: Archive PL/Alamy Stock Photo
Clara Bow: Everett Collection
Sue Carol: Courtesy of The New York Public Library
Vera Reynolds: RGR Collection/Alamy Stock Photo

1928
Marceline Day: Courtesy of the Library of Congress
Josephine Lovett: Everett Collection
Dorothy Arzner: Hulton Archive/Getty Images
Constance Collier: Courtesy of The New York Public Library
Helene Costello: ullstein bild Dtl./Getty Images
Olga Baclanova: Photo 12/Alamy Stock Photo
Evelyn Brent: Courtesy of the Library of Congress
Eleanor Boardman: Courtesy of the Library of Congress

1929
Joan Bennett: Pictorial Press Ltd/Alamy Stock Photo
Jeanette MacDonald: Everett Collection
Hallelujah Poster: AF archive/Alamy Stock Photo
Nina Mae McKinney: Pictorial Press Ltd/Alamy Stock Photo
Louise Brooks: Courtesy of the Library of Congress

Gloria Swanson: Edward Steichen/Condé Nast via Getty Images

Lina Basquette: George Rinhart/Corbis via Getty Images

Doris Anderson: John Mahler/Toronto Star via Getty Images

Janet Gaynor (left): Courtesy of the Library of Congress

Janet Gaynor (right): Everett Collection

Page 108

Greta Garbo: Archive PL/Alamy Stock Photo

1930

Beryl Mercer: Glasshouse Images/Alamy Stock Photo

Polly Moran: PD-US

Bessie Love: Courtesy of the Library of Congress

Joan Blondell: Wikipedia

Bess Meredyth: John Springer Collection/CORBIS/Corbis via Getty Images

Beatrice Van: Wikipedia

Corinne Griffith: Courtesy of the Library of Congress

Jean Harlow: George Hurrell/John Kobal Foundation/Getty Images

1931

Frances Marion: General Photographic Agency/Getty Images

Norma Shearer: Courtesy of the Library of Congress

Dorothy Howell: Wikipedia

Dana Suesse: Used by the permission of the University of Missouri-Kansas City Libraries, Dr. Kenneth J. LaBudde Department of Special Collections

Mae Questel: John Springer Collection/CORBIS/Corbis via Getty Images

Thelma Todd: Wikipedia

Heather Angel: Courtesy of The New York Public Library

Maude Fulton: University of Washington Libraries, Special Collections, JWS20432

Greta Garbo: Donaldson Collection/Getty Images

Marlene Dietrich: Clarence Sinclair Bull/John Kobal Foundation/Getty Images

Maude Adams: Courtesy of the Library of Congress

1932

Marie Dressler (left): PD-US

Marie Dressler (right): Everett Collection

Irene Dunne: Courtesy of The New York Public Library

Mae West: Everett Collection

Dorothy Gulliver: Historic Collection/Alamy Stock Photo

Marian Nixon: cineclassico/Alamy Stock Photo

Iris Barry: Sasha/Getty Images

1933

Jane Murfin: Wikipedia

Gracie Allen: Courtesy of The New York Public Library

Helen Ferguson: Courtesy of the Library of Congress

Adela Rogers St. Johns: John Springer Collection/CORBIS/Corbis via Getty Images

Zoe Akins: Wikipedia

Ruby Keeler: Wikipedia

Lupe Velez: Wikipedia

Fay Wray: Hulton Archive/Getty Images

Helen Hayes: Courtesy of the Library of Congress

1934

Sarah Y. Mason: PD-US

Katharine Hepburn: RKO Radio Pictures/Getty Images

Vera West: Everett Collection

Lillian Friedman (Astor): Wikipedia

Adrienne Ames: Glasshouse Images/Alamy Stock Photo

Virginia Van Upp: Wikipedia

Jane Withers: © 20th Century Fox Film Corp./Courtesy of the Everett Collection

Albertina Rasch: Courtesy of the Library of Congress

Louise Beavers (left): John Springer Collection/CORBIS/Corbis via Getty Images

Louise Beavers (right): PD-US

Myrna Loy: Wikipedia

1935

Jean Arthur: Wikipedia

Shirley Temple Black: Album/Alamy Stock Photo

Mary C. McCall Jr.: PD

Salka Viertel: PD-US

Claire Parker: PD-US

Frances Goodrich: Everett Collection

Claudette Colbert (left): John Kobal Foundation/Getty Images

Claudette Colbert (right): PD-US

Gladys Unger: APIC/Getty Images

Florabel Muir: Ed Clark/The LIFE Picture Collection/Getty Images

Marion Morgan: Everett Collection Historical/Alamy Stock Photo

1936

Kay Brown Barrett: Courtesy of Kate R. Barrett

Margaret Herrick (Gledhill): Courtesy of The American Society of Cinematographers

Paulette Goddard: Everett Collection

Bette Davis: WARNER BROTHERS/Album/Alamy

Ethel Merman: Wikipedia

Margaret Booth: Everett Collection

1937

Adele Comandini: PD-US

Joyce Compton: Album/Alamy Stock Photo

Lucille LaVerne: Courtesy of The New York Public Library

Carole Lombard: Wikipedia

Luise Rainer (left): PictureLux/The Hollywood Archive/Alamy Stock Photo

Luise Rainer (right): Wikipedia

Dorothy Fields: Courtesy of the Library of Congress

Lucille Ball: Silver Screen Collection/Hulton Archive/Getty Images

Gale Sondergaard: Everett Collection

1938

Hedy Lamarr: Collection Christophel/RnB © Warner Bros/Alamy

Alice Faye: Hulton Archive/Getty Images

Barbara Stanwyck: Bettmann/Getty Images

Hedda Hopper: Courtesy of the Library of Congress

Alice Brady: Courtesy of the Library of Congress

Olive Cooper: Everett Collection

Helen Thurston: Everett Collection

Dorothy Parker: Courtesy of The New York Public Library

1939

Katharine Blodgett: Wikipedia

Blanche Sewell: Everett Collection

Lenore Coffee: W. F. Seely/Margaret Chute/Getty Images

Sonja Henie: Archive PL/Alamy Stock Photo

Florence Ryerson: Wikipedia

Ethel Hill: PD-US

Deanna Durbin: PD-US

Maureen O'Hara: Everett Collection

Claire Trevor: Wikipedia

Mary Boland: Courtesy of the Library of Congress

Fay Bainter: Courtesy of the Library of Congress

Billie Burke: Everett Collection

Natalie Kalmus: RGR Collection/Alamy Stock Photo

Kay Van Riper: MGM/Ronald Grant Archive/Alamy Stock Photo

Page 140

Judy Garland: Silver Screen Collection/Getty Images

1940

Vivien Leigh: Everett Collection

Betty Grable: Silver Screen Collection/Hulton Archive/Getty Images

Judy Garland: Pictorial Press Ltd/Alamy Stock Photo

Mary Ellen Bute: Everett Collection

Hattie McDaniel: Everett Collection

Dorothy Lamour: Ronald Grant Archive/Alamy Stock Photo

1941

Ida Lupino: Wikipedia

Marjorie Rambeau: Wikipedia

Bella Spewack: Courtesy of The New York Public Library

Anne Bauchens: Alfred Eisenstaedt/Pix Inc./The LIFE Picture Collection/Getty Images

Jane Darwell: Copyright © 20th Century-Fox Film Corp./Everett Collection

Alma Reville: Bettmann/Getty Images

Evelyn Finley: Everett Collection

Ginger Rogers: Hulton Archive/Getty Images

Joan Harrison: Everett Collection

1942

Retta Scott (left): Courtesy of Robert Sommers

Retta Scott (right): © Disney

Mary Astor: Popperfoto/Getty Images

Joan Fontaine: Album/Alamy Stock Photo

Lillian Hellman: Wikipedia

Irene Morra: Bison Archives/HollywooHistoricPhotos.com

Julia Heron: Everett Collection

1943

Agnes Moorehead: Wikipedia

Greer Garson: Everett Collection

Lillie Hayward: Copyright © 20th Century Fox Film Corp./Courtesy of the Everett Collection

Gladys Cooper: Courtesy of the Library of Congress

Teresa Wright: Wikipedia

Jane Russell: Pictorial Press Ltd/Alamy Stock Photo

Madame Sul-Te-Wan: Everett Collection

Rosalind Russell: Silver Screen Collection/Getty Images

1944
Lauren Bacall: Herbert Dorfman/Corbis via Getty Images
Jennifer Jones: Wikipedia
Betty Hutton: Wikipedia
Katina Paxinou: INTERFOTO/Alamy Stock Photo
Mai Zetterling: Everett Collection

1945
Margaret O'Brien: AF archive/Alamy Stock Photo
Gladys Lehman: Everett Collection
Elizabeth Reinhardt: PD-US
Ethel Barrymore: Courtesy of the Library of Congress
Ingrid Bergman: Silver Screen Collection/Getty Images
Barbara McLean: Jean Howard/Condé Nast via Getty Images
Angela Lansbury: Courtesy of the Library of Congress

1946
Peggy Ann Garner: Film Favorites/Getty Images
Joan Crawford: Courtesy of the Library of Congress
Rita Hayworth: ScreenProd/Photononstop/Alamy Stock Photo
Ann Ronell: Courtesy of the Library of Congress
Ava Gardner: Silver Screen Collection/Getty Images
Tess Slesinger: Courtesy of Peter Davis
Mary Blair: Hart Preston/The LIFE Picture Collection/Getty Images
Leigh Brackett: AF archive/Alamy Stock Photo
Anne Revere: Everett Collection

1947
Anne Baxter: Copyright © 20th Century Fox Film Corp. All rights reserved/Courtesy of the Everett Collection
Olivia de Havilland: Everett Collection
Sally Benson: Everett Collection
Muriel Box: Everett Collection
Polly Burson: Rothschild Photo, Herald-Examiner Collection/Los Angeles Public Library
Maya Deren: Everett Collection

1948
Celeste Holm: Everett Collection
Harriet Parsons: Everett Collection
Loretta Young: Herbert Dorfman/Corbis via Getty Images
Katherine Dunham: Gjon Mili/The LIFE Picture Collection/Getty Images

1949
Irma von Cube: Mary Evans/Warner Bros/Ronald Grant/Everett Collection
Jean Simmons: John Kobal Foundation/Getty Images
Irene: Everett Collection
Jane Wyman: Everett Collection
Stella Adler: Everett Collection
Vera Caspary: Everett Collection
Barbara Bel Geddes: Wikipedia
Ayn Rand: Julius Shulman/Conde Nast via Getty Images
Dorothy Jeakins: Everett Collection
Carmen Dillon: Mary Evans/Ronald Grant/Everett Collection
Esther Williams: Slim Aarons/Getty Images

Page 168
Audrey Hepburn: Norman Parkinson Achive/Iconic Images/Getty Images

1950
Clare Boothe Luce: Cecil Beaton/Condé Nast via Getty Images
Helen Levitt: © Film Documents LLC
Lucille Bliss: PD-US
Ruby Dee: Courtesy of the Library of Congress
Leah Rhodes: Mary Evans/Ronald Grant/Everett Collection
Mercedes McCambridge: Everett Collection
Edith Head: Allan Grant/The LIFE Picture Collection/Getty Images
Ethel Waters: Courtesy of the Library of Congress
Deborah Kerr: Silver Screen Collection/Getty Images
Marjorie Best: Everett Collection
June Foray: Everett Collection

1951
Thelma Ritter: AF archive/Alamy Stock Photo
Edna Anhalt: Wikipedia
Judy Holliday: Silver Screen Collection/Getty Images
Josephine Hull: Album/Alamy Stock Photo
Gwen Wakeling: Copyright ©20th Century Fox Film Corp. All rights reserved/Courtesy of The Everett Collection
Elois Jenssen: Everett Collection
Eleanor Parker: Bettmann/Getty Images

1952
Irene Sharaff: Entertainment Pictures/Alamy Stock Photo
Kim Hunter: Sam Shaw/Shaw Family Archives/Getty Images

1953
Donna Hall: Underwood Archives/Getty Images
Phyllis Craig: MARKA/Alamy Stock Photo
Shirley Booth: G. K. Livitsanos/Archive Photos/Getty Images
Gina Kaus: Stephanie Brandl/ullstein bild via Getty Images
Helen Rose (left): Everett Collection
Helen Rose (right): Everett Collection
Gloria Grahame: Silver Screen Collection/Getty Images

1954
Betty Comden: Courtesy of The New York Public Library
Ruth Orkin: Keith Beaty/Toronto Star via Getty Images
Sylvia Fine: Victor Blackman/Daily Express/Hulton Archive/Getty Images
Donna Reed (left): Silver Screen Collection/Getty Images
Donna Reed (right): Herbert Dorfman/Corbis via Getty Images
Audrey Hepburn: Donaldson Collection/Michael Ochs Archives/Getty Images

1955
Mary Loos: PD-US
Dorothy Kingsley: PD-US
Eva Marie Saint: Archive Photos/Getty Images

Kim Novak: Pictorial Press Ltd/Alamy Stock Photo
Grace Kelly: Courtesy of the Library of Congress
Dorothy Dandridge: Silver Screen Collection/Getty Images

1956
Natalie Wood: Harry Warnecke/NY Daily News Archive via Getty Images
Sonya Levien: Hulton Archive/Getty Images
Anna Magnani: World History Archive/Alamy Stock Photo
Nancy Hamilton: Courtesy of the Library of Congress
Jo Van Fleet: Earl Leaf/Michael Ochs Archives/Getty Images
Marni Nixon: Everett Collection
Isobel Lennart: PD-

1957
Marie Menken: Wikipedia
Dorothy Malone: Silver Screen Collection/Getty Images
Sandra Dee: Silver Screen Collection/Getty Images
Hazel George: George Karger/The LIFE Images Collection/Getty Images

1958
Miyoshi Umeki: Earl Leaf/Michael Ochs Archives/Getty Images
Joanne Woodward: John Springer Collection/CORBIS/Corbis via Getty Images
Viola Lawrence: Bison Archives/HollywooHistoricPhotos.com
Lana Turner: Silver Screen Collection/Getty Images

1959
Pearl Bailey: Everett Collection
Wendy Hiller: AF archive/Alamy Stock Photo
Maureen Stapleton: Everett Collection
Susan Hayward: Silver Screen Collection/Getty Images
Marilyn Monroe: Michael Ochs Archives/Getty Images
Fay Kanin: Bettmann/Getty Images

Page 190
Julie Andrews: Silver Screen Collection/Getty Images

1960
Alice Davis: Angela Weiss/Getty Images
Juanita Moore: John D. Kisch/Separate Cinema Archive/Getty Images
Simone Signoret: Jean-Regis Rouston/Roger Viollet/Getty Images
Shelley Winters: John Springer Collection/CORBIS/Corbis via Getty Images
Doris Day: Silver Screen Collection/Getty Images
Ruby Levitt: Bill Eppridge/The LIFE Picture Collection/Getty Images
Shirley Clarke: Robert R. McElroy/Getty Images
Elizabeth Haffenden: Everett Collection

1961
Haley Mills: Tom Nebbia/CORBIS/Corbis via Getty Images
Ann-Margret: Hulton Archive/Getty Images
Shirley Jones: Silver Screen Collection/Getty Images

Janet Leigh: Archive Photos/Getty Images
Elizabeth Taylor: Bettmann/Getty Images
Lorraine Hansberry: David Attie/Getty Images
Dory Previn: CBS via Getty Images

1962
Piper Laurie: Frederic Lewis/Archive Photos/Getty Images
Una Merkel: PARAMOUNT/AF archive/Alamy Stock Photo
Sophia Loren: John Springer Collection/CORBIS/Corbis via Getty Images
Rita Moreno: Silver Screen Collection/Getty Images

1963
Faith Hubley: Gary Friedman/Los Angeles Times via Getty Images
Anne V. Coates: Ken Hively/Los Angeles Times via Getty Images
Mary Wills (left): Courtesy of the Christian Esquevin Collection
Mary Wills (right): Courtesy of the Christian Esquevin Collection
Anne Bancroft: Photo 12/Alamy Stock Photo
Patty Duke: ZUMA Press, Inc./Alamy Stock Photo

1964
Edith Evans: Everett Collection
Margaret Rutherford: Silver Screen Collection/Getty Images
Jocelyn Herbert: Gemma Levine/Hulton Archive/Getty Images
Patricia Neal: Silver Screen Collection/Getty Images
Renié: Pictorial Press Ltd/Alamy Stock Photo

1965
Lila Kedrova: Photo 12/Alamy Stock Photo
Pauline Kael: Erin Combs/Toronto Star via Getty Images
Julie Andrews: Bettmann/Getty Images
Debbie Reynolds: Archive Photos/Getty Images

1966
Phyllis Dalton: Everett Collection
Julie Christie: Silver Screen Collection/Getty Images
Rona Barrett: Everett Collection
Julie Harris: Karen Radkai/Condé Nast via Getty Images

1967
Sandy Dennis: Photoshot/Getty Images
Joan Bridge: Everett Collection
Lynn Redgrave: AF archive/Alamy Stock Photo

1968
Estelle Parsons: Bettmann/Getty Images
Theadora Van Runkle: Everett Collection
Carol Channing: Photoshot/Getty Images
Katharine Ross: Bert Stern/Condé Nast via Getty Images
Beah Richards: John D. Kisch/Separate Cinema Archive/Getty Images

1969
Jeannie Epper: Everett Collection
Martha Raye: Margaret Bourke-White/The LIFE Picture Collection/Getty Images
Ruth Gordon: Everett Collection
Marilyn Bergman: Bettmann/Getty Images

Barbra Streisand: Steve Schapiro/Corbis via Getty Images
Onna White: Warner Bros/Ronald Grant Archive/Alamy Stock Photo
Page 212
Carrie Fisher: From *A New Hope* Directed by George Lucas Film Company Lucasfilm 25/AF archive/Alamy Stock Photo

1970
Francoise Bonnot: RGR Collection/Alamy Stock Photo
Maggie Smith: Silver Screen Collection/Getty Images
Dyan Cannon: Alexis Waldeck/Condé Nast via Getty Images
Margaret Furse: Bettmann/Getty Images
Goldie Hawn: Bert Stern/Condé Nast via Getty Images
Barbara Loden: Time Life Pictures/Pix Inc./The LIFE Picture Collection/Getty Images

1971
Jane Alexander: TM and Copyright © 20th Century Fox Film Corp. All rights reserved/Courtesy of the Everett Collection
Ali MacGraw: Sante Forlano/Condé Nast via Getty Images
Glenda Jackson: Jack Robinson/Hulton Archive/Getty Images
Karen Black: Collection Christophel/RnB © BBS Productions/Columbia Pictures Corporation/Raybert Productions

1972
Jane Fonda: Richard Markell/Courtesy of the Everett Collection
Yvonne Blake: Everett Collection
Maya Angelou: Granamour Weems Collection/Alamy Stock Photo
Cloris Leachman: CBS via Getty Images

1973
Suzanne de Passe: © ABC/Courtesy of the Everett Collection
Liv Ullmann: Julian Wasser/The LIFE Images Collection/Getty Images
Eileen Heckart: Everett Collection
Sarah Kernochan: Barbara Alper/Getty Images
Ann Guenther: Stephen Shugerman/Getty Images
Cicely Tyson: Michael Ochs Archives/Getty Images
Jay Presson Allen: © Warner Bros/Courtesy of the Everett Collection
Liza Minnelli: Bert Stern/Condé Nast via Getty Images
Diana Ross: Harry Langdon/Getty Images

1974
Marcia Nasatir: Jerod Harris/Getty Images
Molly Haskell: Reg Innell/Toronto Star via Getty Images
Julia Phillips: Columbia TriStar/Courtesy of Getty Images
Gloria Katz: © Universal/Courtesy of the Everett Collection
Madeline Kahn: Archive PL/Alamy Stock Photo
Marsha Mason: © Orlando/Globe Photos/ZUMAPRESS.com
Suzanne Schiffman: Didier Baverel/Sygma via Getty Images

Linda McCartney: David Montgomery/Getty Images
Tatum O'Neal: Collection Christophel/Alamy Stock Photo
Pam Grier: AF archive/Alamy Stock Photo

1975
Joan Tewkesbury: AVCO/Getty Images
Judy Collins: Michael Ochs Archives/Getty Images
Diane Ladd: Everett Collection
Kitty O'Neil: Bettmann/Getty Images
Theoni Aldredge: Michael Montfort/Michael Ochs Archives/Getty Images
Joan Micklin Silver: Tristar Pictures/Ronald Grant Archive/Alamy Stock Photo
Talia Shire: Everett Collection
Susan Backlinie: Universal/AF archive/Alamy Stock Photo
Gena Rowlands: Bettmann/Getty Images
Ellen Burstyn: Everett Collection
Diahann Carroll: Everett Collection

1976
Dede Allen: © Paramount/Courtesy of the Everett Collection
Louise Fletcher: Giancarlo BOTTI/Gamma-Rapho via Getty Images
Milena Canonero: Ron Galella/WireImage
Lily Tomlin: Steve Schapiro/Corbis via Getty Images
Joan Didion: Henry Clarke/Conde Nast via Getty Images
Leslie Hoffman: Courtesy of Leslie Hoffman
Lee Grant: Michael Ochs Archives/Getty Images
Lynzee Klingman: © Sylvia Norris/Globe Photos/ZUMA Wire/Alamy Live News

1977
Caroline Leaf: Stephen Shugerman/Getty Images
Daniele Thompson: © Miramax/Courtesy of the Everett Collection
Lina Wertmuller: Everett Collection
Faye Dunaway: Warner-Seven Arts/AF archive/Alamy Stock Photo
Carrie Fisher: Twentieth Century Fox Pictures/Sunset Boulevard/Corbis via Getty Images
Beatrice Straight: Everett Collection
Lynne Littman: Michael Buckner/Getty Images
Barbara Myerhoff: Wikipedia
Barbara Kopple: Everett Collection

1978
Vanessa Redgrave: Mary Evans/20th Century Fox/Ronald Grant/Everett Collection
Diane Keaton: © Columbia/Courtesy of the Everett Collection
Julia Reichert: Brian Ach/WireImage
Elaine May: Everett Collection

1979
Claudia Weill: ©Warner Bros/Courtesy of the Everett Collection
Sheila Nevins: ZUMA Press, Inc./Alamy Stock Photo
Frances Williams: © Viacom/Courtesy of the Everett Collection
Jill Clayburgh: Stanley Bielecki Movie Collection/Getty Images
Nancy Dowd: Reg Innell/Toronto Star via Getty Images
Jadie David: Courtesy of Jadie David

Page 240

Oprah Winfrey: Everett Collection

1980

Diane Johnson: Sophie Bassouls/Sygma/Sygma via Getty Images
Bette Midler: Photo 12/Alamy Stock Photo
Patricia Resnick: Ryan Miller/Getty Images
Sandra Lee Gimpel: WENN Ltd/Alamy Stock Photo
Sally Field: Douglas Kirkland/Corbis via Getty Images
Sharon Schaffer: Courtesy of Sharon Schaffer
Meryl Streep: Jack Mitchell/Getty Images
Kathleen Collins: Courtesy of Nina Lorez Collins and Milestone Films
Sherry Lansing: Ronald Grant Archive/Alamy Stock Photo

1981

Mary Steenburgen: © Universal/Courtesy of the Everett Collection
Paula Weinstein: Gonzalo Marroquin/Patrick McMullan via Getty Images
Marjorie Baumgarten: Mary Sledd/WireImage
Lesley Gore: Ebet Roberts/Redferns
Sissy Spacek: Mary Evans/Universal/Ronald Grant/Everett Collection
Heidi von Beltz: Everett Collection
Jessie Maple: © Leroy Patton/Courtesy of the Indiana University Black Film Center/Archive
Thelma Schoonmaker: Mary Evans/Wadleigh-Maurice/Ronald Grant/Everett Collection
Jane Wagner: © Universal/Courtesy of the Everett Collection
Dolly Parton: Steve Schapiro/Corbis via Getty Images
Mary Tyler Moore: Francesco Scavullo/Condé Nast via Getty Images

1982

Ayoka Chenzira: Jett Bagley
Rita Egleston: Valerie Macon/Getty Images
Amy Heckerling: RGR Collection/Alamy Stock Photo
Carole Bayer Sager: Ebet Roberts/Redferns

1983

Eurlyne Epper: Vince Bucci/Getty Images
Kathleen Kennedy: Bertrand Laforet/Gamma-Rapho via Getty Images
Jessica Lange: Douglas Kirkland/Corbis via Getty Images
Nancy Meyers: Francois Duhamel/© Warner Bros./Courtesy Everett Collection
Melissa Mathison: Bruce McBroom/Sygma via Getty Images
Carol Littleton: Max Morse/WireImage
Glenn Close: Lynn Goldsmith/Corbis/VCG via Getty Images
Buffy Sainte-Marie: Jack Robinson/Condé Nast via Getty Images
Debra Winger: Mary Evans/Paramount Pictures/Ronald Grant/Everett Collection

1984

Polly Platt: Everette Collection
Nora Ephron: © Warner Bros./Courtesy of the Everett Collection
Barbara Benedek: Frazer Harrison/Getty Images
Donna Keegan: Albert L. Ortega/Getty Images
Gale Anne Hurd: © Universal/Courtesy of the Everett Collection

Shirley MacLaine: © Paramount/Courtesy of the Everett Collection
Irene Cara: Chris Walter/WireImage/Getty Images
Marian Green: Publicity Photograph via iStunt
Alfre Woodard: © Paramount/Courtesy of the Everett Collection
Linda Hunt: The LIFE Picture Collection/Getty Images

1985

Kym Washington Longino: Courtesy of Kym Washington Longino
Patrizia von Brandenstein: Stephen Lovekin/WireImage/Getty Images
Leora Barish: Dario Cantatore/Getty Images
Christine Lahti: © Warner Brothers/courtesy Everett Collection
Peggy Ashcroft: Gemma Levine/Getty Images
Neema Barnette: Entertainment Pictures/Alamy Stock Photo
Lauren Shuler Donner: © Columbia Pictures/courtesy Everett Collection
Bonnie Happy: Courtesy of Bonnie Happy

1986

Victoria Mudd and Maria Florio: ABC Photo Archives/ABC via Getty Images
Shinobu Muraki: Greenwich Film Productions/Ronald Grant Archive/Mary Evans/Everett Collection
Joyce Chopra: Douglas Kirkland/Corbis via Getty Images
Geraldine Page: © Island Pictures/Courtesy of The Everett Collection.
Aida Bortnik: Historic Collection/Alamy Stock Photo
Emi Wada: Bryan Chan/Los Angeles Times via Getty Images
Anjelica Huston: Harry Langdon/Getty Images
Oprah Winfrey: ©Warner Bros./courtesy Everett Collection
Randa Haines: Vince Bucci/Getty Images for DGA
Barbara De Fina: Ron Galella/WireImage
Josie MacAvin: Independent News and Media/Getty Images

1987

Dawn Steel: WENN Ltd/Alamy Stock Photo
Kathleen Turner: Sunset Boulevard/Corbis via Getty Images
Alison Reid: Courtesy of Alison Reid
Stephanie Finochio: Bobby Bank/WireImage
Susan E. Morse: ZUMA Press, Inc./Alamy Stock Photo
Brigitte Berman: Dick Loek/Toronto Star via Getty Images
Leslie Dixon: Roy Rochlin/FilmMagic/Getty Images
Vivienne Verdon-Roe: The LIFE Picture Collection/Getty Images
Marlee Matlin: Entertainment Pictures/Alamy Stock Photo
Jenny Beavan (left): Entertainment Pictures/Alamy Stock Photo
Jenny Beavan (right): Stephen Shugerman/Getty Images
Cynthia Weil: Michael Ochs Archives/Getty Images
Claire Simpson: Bettmann/Getty Images
Ruth Prawer Jhabvala: Mikki Ansin/Getty Images
Dianne Wiest: Christophe D Yvoire/Sygma via Getty Images

Carol Joffe: Moviestore collection Ltd/Alamy Stock Photo
Sigourney Weaver: Terry O'Neill/Iconic Images/Getty Images

1988

Joanne Woollard: PA Images/Alamy Stock Photo
Deborah Dickson: Fred Hayes/WireImage/Getty Images
Mary Agnes Donoghue: United Archives GmbH/Alamy Stock Photo
Jana Sue Memel: Andrea Cimini/Courtesy of Jana Sue Memel
Amy Holden Jones: © Hollywood Pictures/Courtesy of the Everett Collection
Cher: Courtesy of the Library of Congress
Pamela Conn and Sue Marx: John Barr/Liaison/Getty Images
Gabriella Cristiani: John Barr/Liaison/Getty Images
Olympia Dukakis: Dominic Chavez/The Boston Globe via Getty Images
Penny Marshall: AF archive/Alamy Stock Photo
Diane Warren: Everett Collection

1989

Anne Spielberg: Rodrigo Vaz/FilmMagic/Getty Images
Christine Choy: State Archives of Florida, Florida Memory
Michelle Pfeiffer: © Warner Bros/courtesy Everett Collection
Carly Simon: Ed Caraeff/Getty Images
Ve Neill: Nicole Wilder/©Syfy/courtesy Everett Collection
Linda Fetters Howard: Jeff Kravitz/FilmMagic, Inc/Getty Images
Bari Dreiband-Burman: Vince Bucci/Getty Images
Geena Davis: Douglas Kirkland/Corbis via Getty Images
Euzhan Palcy: PA Images/Alamy Stock Photo
Jodie Foster: Douglas Kirkland/Corbis via Getty Images
Anna Hamilton Phelan: Ginny Winn/Michael Ochs Archives/Getty Images

Page 278

Judi Dench: David Montgomery/Getty Images

1990

Anne Kuljian: Stephen Shugerman/Getty Images
Lili Fini Zanuck: Annie Wells/Los Angeles Times via Getty Images
Laura Ziskin: AF archive/Alamy Stock Photo
Anette Haellmigk: Michael Buckner/Getty Images For Women In Film Crystal + Lucy Awards
Liz (Elizabeth) Ziegler: Gisela Schober/Getty Images
Melissa Stubbs: Courtesy of Melissa Stubbs
Denise Di Novi: ©Warner Bros./courtesy Everett Collection
Meg Ryan: © Columbia/courtesy Everett Collection
Caroline Thompson: ©Columbia Pictures/courtesy Everett Collection
Jessica Tandy: AF archive/Alamy Stock Photo
Brenda Fricker: Everett Collection
Christine Anne Baur: Courtesy of Christine Anne Baur

1991

Annette Bening: Aaron Rapoport/Corbis Outline/Corbis via Getty Images

Marguerite Happy: Courtesy of Marguerite Happy
Franca Squarciapino: Marco Secchi/Getty Images
Linda Woolverton: Jeff Spicer/Getty Images
Debbie Evans: Courtesy of Debbie Evans
Sonia Izzolena: Courtesy of Sonia Izzolena
Whoopi Goldberg: Nancy R. Schiff/Getty Images
Cecelia Hall: Noel Vasquez/Getty Images
Betzy Bromberg: Jemal Countess/WireImage/Getty Images
Kathy Bates: Larry Busacca/NBC/NBC via Getty Images
Julie Dash: Everett Collection
Martha Coolidge: © Buena Vista/courtesy Everett Collection

1992

Penelope Spheeris: © Paramount Pictures/Courtesy of the Everett Collection
Mercedes Ruehl: © Columbia Pictures/Courtesy of the Everett Collection
Leslie Harris: Eric Robert/Sygma/Sygma via Getty Images
Allie Light: Byron Gamarro/Getty Images
Barbara Hammer: Everett Collection
Debra Chasnoff: Byron Gamarro/Getty Images
Nancy Haigh: Ron Galella, Ltd./Getty Images
Agnieszka Holland: Larry Busacca/Getty Images
Callie Khouri: Liz O. Baylen/Los Angeles Times via Getty Images
Lynda Obst: © Paramount/Courtesy of the Everett Collection
Wendy Tilby: Kevork Djansezian/Getty Images
Fannie Flagg: Everett Collection
Laura Dern: Mike Windle/Getty Images for American Lung Association

1993

Eiko Ishioka: © Relativity Media/Courtesy of the Everett Collection
Lisa Henson: Mathew Imaging/WireImage/Getty Images
Linda Thompson: Harry Langdon/Getty Images
Joan Gratz: Ron Galella, Ltd./WireImage/Getty Images
Gerardine Wurzburg: Jeff Kravitz/FilmMagic, Inc/Getty Images
Luciana Arrighi: Moviestore collection Ltd/Alamy Stock Photo
Joey Forsyte: Rebecca Sapp/WireImage/Getty Images
Michaela Pavlatova: Courtesy of Michaela Pavlatova
Marisa Tomei: Lynn Goldsmith/Corbis/VCG via Getty Images
Emma Thompson: Terry O'Neill/Iconic Images/Getty Images
Ruth E. Carter: J. Countess/Contour by Getty Images

1994

Janet Jackson: © Columbia/Courtesy of the Everett Collection
Pearl Bowser: Astrid Stawiarz/Getty Images
Janet Patterson: © Gramercy Pictures /Courtesy of the Everett Collection
Yolanda Toussieng: Stephen Shugerman/Getty Images
Margaret Lazarus: Rebecca Sapp/Getty Images for Santa Barbara International Film Festival
Rosie Perez: Desiree Navarro/WireImage/Getty Images

Jane Campion: John Stoddart/Getty Images
Susan Raymond: Everett Collection
Susan Seidelman: © Orion/Courtesy of the Everett Collection
Anna B. Sheppard: Mary Evans/Amblin Entertainment/Universal Pictures/Ronald Grant/Everett Collection
Gillian Armstrong: © Columbia Pictures/Courtesy of the Everett Collection
Anna Paquin: Collection Christophel/Alamy Stock Photo
Holly Hunter: J. Vespa/WireImage/Getty Images
Gabriella Pescucci: Franco Origlia/Getty Images

1995

LaFaye Baker: Courtesy of LaFaye Baker
Sharon Calahan: Alberto E. Rodriguez/WireImage
Lizzy Gardiner: Photo 12/Alamy Stock Photo
Wendy Finerman: © TriStar Pictures/Courtesy of the Everett Collection
Drew Barrymore: Martin Godwin/Getty Images
Sally Menke: Jeff Vespa/Getty Images
Freida Lee Mock: J. Vespa/WireImage/Getty Images
Ruth Kenley-Letts: David M. Benett/Dave Benett/Getty Images
Patty Smyth: Lynn Goldsmith/Corbis/VCG via Getty Images
Peggy Rajski: © Paramount/Courtesy of the Everett Collection

1996

Susan Sarandon: United Archives GmbH/Alamy Stock Photo
Lois Burwell: Valerie Macon/Getty Images
Lynn Salvatori: Courtesy of Lynn Salvatori
Nancy Lee Thurston: Courtesy Of Nancy Lee Thurston
Joan Allen: J. Vespa/WireImage/Getty Images
Jennifer Lamb: Publicity Photograph via iStunt
Cheryl Carasik: © Paramount/Courtesy of the Everett Collection
Anna Foerster: ©Screen Gems/Courtesy of the Everett Collection
Mira Sorvino: Aaron Rapoport/Corbis via Getty Images

1997

Sophia Crawford: Courtesy of Sophia Crawford
Ann Roth: Michel Boutefeu/Getty Images
Jessica Yu: J. Vespa/WireImage for Sundance Film Festival/Getty Images
Kasi Lemmons: © RTRoth/MediaPunch
Leigh Hennessy: Courtesy of Leigh Hennessy
Frances McDormand: J. Vespa/WireImage/Getty Images
Rachel Portman: PA Images/Alamy Stock Photo
Juliette Binoche: Christophe D Yvoire/Sygma via Getty Images
Dorenda Moore (left): Joe Romeiro/Courtesy of Dorenda Moore
Dorenda Moore (right): Bazza J Holmes/Courtesy of Dorenda Moore
Stephanie McMillan: Stephen Shugerman/Getty Images

1998

Helena Bonham Carter: Terry O'Neill/Iconic Images/Getty Images
Helen Hunt: Ronald Grant Archive/Alamy Stock Photo

Lynn Ahrens: Walter McBride/Getty Images
Jeannine Claudia Oppewall: Neilson Barnard/Getty Images for Persol
Delia Ephron: Gregory Pace/FilmMagic
Lisa Westcott: PA Images/Alamy Stock Photo
Donna Dewey: Courtesy of Donna Dewey
Deborah Lynn Scott: Brian To/FilmMagic/Getty Images
Deborah Lurie: Fred Hayes/WireImage/Getty Images
Anne Dudley: JEP Live Music/Alamy Stock Photo
Kim Basinger: © Warner Bros. Pictures/courtesy Everett Collection
Danielle Feinberg: © Walt Disney Co. Courtesy of the Everett Collection

1999

Allison Moorer: Harry Scott/Redferns/Getty Images
Alisa Lepselter: Mike Coppola/Getty Images
Jenny Shircore: Jesse Grant/Getty Images
Judi Dench: Miramax/Laurie Sparham/Getty Images
Gwyneth Paltrow: AF archive/Alamy Stock Photo
Sandy Powell: Eamonn M. McCormack/Getty Images for Doha Film Institute
Donna Gigliotti: Roy Rochlin/FilmMagic/Getty Images
Keiko Ibi: ZUMA Press, Inc./Alamy Stock Photo
Jill Quertier: PA Images/Alamy Stock Photo
Yvonne Welbon: Courtesy of Yvonne Welbon
Mary Sweeney: © Buena Vista Pictures/Courtesy Everett Collection
Judianna Makovsky: Lawrence K. Ho/Los Angeles Times via Getty Images
Gloria Foster: AF archive/Alamy Stock Photo
Patricia Rozema: Neville Elder/Corbis via Getty Images

Page 314

Amy Adams: Alberto E. Rodriguez/Getty Images

2000

Aimee Mann: Dan Tuffs/Getty Images
Mimi Leder: Pictorial Press Ltd/Alamy Stock Photo
Angelina Jolie: Kevin Winter/Getty Images
Hilary Swank: Matt Carr/Getty Images
Eileen Weisinger: Courtesy of Eileen Weisinger
Lucy Liu: Bruce Glikas/FilmMagic/Getty Images
Susan Hannah Hadary: Angela Weiss/Getty Images
Lindy Hemming: Jack Taylor/Getty Images
Gloria O'Brien: Courtesy of Gloria O'Brien
Laurie Creach: Courtesy of Laurie Creach
Eve Stewart: Frederick M. Brown/Getty Images
Lisa Rinzler: ©Maya Entertainment/Courtesy of the Everett Collection
Amanda Forbis: Frazer Harrison/Getty Images
Lisa Zeno Churgin: Toby Canham/Getty Images

2001

Laura Linney: Vera Anderson/WireImage/Getty Images
Marcia Gay Harden: Jason LaVeris/FilmMagic/Getty Images
Susannah Grant: AF archive/Alamy Stock Photo
Julia Roberts: Album/Alamy Stock Photo
Jacqueline West: © Paramount/Courtesy Everett Collection
Janty Yates: David McNew/Getty Images
Tracy Seretean: Angela Weiss/Getty Images
Deborah Oppenheimer: Lawrence K. Ho/Los Angeles Times via Getty Images

2002

Jill Bilcock: Jemal Countess/Getty Images

Lisa Blount: © New World Television/courtesy Everett Collection

Brigitte Broch: TIMOTHY A. CLARY/AFP/Getty Images

Dody Dorn: Publicity Photograph

Enya: Pictorial Press Ltd/Alamy Stock Photo

Catherine Martin: Andrew Toth/FilmMagic/Getty Images

Lucy Fisher: © Universal/Courtesy of the Everett Collection

America Georgine Ferrera: Christopher Polk/NBC/NBCUPhotoBank via GettyImages

Halle Berry: Vera Anderson/WireImage

Jennifer Connelly: Matt Carr/Getty Images

2003

Giselle Chamma (left): Jessica Miglio/Courtesy of Giselle Chamma

Giselle Chamma (right): Courtesy of Giselle Chamma

Queen Latifah: Monty Brinton/CBS via Getty Images

Nia Vardalos: Larry Busacca/Getty Images

Beatrice De Alba: KMazur/WireImage/Getty Images

Caroline Link: © IFC Films/courtesy Everett Collection

Mie Andreasen: Robert Mora/Getty Images

LisaGay Hamilton: Emma McIntyre/Getty Images

Zoe Bell: Donato Sardella/Getty Images for HL Group

Stacey Carino: Publicity Photograph via iStunt

Catherine Zeta-Jones: Paul Hawthorne/Getty Images

Julie Taymor: © Miramax Films/courtesy Everett Collection

Colleen Atwood: © Columbia Pictures/Courtesy of the Everett Collection

Nicole Kidman: Vera Anderson/WireImage/Getty Images

Lisa Hoyle: Publicity Photograph via iStunt

2004

Kerry Washington: Moviestore collection Ltd/Alamy Stock Photo

Annette O'Toole: Michael Bezjian/WireImage for BWR Public Relations/Getty Images

Maryann DeLeo: PA Images/Alamy Stock Photo

Fran Walsh: © New Line/courtesy Everett Collection

Philippa Boyens: Brian To/WENN.com/Alamy

Ngila Dickson: © New Line/courtesy Everett Collection

Annie Lennox: Brian Rasic/Getty Images

Renee Zellweger: Stephane Cardinale-Corbis/Corbis via Getty Images

Charlize Theron: Andrea Raffin/Alamy Stock Photo

Sofia Coppola: ©Sony Pictures/courtesy Everett Collection

Naomi Watts: © Universal/courtesy Everett Collection

2005

Celia Bobak: © Warner Bros/Courtesy of the Everett Collection

Jennifer Caputo: Tasia Wells/Getty Images

Zana Briski: J. Vespa/WireImage/Getty Images

Valli O'Reilly: Frank Micelotta/Getty Images

Cate Blanchett: Christopher Polk/Getty Images

Francesca Lo Schiavo: Giuseppe Andidero/Alamy Stock Photo

Julie Delpy: Jean-Christian Bourcart/Gamma-Rapho via Getty Images

Andrea Arnold: AF archive/Alamy Stock Photo

2006

Michelle Williams: Steve Granitz/WireImage/Getty Images

Tami Lane: Barry King/Alamy Stock Photo

Amy Adams: John Phillips/John Phillips/Getty Images

Rosario Dawson: Laurent KOFFEL/Gamma-Rapho via Getty Images

Cathy Schulman: Arun Nevader/WireImage/Getty Images

Amy Pascal: Jeff Vespa/Getty Images

Reese Witherspoon: TM & Copyright © 20th Century Fox Film Corp./Everett Collection

Natascha Hopkins: Courtesy of Natascha Hopkins

Gretchen Rau: Photo 12/Alamy Stock Photo

Sarah Greenwood and Katie Spencer: WENN Ltd/Alamy Stock Photo

Rachel Weisz: Collection Christophel/Alamy Stock Photo

Diana Ossana: Ann Summa/Getty Images

Kathleen York: Michael Bezjian/WireImage/Getty Images

Corinne Marrinan: Kevin Winter/Getty Images

2007

Siedah Garrett: Kevork Djansezian/Getty Images

Iris Yamashita: © Warner Bros./Courtesy of the Everett Collection

Polly Morgan: Darren Gerrish/WireImage/Getty Images

Melissa Etheridge: Business Wire via Getty Images

Anne Preven: Everett Collection Inc/Alamy Stock Photo

Pilar Revuelta (left): © Picturehouse/Courtesy of the Everett Collection

Pilar Revuelta (right): Jeff Kravitz/FilmMagic, Inc/Getty Images

Helen Mirren: Terry O'Neill/Iconic Images/Getty Images

Jennifer Hudson: AF archive/Alamy Stock Photo

Dana Glauberman: Everett Collection Inc/Alamy Stock Photo

Ruby Yang: Everett Collection Inc/Alamy Stock Photo

Frances-Anne Solomon: Storms Media Group/Alamy Stock Photo

Torill Kove: Aaron Harris/WireImage/Getty Images

2008

Kimberly Shannon Murphy: Sheryl Nields/Courtesy of Kimberly Shannon Murphy

Tilda Swinton: Ian Gavan/Getty Images

Eva Orner: John Phillips/Getty Images for BFI

Gina Prince-Bythewood: Jeff Vespa/WireImage/Getty Images

Marion Cotillard: Andreas Rentz/Getty Images

Diablo Cody: ©Fox Searchlight. All rights reserved/courtesy Everett Collection

Darnell Martin: Ann Summa/Getty Images

Reed Morano: Desiree Navarro/Getty Images

Abigail Disney: Zach Hyman/Patrick McMullan via Getty Image

Alexandra Byrne: Vittorio Zunino Celotto/Getty Images for DIFF

Marjane Satrapi: Ernesto Ruscio/Getty Images

Cynthia Wade: J. Vespa/WireImage for Sundance Film Festival

Kelly Reichardt: © Oscilloscope Pictures/Courtesy of the Everett Collection

Catherine Hardwicke: Franco S. Origlia/Getty Images

Saoirse Ronan: Larry Busacca/Getty Images

Suzie Templeton: Michael Caulfield/WireImage/Getty Images

Luci Romberg: Chad Bonanno/Courtesy of Luci Romberg

Marketa Irglova: Fred Hayes/WireImage for Sundance Film Festival

Karen Baker Landers: Vince Bucci/Getty Images

2009

Taraji P Henson: AF archive/Alamy Stock Photo

Kristina Johnson: Courtesy of Kristina Johnson

Ellen Kuras: dpa picture alliance/Alamy Stock Photo

Megan Mylan: Everett Collection

Maya Arulpragasam: Geisler-Fotopress GmbH/Alamy Stock Photo

Angela Meryl: Publicity Photograph via iStunt

Paula DuPre Pesmen: Tibrina Hobson/FilmMagic/Getty Images

Kate Winslet: Michael Ochs Archives/Getty Images

Penelope Cruz: Mike Marsland/Mike Marsland/WireImage/Getty Images

Page 348

Ava DuVernay: Charley Gallay/Getty Images

2010

Sandra Bullock: Christopher Polk/Getty Images for PCA

Gwendolyn Yates Whittle: Courtesy of Gwendolyn Yates Whittle

Mo'Nique: Charley Gallay/Getty Images for NAACP

Anna Kendrick: Jace Downs/TM & copyright © Fox Searchlight Pictures. All rights reserved./Courtesy of the Everett Collection

Mindy Hall: Jesse Grant/Getty Images

Elinor Burkett: Kevin Mazur/WireImage

Kathryn Bigelow: Jonathan Olley /© Summit Entertainment/Courtesy of the Everett Collection

2011

Uta Briesewitz: E. Charbonneau/WireImage for PMK/HBH/Getty Images

Amy Vincent: © Paramount Classics/courtesy Everett Collection

Hillary Lindsey: ZUMA Press, Inc./Alamy Stock Photo

Dido: Brian Aris/Live 8 via Getty Images

Anne Rosellini: Mike Pont/Getty Images

Melissa Leo: Larry Busacca/Getty Images for Sundance Film Festival

Chrissy Weathersby Ball: Courtesy of Chrissy Weathersby Ball

Pamela Martin: Everett Collection Inc/Alamy Stock Photo

Lynne Ramsay: Vittorio Zunino Celotto/Getty Images for DIFF

Audrey Marie Marrs: Valerie Macon/Getty Images

Dee Rees: George Pimentel/Getty Images

Darla Anderson: Jesse Grant/Getty Images for Disney

Debra Granik: Sebastian Mlynarski/© Roadside Attractions/Courtesy of the Everett Collection

Karen Goodman: Michael Courtesy of the Library of Congresscisano/Getty Images for HBO

Natalie Portman: © Fox Searchlight Pictures. All rights reserved./Courtesy of the Everett Collection

Lora Hirschberg: Jason Merritt/Getty Images

2012

Sharmeen Obaid-Chinoy: Emma Hardy/© Broad Green Pictures/Courtesy Everett Collection

Octavia Spencer: Robby Klein/Getty Images

Jessica Chastain: Dale Robinette/© Walt Disney Studios Motion Pictures/Courtesy Everett Collection

Annie Mumolo and Kirsten Wiig: Michael Buckner/Getty Images

Deb Adair: Steve Granitz/WireImage/Getty Images

Oorlagh Marie George: Kevork Djansezian/Getty Images

Jennifer Yuh Nelson: WENN Ltd/Alamy Stock Photo

2013

Megan Ellison: Michael Kovac/Getty Images for AFI

Jennifer Lawrence: JoJo Whilden/© Weinstein Company/Courtesy of the Everett Collection

Christina Voros: Tiffany Rose/Getty Images for Canon

Andrea Nix Fine: Kevork Djansezian/Getty Images

Lorelay Bove: Carlos R. Alvarez/WireImage/Getty Images

Brenda Chapman: Matt Winkelmeyer/Getty Images

Adele: Graham Denholm/Getty Images

Amma Asante: David Appleby/TM and Copyright/© Fox Search

Jacqueline Durran: Dave J Hogan/Getty Images for The V&A

Anne Hathaway: Photo 12/Alamy Stock Photo

Jane Gaines: Courtesy of Jane Gaines

2014

Lupita Nyong'o: Jaap Buitendijk/TM and Copyright © Fox Searchlight Pictures. All rights reserved./Courtesy of the Everett Collection

Natasha Braier: © Broad Green Pictures/Courtesy of the Everett Collection

Beverly Dunn: AF archive/Alamy Stock Photo

Dede Gardner: Steve Granitz/WireImage/Getty Images

Lauren MacMullan and Dorothy McKim: Kevin Winter/Getty Images

Kristen Anderson-Lopez: Alberto E. Rodriguez/Getty Images

Sally Hawkins: PictureLux/The Hollywood Archive/Alamy Stock Photo

Jennifer Lee: Vera Anderson/WireImage/Getty Images

Caitrin Rogers: Valerie Macon/Getty Images

Karen O: Stefanie Keenan/Getty Images for CHANEL

Kristine Belson: Ethan Miller/Getty Images for CinemaCon

Adruitha Lee and Robin Mathews: Elizabeth Goodenough/Everett Collection

2015

Amanda Silver: Everett Collection Inc/Alamy Stock Photo

Danielle Brisebois: Vincent Sandoval/WireImage/Getty Images

Sandra Adair: Jeff Vespa/Getty Images

Frances Hannon: Robin Marchant/WireImage/Getty Images

Becky Sullivan: Jason Kempin/Getty Images for WIF & Perrier-Jouet

Kristina Reed: Tommaso Boddi/WireImage/Getty Images

Patricia Arquette: © IFC Films/courtesy Everett Collection

Bonnie Arnold: Stefanie Keenan/Getty Images for TCM

Mathilde Bonnefoy: Smallz & Raskind/Getty Images

Ellen Goosenberg Kent and Dana Perry: Frederic J. Brown/AFP/Getty Images

Laura Poitras: Smallz & Raskind/Getty Images

Julianne Moore: Sydney Alford/Alamy Stock Photo

Anna Pinnock: James Atoa/Everett Collection

2016

Alicia Vikander: © Focus Features/Courtesy of the Everett Collection

Blye Pagon Faust and Nicole Rocklin: Jeff Vespa/WireImage/Getty Images

Kirsten Johnson: Lynsey Addario /© Janus Films/Courtesy of the Everett Collection

Lesley Vanderwalt and Elka Wardega: C Flanigan/FilmMagic/Getty Images

Nicole Paradis Grindle: WENN Ltd/Alamy Stock Photo

Lillian Benson: Alison Buck/WireImage/Getty Images

Maryann Brandon and Mary Jo Markey: Frazer Harrison/Getty Images

Rosa Tran: Vivien Killilea/Getty Images for SCAD aTVfest 2018

Margaret Sixel: Byron Purvis/AdMedia/ZUMA Wire/Alamy Live News

Anohni: Ragnar Singsaas/Redferns via Getty Images

Lisa Thompson: Ted Soqui/Corbis via Getty Images

Brie Larson: AF archive/Alamy Stock Photo

Meg LeFauve: Joe Scarnici/WireImage/Getty Images

Rachel McAdams: AF archive/Alamy Stock Photo

Serena Armitage: Jennifer Lourie/Getty Images

Lady Gaga: Samir Hussein/Samir Hussein/WireImage/Getty Images

Sara Bennett: Adrian Sanchez-Gonzalez/AFP/Getty Images

2017

Viola Davis: David Lee/© Paramount Pictures/courtesy Everett Collection

Patty Jenkins: Clay Enos/© Warner Bros/Courtesy of the Everett Collection

Sandy Reynolds-Wasco: Kevin Winter/Getty Images

Emma Stone: Rune Hellestad-Corbis/Corbis via Getty Images

Mica Levi: Dave M. Benett/Dave Benett/Getty Images

Joanna Natasegara: PictureLux/The Hollywood Archive/Alamy Stock Photo

Caroline Waterflow: Kevork Djansezian/Getty Images

Arianne Sutner: Frederick M. Brown/Getty Images

Adele Romanski: Pascal Le Segretain/Getty Images

Anna Udvardy: David Crotty/Patrick McMullan via Getty Images

Ava DuVernay: Atsushi Nishijima/© Walt Disney Studios Motion Pictures/Courtesy Everett Collection

Joi McMillon: Emma McIntyre/Getty Images for Film Independent

Carla Hacken: E. Charbonneau/WireImage for 20th Century Fox Studios

Mildred Iatrou Morgan and Ai-Ling Lee: Kevin Winter/Getty Images

2018

Lucy Sibbick: Frederick M. Brown/FilmMagic/Getty Images

Mary H. Ellis: WENN Ltd/Alamy Stock Photo

Vanessa Taylor: Albert L. Ortega/Getty Images

Greta Gerwig: ©A24/courtesy Everett Collection

Rachel Morrison: Steve Dietl/© Netflix/Courtesy of the Everett Collection

Allison Janney: Eli Winston/Everett Collection

Rachel Shenton: Ian West/PA Images via Getty Images

Mary J. Blige: Cindy Ord/Getty Images for Casa Reale

Taura Stinson: Valerie Macon/AFP/Getty Images

Agnes Varda: © Cohen Media Group/Courtesy of the Everett Collection

Page 378

Piper Laurie: Loomis Dean/The LIFE Picture Collection/Getty Images

ACKNOWLEDGMENTS

Our gratitude and appreciation go to all of our friends and family who gave us tireless enthusiasm throughout the process of writing this book. In particular we would like to thank:

Our book agent, Sandra Bond, for seeing this book's possibilities and for providing unflagging assistance throughout.

Rick Rinehart and Ellen Urban, our editors at Rowman & Littlefield, for believing in this project.

Our book designer, Laura Klynstra, whose vision brought beauty and life to the book, inside and out.

Our copy editor, Deirdre Langeland, for her thorough understanding of words, punctuation, transitions and omissions.

To Abby Disney, for her friendship and for her support of this book, bringing to it her thoughts about women and film.

To all of the women who are in this book, for all that they are doing and have done to create the movies that we love.

To David Tietjen, Jill's husband, for his patience, love and support.

To Barbara's son, Jeff Bridges, for his knowledge of computers and his generous help when needed.

To Gerry Hammond, for his patience and encouragement.

ABOUT THE AUTHORS

JILL S. TIETJEN, P.E. is an author, speaker, and electrical engineer. She is the co-author of *Her Story: A Timeline of the Women Who Changed America*, which received the Daughters of the American Revolution History Award Medal. Jill has conducted research into historical women around the world for the past thirty years, and speaks around the country about women's contributions to history. One of the top historians on women across all fields of endeavor in the U.S., she works to bring more visibility to women through her continual nominations of historical and living women for national, state and local awards. Her nominees have been successfully inducted into the National Women's Hall of Fame, the National Inventor's Hall of Fame, and a number of state women's halls of fame. Jill is often profiled and quoted in the media, and her articles have been printed in a wide variety of publications. She has received numerous awards and has been inducted into the Colorado Women's Hall of Fame.

BARBARA BRIDGES has spent much of her life as an entrepreneur and businesswoman. In 2006, she founded Women+Film, a program in partnership with the Denver Film Society, where she has been bringing audiences together with films, by and about women, that ignite discussions around global issues facing women today. With the annual Women+Film Festival, a section of movies in the Denver Film Festival and movie screenings throughout the year, it is a popular film program that not only entertains, but educates and inspires as well. Barbara speaks to various groups about the role of women in the movies and has been involved with various film festivals. The *Denver Post* named her one of Colorado's Top Thinkers in Arts and Culture. Barbara has served on the boards of several women's organizations, both locally and nationally, and has received numerous awards as a result.